BRITISH URBAN POLICY AND THE URBAN DEVELOPMENT CORPORATIONS

edited by
Rob Imrie and Huw Thomas

P·C·P
Paul Chapman
Publishing Ltd

Editorial material and Chs. 1 and 5, copyright © 1993 Imrie R., and Thomas, H. All other material © 1993 Paul Chapman Publishing, unless otherwise credited.

Paul Chapman Publishing Ltd
144 Liverpool Road
London
N1 1LA

British Library Cataloguing in Publication Data

British Urban Policy and the Urban
Development Corporations
 I. Imrie, Rob II. Thomas, Huw
 711.40941

ISBN 1-85396-207-4

Typeset by Best-set Typesetter Ltd., Hong Kong
Printed and bound by Athenaeum Press Ltd, Newcastle upon Tyne

A B C D E F G H   9 8 7 6 5 4 3

CONTENTS

The Editors

Rob Imrie teaches economic geography and regional development courses in the Department of Geography at Royal Holloway University of London. His research interests include industrial linkages and buyer–supplier relations, urban policy and planning, and, most recently, disablism and access in local planning. He is co-author of *Transforming Buyer–Supplier Relations* (Macmillan, 1992) and has published widely on urban policy in a number of international journals. He is presently working with Huw Thomas on an ESRC project, investigating the implementation and effects of business relocation policies.

Huw Thomas is a lecturer at the School of Planning, Oxford Brookes University. His research interests include a detailed study of the changing focus of urban renewal in Cardiff, South Wales, in the early 1980s, while he has recently completed a major study of how to sensitize planning policies and practices to the needs and aspirations of black and ethnic minorities. He has published widely in a range of international journals and is editor of two books on ethics and values in planning.

LIST OF CONTRIBUTORS

Sue Brownill is currently a senior lecturer at the School of Planning, Oxford Brookes University. Previously she worked for the Docklands Forum, a community planning organization in London's Docklands. She is author of *Developing London's Docklands: Another Great Planning Disaster?*, published by Paul Chapman in 1991.

Paul Burton is a research fellow in the School for Advanced Urban Studies, University of Bristol. He is a specialist on urban policy and has written extensively on Urban Development Corporations and a range of government policy initiatives.

David Byrne is senior lecturer in Social Policy at the University of Durham and previously worked in Northern Ireland and for the North Shields Community Development Project. He is a native of South Shields and a Labour councillor in Gateshead.

Bob Colenutt has a background in urban geography with a long-standing interest in the property market and its effects on local communities. For the past 20 years he has worked in London for community groups in North Southwark and Docklands. He later worked for the GLC Industry and Employment Department, was a councillor on the London Borough of Lambeth, and is presently the Head of the Docklands Consultative Committee Support Unit, a local authority monitoring and research organization for Docklands.

Andrew Coulson, senior lecturer at the Institute of Local Government Studies, University of Birmingham, coordinated a network of local authorities with Urban Development Corporations in their areas between 1988 and 1992. He is a specialist on local economic development, and previously worked as an economic development officer for Sheffield City Council.

Gordon Dabinett is a senior lecturer in Urban Policy at the School of Urban and Regional Studies, Sheffield Hallam University. Previously he worked for Sheffield City Council. He works on different aspects of urban economic development and policy evaluation within the Centre for Regional Economic and Social Research.

Richard Meegan is a lecturer in the Department of Geography at the University of Liverpool. He joined the University after working as a full-time researcher at the independent, non-profit research centre, CES Ltd, in London. He has also had the honour of having worked at two institutions deemed worthy of closure by Conservative central government administrations, the Greater London Council and the Centre for Environmental Studies. He is the co-author, with Doreen Massey, of *The Geography of Industrial Reorganization, The Anatomy of Job Loss*, and the editor, with Doreen Massey, of *Politics and Method*.

Brendan Nevin is a research fellow based in the Built Environment Development Centre, at the University of Central England in Birmingham. He has extensive experience of researching Urban Development Corporations and in assessing more generally the impact of central government urban initiatives in the Birmingham area. He has previously worked for local authorities in Dudley and Sandwell.

Nick Oatley is currently based at the University of the West of England (UWE), Bristol, and the Planning and Development Directorate at Bristol City Council. He teaches a range of planning-related courses in the School of Planning in the new Faculty of the Built Environment at UWE and has worked on employment issues and the Bristol Local Plan at the City Council. His research interests include employment policy in Local Plans, urban policy, and local economic development.

Peter Ramsden is a senior lecturer in Urban Policy at the School of Urban and Regional Studies, Sheffield Hallam University. Previously he worked in London for a community development agency. His major research interests are in the field of industrial and urban regeneration and he has written and published widely on Sheffield's Lower Don Valley.

Peter Roberts is Professor of Urban Planning and Associate Dean at the Leeds School of the Environment, Leeds Metropolitan University. He has taught and researched at a number of UK academic institutions and was the Senior Research Manager for ECOTEC. His particular interests are in strategic planning and management, urban and regional development and the environment and business relationship.

Mo O'Toole is a lecturer in the School for Advanced Urban Studies, University of Bristol. Previously she taught and studied at the University of Newcastle-upon-Tyne. She is active in local politics and has published numerous articles on contemporary urban politics and policy.

David Whitney is Assistant Dean at the Leeds School of the Environment, Leeds Metropolitan University. He joined the staff at Leeds having gained practice experience in Liverpool and Wakefield. His main interests are in local planning, urban development, and partnership modes of operation.

PREFACE

This book documents a traumatic and contested period of British urban policy. Since 1981, the Urban Development Corporations (UDCs) have symbolized the ideological and political values of successive Conservative governments, the rhetoric of the market over planning, and the propagation of a property, in distinction to people, based approach to urban regeneration. In particular, the UDCs have proffered a conception of inner city land uses which are inextricably linked to wider global restructuring processes. The city spaces in Britain and beyond reflect the legacies of productive decentralization, the rapid growth, globally, of new industrial sectors, and new forms of interregional and international competition for mobile capital. Amidst all of this, urban policy remains controversial in underpinning the socio-political and economic transformation of the cities.

In September 1991, with the financial support of the Nuffield Foundation, a two-day seminar was held in Cardiff to discuss the changing nature of the UDC initiative and its future in British urban policy. Despite the considerable volume of academic research and reporting on the UDCs, relatively few attempts have been made to document, and assess, the range of UDC policies and practices. The UDCs have been submerged under stereotypical conceptions which variously portray them as 'executives' of the central state, 'puppets' for global corporate capital, and mechanisms for overriding local democratic institutions. Yet, as the chapters in this book will illustrate, no single UDC rigidly conforms to the contours outlined above, while it is clear that there are significant variations in their modes of operation. In particular, it is increasingly clear that there is imperfect understanding of the localized development and delivery of national urban policy, and of how its wider development objectives are sustained, modified, or contradicted, by local socio-political milieux.

Thus, the starting point, common to all contributors, is the likelihood of significant variation in the delivery and implementation of urban policy, its unevenness, whatever the stated objectives of national government. We collectively identify three significant issues which provide the focal points for the case study chapters in Part Two of the book. First, how do UDCs develop and formulate policies and programmes in relation to the opportunities and constraints of their locales? Second, what is the nature, extent, and influence, of institutional innovation, interaction, and collaboration, between the UDCs and local participants in development? Finally, in what ways can the UDCs contribute to 'best practice' in urban policy? Discussion of these themes is organized into three parts. Part One of the book places the UDCs in their wider socio-political context and traces many of the political tensions and social disputes which have followed in their wake. In Part Two, detailed case studies of eight of the British UDCs are presented. In Part Three, the chapters reflect on UDC policies and programmes and examine the transferability of their approaches and the likelihood of their survival as an element of future urban policy.

In bringing this project to fruition, we wish to acknowledge, with grateful thanks, the financial support of the Nuffield Foundation who made the overall project possible. We also wish to thank Justin Jacyno for drawing the figures in Chapters 1, 5 and 6, and Mark Lloyd for providing us with invaluable assistance in the final production of the book. Finally, we are grateful to the Department of Geography, Royal Holloway University of London, for providing a whole range of back-up assistance and materials.

Rob Imrie
University of London

Huw Thomas
Oxford Brookes University

October, 1992

PART ONE

Urban Development Corporations in Context

1

URBAN POLICY AND THE URBAN DEVELOPMENT CORPORATIONS

Rob Imrie and Huw Thomas

Introduction

In August 1992, John Redwood, the Local Government minister, confirmed the continuing importance for one of the more controversial urban policy instruments of the last decade, the Urban Development Corporations (UDCs), in commenting that, 'we're committed to backing the UDCs' (Redwood, 1992). In proclaiming his faith in the UDCs, Redwood was endorsing over ten years of Conservative government urban policy, comprising a range of programmes which the Audit Commission (1989) concluded were 'a patchwork quilt of complexity and idiosyncracy with few resources to match the scale of the attendant problems' (p. 4). Indeed, since the early 1980s, government policy towards the protracted problems of the inner cities has brought forward many initiatives, such as, Business in the Community, Task Forces, City Grants, and City Challenge, yet arguably none has matched the level of resourcing, or political zeal, which has underpinned the government's support for the UDCs. In these, and other senses, many authors, quite rightly, concur that the UDCs represent the flagship, the jewel in the crown, of Conservative government urban policy (Boyle, 1988; Lawless, 1989, 1991; Robson, 1988).

Yet, despite the proliferation of comments, articles, and outpourings on the UDCs, the Centre for Local Economic Strategies (CLES, 1990b, 1992) recently concluded that there is little systematic evaluation or monitoring of the UDCs. In particular, a number of key issues have been remarkably underdeveloped, and even overlooked, by researchers of urban policy, including little evaluation of the institutional dynamics of UDC policy formation, the links between UDCs and other agencies of regeneration, and the distributive costs of UDC policy (for exceptions see Imrie and Thomas, 1992). More importantly, while policy studies literature generally accepts the notion that policy processes differ considerably within and between policy domains, much research on the UDCs has tended to take a reductionist line in portraying them as invariant, undifferentiated, policy vehicles, instruments of both central government and the imperatives of global capital (Anderson, 1991; Atkinson and Coleman, 1992). Yet, as the various chapters in this book argue, such ideas are problematical in denying the institutional and political specificities, and autonomy, of the UDCs, while, simultaneously, precluding systematic discussion of how organizations like UDCs may differ in operation, objectives, and policy.

The UDCs were created by the 1980 Local Government, Planning and Land Act and have since become a significant instrument for the formulation, development, and implementation of urban policy in England and Wales. Their remit was originally outlined by Michael Heseltine (the then Secretary of State for the Environment) in 1979, who saw the UDCs as both a political and economic mechanism for unlocking the 'development' potential of the inner cities. In economic terms, the objectives of the UDCs were clearly signalled by Section 136 of the Act, 'to secure the regeneration of its area, by bringing land and buildings into effective use, encouraging the development of existing and new industry and commerce'. The UDCs were forerunners in reorienting urban policy towards new economic imperatives in urban regeneration with the objective of pump-priming inner city land values through infrastructure projects, creating, and enabling, the new spaces of production and consumption, and utilizing private sector capital as a mechanism for revitalizing the cities.

The UDCs were also born at a time of great upheaval for local government, where the very *raison d'être* of local authorities was being questioned (Gyford, 1985; Stoker, 1991). Indeed, up until 1979, it was widely, although not exclusively, accepted that local authorities were the natural agencies for the propagation of urban policy, yet by 1980 their role, at the heart of both devising and delivering policies for the regeneration of the cities, was being transformed. In particular, government concern was premised on an ideological distaste of public sector intervention, and, in its early years, the Thatcher administration was particularly zealous in seeking to privatize public policy and reduce the role of what was being presented as 'the interfering state' (Gurr and King, 1987; Stoker, 1991). Such ideas were crystallized by Michael Heseltine in 1979, who held up the UDCs as an alternative model in noting that 'there is a need for a single minded determination not possible for the local authorities concerned with their much broader responsibilities' (DOE, 1979). In essence, the UDCs were to represent the future, an amalgam of free-enterprise, deregulated decision making, and streamlined bureaucracy.

The introduction of the UDCs in 1980 reflected these new political priorities and they have undoubtedly come to symbolize the times, as non-elected agencies, ultimately responsible to, and controlled by, central government, with an emphasis on market-led, property-based regeneration. Indeed, what marks out the UDCs as a particular policy phenomenon of the last decade, a kind of watershed, is their embodiment of the post-modern city, an embellishment of fragmented institutions, new development alliances, and, most crucially, an apparent diminution in the role of state managerialism (Harvey, 1987; Imrie and Thomas, 1992, 1993a). In particular, a range of authors concur that the UDCs have proffered a new institutional context for the development and delivery of urban policy, a single agency debureaucratized forum (Burton, 1986; Coulson, 1990; Imrie and Thomas, 1992). As Harvey (1987) notes, organizations like the UDCs represent new forms of urban governance, predicated on entrepreneurial activity, with the state increasingly residualized to the role of 'strategic enabler', in practice, a passive fragmented player in the restructuring of the cities.

Yet, as the chapters in this book will indicate, such views tend to ignore the complex and multi-layered policy networks which characterize the operational environments of the UDCs, and other urban policy instruments. Too often, discussion of the UDCs is predicated on the 'withering away of the state' thesis, that state involvement in urban regeneration is markedly reducing. Yet this belies the evidence on the emergence of public–private partnerships and the close alignments which are occurring between many local authorities and the private sector (Boyle, 1988, 1989; Harding, 1991). As the chapters in this book note, the local embeddedness of the UDCs, forging links variously with local politicians, community groups, and local civil servants, is both unavoidable and a necessary condition for the successful formation and implemention of UDC policy and strategy (Coulson, 1990; Stoker, 1991). UDCs themselves may see such processes as legitimation exercises, but, if so, they can be ones which have tangible impacts on their working practices and policies. In this sense, a full understanding of UDCs needs to recognize their involvement in webs of interaction and collaboration with local participants in the development process, processes which are integral to the shaping, containment, and development of UDC strategy and policy.

Moreover, evidence from chapters in this book brings into question the stereotypical notion that the UDCs represent, in Heseltine's words, 'single-minded determination', a shift from the rigidities of the bureaucratic (local) state. While the UDCs have particular powers which enable them to circumvent local democratic channels, there are still many senses in which 'bureaucracy', 'red-tape', even accountability, have not been emasculated. Some UDCs actively forge relations with local authorities, developing new joint committees and committee cycles, and entering into partnership agreements while utilizing shared budgets, strategies which fly in the face of government exhortations concerning the apparent inertia of the local state. Indeed, at least some UDCs are more critical of the ties and controls exercised by what one Chief Executive termed 'that interfering central government'. For example, as one senior official in the Cardiff Bay Development Corporation has commented, on its relations with the Welsh Office, 'they've got us pinned down and fiscal control, centrally, is really preventing us from getting on with the job'.

In this opening chapter we critically discuss the significance of the UDCs as a central component of contemporary policies for urban regeneration. We divide the rest of the chapter into three. In the next section we provide an overview of the main transformations in urban policy since the late 1970s, particularly focusing on changes in the organizational and fiscal context of central–local government relations. We then provide an outline of the UDC initiative, commenting on its origins, objectives, and financing, while also providing an assessment of some of the main transformations and continuities in UDC strategy and policy since the early 1980s. The final section outlines the main themes and issues of the book by calling for more sensitized, or contextualized, evaluations of urban programmes and policies.

The Changing Dimensions of Urban Policy

In the last ten years a wide range of policy measures have been adopted by both central and local government in attempts to combat the worst consequences of urban decline. While a complex, multi-dimensional, inner city problem was officially recognized in the 1970s, policy frameworks have changed significantly with the onus moving from exclusively public sector initiatives to market based, or private, solutions. In particular, the term 'urban regeneration' has been coined to signal a new era of urban policy based on property-led answers to urban problems (Healey, 1992; Moore and Richardson, 1989; Turok, 1992). As CLES (1990b) suggest, the term 'urban regeneration' is an American import which describes a particular approach to city revitalization, the physical regeneration of localities, investment in buildings and infrastructure. Boyle (1988) summarizes the key features of this approach to inner city decline, as market-led strategies to lever in private property investment, with an effective transfer of policy making from public to private sectors.

Yet the role of the local authorities, as the 'natural agencies' of inner city reconstruction and policy, was enshrined in the 1978 Inner Urban Areas Act which stressed that private sector disinvestment, consequent upon structural changes in the economy, was the primary cause of inner city decline. In particular, it was argued that an expanded role for the local state was a prerequisite in overcoming urban decline, a position clearly outlined years later by the Association of Metropolitan Authorities (1986), who argued that local government is uniquely positioned to be sufficiently responsive to the needs and problems of all sections of the community. As Lawless (1991) notes, a number of broad themes dominated much of the early thinking on the inner cities, especially a recognition that inner city deprivation was primarily caused by declining personal household and community income due to diminishing job opportunities and inadequate social welfare services (p. 16). Indeed, the 1977 White Paper, *Policy for the Inner Cities*, concluded that 'any effective urban policy would require central and local government to make funds available for the inner cities' (p. 5).

This interventionist ethos also underpinned the Urban Programme, introduced in 1968. However, this earlier programme differed from the structural analysis of the 1977 White Paper, being based on social pathological reasoning, that the problems of the inner cities, crime, poverty, poor housing, and inadequate health, welfare, and community facilities, were somehow linked to the personal and familial inadequacies of the resident populations (Lawless, 1989; Robson, 1988). The early focus of the Urban Programme was on social and community programmes, with central government funding 75% of project costs, although, as Lawless (1989) notes, it was evident by the mid 1970s that little headway was being made in stemming the continuing job and population losses from the cities. Thus, by the late 1970s, the overt concerns of the Programme were beginning to focus on job creation and the economy, an orientation which was clearly specified by a Department of the Environment (DOE, 1981) guideline which stated that there 'must be a presumption in favour of projects which have as their objective the stimulation of economic activity appropriate to the area'.

This orientation, with its recognition that changes in the economic base of inner areas were crucial in explaining their characteristics, was crystallized in the 1977 White Paper, which recommended the creation of the Inner City Partnerships (ICPs), joint central–local state initiatives, in conjunction with private sector interests, to develop projects aimed at the economic revival of the inner cities (see Gurr and King, 1987). In particular, the Partnerships were an attempt to develop a common approach to seven of the most deprived localities in England, utilizing the expertise of a wide range of constituent interests, including local government, the police, voluntary groups, the DOE, and the private sector. Yet, as Lawless (1991) and others have noted, the ICPs failed to agree a corporate approach, and the little coordination which was achieved tended to be short-lived by 'dissolving into its component parts' (Parkinson and Wilks, 1985, p. 302). Indeed, by the early 1980s, the Conservative government had rejected the idea that local government should be a major player in urban policy and, as Lawless (1991) notes, a shift towards the liberalization and deregulation of urban policy ensued.

The ensuing transformations in the institutional and fiscal context of urban policy have been linked to national government objectives concerned with enhancing central state control over local government policy making (Duncan and Goodwin, 1988). Throughout the 1980s, the Conservative government introduced a wide range of financial, legislative, and administrative measures (of which the UDCs were but one) aimed at minimizing the role of local authorities in favour of private sector enterprise. As Heseltine argued in 1979,

The Government is committed to take a radical look at the way in which bureaucratic institutions affect our industrial and economic performance. We see the need to redefine the frontier between the public and the private sector.

(Hansard, 13 September, 1979)

This line of argument was more forcibly developed by the Minister for Local Government, Tom King, who provided a rationale for the utilization of the private sector:

The Urban Development Areas, like much of the rest of our inner urban areas, desperately need the private sector's energy and resources . . . so do the Enterprise Zones which we have created. In these too we must encourage and enlist the flair, drive, and initiative of the private sector as the only possible way of restoring lasting prosperity to the decaying areas of some of our towns and cities.

(quoted in Duncan and Goodwin, 1988)

By the mid-1980s, the UDCs were promoted as exemplars of the more general approach increasingly being adopted towards urban policy, particularly the utilization of business leaders to take over the agenda of public policy, a trend which Colenutt, in Chapter 11 of this volume, argues is gaining strength in the 1990s.

As Robinson and Shaw (1991) note, the privatization of public policy chimed with the political objectives of central government, objectives which were indicative of a simultaneous shift from a state-controlled, public sector-led approach, and from a decentralized, fragmented, local structure to a centralized national structure (also see Meager, 1991). The privatization of urban policy has been utilized as a mechanism to achieve 'value for money', based on the assumption that resources are best utilized in a private sector culture, and a whole range of urban policy measures have been co-opted by business leaders who, as Shaw (1990) notes, find themselves bringing their 'vision' and 'leadership' to the Boards of UDCs, Training and Enterprise Councils,

Enterprise Agencies, and Regional Development Companies. As Robinson and Shaw (1991) argue, the 'new leaders' seem to constitute an empowered urban elite akin to the philanthropic businessmen of the Victorian era, yet, as CLES (1992) and others have noted, their power base is partial and their development objectives narrowly construed around commercial returns on projects. Nor is it always the case that, in practice, business leaders (especially if locally based) share the ideological hostility of Conservative governments to the idea of a locally responsive community regeneration (see Colenutt, Chapter 11).

The redrawing of central–local government relations, which has accompanied the privatization of particular facets of policy, has been multi-dimensional, yet with the common objective of a diminution in the power of local government. As Goldsmith (1990) notes, local government finance has shifted from the introduction of expenditure targets for specific local authorities, with sanctions for overspending, to the utilization of local tax-capping with limits placed on the level of local taxes which local government may levy. It is also clear that local government has lost powers in policy formulation and service delivery to a range of sectional interests, including parents, voluntary groups, and, significantly, businesses. The strategy of privatization has involved the withdrawal of key activities from local government, the contracting-out of services, and an increase in legal forms of control over local authorities. Moreover, the focus on business elites, quangos, and other localized forums for policy delivery, has led to a proliferation of non-elected bodies dealing with the socio-economic problems of the British cities. In sum, urban policy has gradually come to be dominated by central directions, with implementation heavily influenced by the private sector and market trends.

This is well exemplified with regard to the financing of urban policy which, as Robson (1988) claims, has been 'piecemeal, *ad hoc*, and subject to the law of one hand taking away what the other was giving' (p. 96). For instance, while the overall level of finance in the Urban Programme (including the UDCs) increased substantially, from £29 million in 1977–78 to £361 million in 1985–86, no additional government spending was actually involved, in that additional spending on the UP was a product of savings made by government cuts in the Rate Support Grant (RSG) to urban councils. Yet, as Duncan and Goodwin (1988) note, the increase in spending on the Urban Programme signalled a shift from local authority controlled Partnership Programmes to the non-elected UDCs and other (privatized) policies. By 1988–89, of the alleged £3 billion that central government had allocated to the cities, only 10%, the Urban Programme, was subject to local government influence (Lawless, 1991, p. 25).

The restrictions on local government discretion, or the framework within which urban policy has been conceived and delivered, have facilitated successive Conservative governments in their efforts to redefine the *content and direction* of urban policy. The idea of a complex interplay of economic, social and environmental factors, each requiring an appropriate response, exemplified by the aspirations, if not reality, of the original inner city partnerships, has also been replaced by a focus on physical transformation, a property-led approach to regeneration. In particular, policy instruments, like City Grants and the UDCs, are exemplars of this approach, investment in buildings and infrastructure, based on the unsubstantiated premise that their supply will (inevitably) generate new jobs and wealth. The simplicity, or crudeness, of this approach has in turn made it easier to involve the private sector, and certainly private sector property development in inner cities has been easier to encourage (with suitable subsidies) than, say, business involvement in city technology colleges.

The involvement of business interests in urban policy has also been facilitated by local government responses to global economic changes and their uneven impact on particular areas. Harvey (1987), Mayer (1989) and others have noted the increase in urban entrepreneurialism, as local authorities and public agencies respond to rapid shifts in international patterns of investment. Places need to compete for mobile investment, and this means, *inter alia*, creating the 'right business climate'. This has many aspects, but of crucial significance is that public agencies, including local government, be seen to be responsive to, and closely working with, businesses in the community. Thus, promotional literature and place marketing is increasingly seen as important. In some parts of Britain, local businesses have organized their own strategies for creating the 'right' conditions for growth. In general, the 1980s, with its 'place marketing', saw closer relationships developing between local government and business interests, irrespective of central government pressure to increase private sector influence. The UDCs, with their private-sector-dominated Boards, represent a logical continuation of this trend.

However, the content and direction of contemporary urban policy, particularly its property-based approach, has attracted much comment and criticism (Imrie and Thomas, 1992, 1993a; Lawless, 1991; Solesbury, 1990; Turok, 1992). In a wide-ranging review, Turok (1992) concludes that property development is hardly a panacea for economic regeneration and, even in physical terms, appears to be deficient. For instance, the Audit Commission (1989) has noted that the rate of reclamation of derelict land during the 1980s failed to keep pace with the growth of new derelict spaces. Similarly, Turok notes that property-based measures ignore some of the crucial dimensions of city revitalization, such as education and training, investment in basic infrastructure (like transport and communications), and the underlying competitiveness of industry (especially the technical bases of production and the innovative capacity of firms). However, the difficulty here is not necessarily the weaknesses of property development *per se*, but the relative absence of additional strategies and measures in revitalizing cities.

It is also apparent that government emphasis on property-led regeneration is, in part, an attempt to facilitate local economic growth. Statements from the DOE have given formal backing to the idea that physical redevelopment provides a major stimulus in economic restructuring, yet evidence suggests that a property-based approach cannot guarantee any rise in the level of economic activity. As Turok (1992) rightly argues, one of the main problems of property-based approaches in facilitating economic regeneration is likely to be that the other preconditions for growth are absent or weak in the target cities. However, Healey (1991) notes that urban policy is increasingly concerned with propagating property development as the purveyor of new rounds of economic growth, solely on the assumption that the new physical spaces will attract in the 'right' mix of investors. Yet, as the recent collapse of the London Dockland's developer, Olympia and York, testifies, many of these assumptions are built on shifting sands.

Others have also criticized the general property-based approach and its distributional consequences. For instance, the Public Accounts Committee in 1988 called for UDCs to place more emphasis on strategic issues, while others have condemned the concept of leverage planning as an ineffectual tool of city revitalization (CLES, 1990a,b; Imrie and Thomas, 1992; Thomas and Imrie, 1989). Brownill (1990), for instance, shows how the haste to maximize private investment has led to developers receiving substantial public subsidies, while others note that the primacy of the approach, in seeking maximum developers' profit, precipitates 'runaway' developments characterized by the absence of strategic infrastructure, like highways and open space. Harding (1991), in a wide-ranging review of regeneration strategies, highlights the fact that property-led strategies appear to ignore local needs.

Yet, the themes of urban competition, regional autarchy, and private sector influence, have, if anything, been strengthened by recent policy initiatives, such as the designation of two new UDCs in 1992, and, as significantly, the City Challenge initiative, introduced by Michael Heseltine, the proponent of the UDCs. This process of competitive bidding for funds, which underpins City Challenge, requires of local authorities that they demonstrate broad-based support and involvement in their renewal strategies. The dominance of the values of the market, taking urban policy to its logical conclusion, has been noted by Gosling (1992) who describes the process as:

a sweepstake dubbed 'Tarzan's tombola' with many officers involved in the bidding complaining that a 'hard sell' presentation is worth more than the quality of the schemes.

(p. 24)

Yet City Challenge typifies over a decade of urban policy, part of a pastiche which is being financed by top-slicing or cutting other Urban Programme funds. Indeed, the Urban Programme was cut by £15 million and housing investment by a further £45 million, in 1991–92, to help finance City Challenge, while a recent Treasury (1992) forecast, on public spending for 1992–93, indicates a significant diminution in the availability of public funds for all spheres of public expenditure.

The future of urban policy also seems crystallized in continuing trends towards the privatization of public policy. Indeed, the 1989 Local Government and Housing Act introduced a so-called 'new balance' of business needs, with the social and political questions which tend to dominate local councils, while specifying restrictions on local authority involvement in activities like the management of land and buildings. Moreover, the government's Housing, Land, and Urban Development Bill, proceeding through Parliament at the time of writing, while seeking to unify many of the disparate strands of urban policy through a new institutional framework, the Urban Regeneration Agency, looks set to continue the centralization of urban policy, although, as Colenutt (Ch. 11) and Burton and O'Toole (Ch. 12) note, in their contributions to this volume, social and community goals in urban regeneration are beginning to work their way back onto the urban policy agenda. Yet, while all is flux in contemporary urban policy, the stable base for the last ten years, the UDCs, remains.

Urban Policy and the Urban Development Corporations: Policies and Practices

There is a wide range of literature describing the origins, ethos, and objectives underlying the British UDCs (Batley, 1989; Brownill, 1991; CLES, 1990a,b; Imrie and Thomas, 1992; Lawless, 1989; Parkinson, 1990; Stoker, 1989; Thornley, 1991). The UDCs have become a central institutional mechanism of contemporary urban policy, and, as Lawless (1991) notes, the UDCs were appointed by central government to oversee the physical regeneration of specified localities, primarily by bypassing the traditional deliverers of urban policy, local government. Their original remit was set out by the 1980 Act, with the focus on property-led regeneration made clear:

> to secure the regeneration of its area by bringing land and buildings into effective use, encouraging the development of existing and new industry and commerce, creating an attractive environment and ensuring that housing and social facilities are available to encourage people to live and work in the area
>
> (Section 136)

Armed with a range of land acquisition and planning control powers, the UDCs claim to have been able to circumvent local government, avoiding controls which, so central government argue, lie at the heart of urban decay in the British cities. In this sense, central government has devised UDCs as 'trouble-shooting' organizations, although various commentators have criticized their methods of evading local democracy, remaining unaccountable to local electorates, and creating inequitable forms of urban development (Fainstein *et al*, 1992; Lawless, 1989; Parkinson and Evans, 1990; Thornley, 1991).

The single agency approach to regeneration has been widely documented, and was extolled in the postwar planning of the New Towns through the New Town Development Corporations, agencies which had extensive powers to acquire and develop land. As Lawless (1989) notes, such was the success of the New Towns programme that the Town and Country Planning Association (1979) made several calls for the designation of development corporations to solve the problems of the inner cities. Such exhortations obviously appealed to the incoming Conservative government of 1979 who drew parallels between independent, centrally appointed development agencies, free from the apparent constraints of local government, and the creation of conducive conditions for the operation of unfettered market forces in securing the reconstruction of the cities.

In particular, a range of authors concur that the UDCs are illustrative of the dominant themes of recent British urban policy, the minimization of local state agencies in urban regeneration and creating a climate conducive to the private investor (Batley, 1989; Stoker, 1991; Thornley, 1991). This ethos was clearly outlined by a House of Lords Select Committee in 1981 which contended that the rationale of the UDCs is 'to remove the political uncertainty and restraints

of local democracy which . . . represents a significant hindrance to the development process and a deterrent to private investment'. Indeed, there is much
evidence to suggest that the UDCs have been at the forefront in the restructuring
of central–local government relations. In reflecting on the designation of the
London Docklands Development Corporation (LDDC), Heseltine noted how

> *we took their powers away from them because they were making such a mess*
> *of it. They are the people who got it all wrong. They had advisory committees*
> *and even discussion committees, but nothing happened . . . UDCs do things*
> *and they are free from the delays of the democratic process.*

By early 1993, there were 13 UDCs in operation in Britain, designated in
five phases (see Figure 1.1). The phase one UDCs, comprising the LDDC
and Merseyside Development Corporation (MDC), were set up in 1981.
Five more followed at the beginning of 1987, comprising Teesside (TDC),
Tyne and Wear (TWDC), Trafford Park (TPDC), the Black Country (BCDC),
and Cardiff Bay (CBDC). These were followed at the end of the year with the
announcement of the 'mini-UDCs' for Central Manchester (CMDC), Bristol

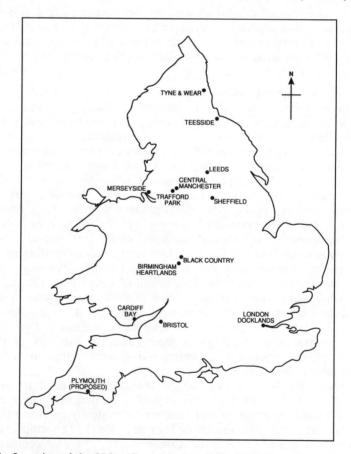

Figure 1.1 Location of the Urban Development Corporations.

Table 1.1   The UDCs at designation

	Area at designation (ha)	Population at designation	Employment at designation
Birmingham Heartlands	1,000	12,500	Not known
Black Country	2,598	35,405	53,000
Bristol	420	1,000	19,500
Cardiff Bay	1,093	500	15,000
Central Manchester	187	500	15,300
Leeds	540	800	NA
London	2,150	40,400	27,213
Merseyside	350	450	1,500
Sheffield	900	300	18,000
Teesside	4,858	400	NA
Trafford Park	1,267	40	24,468
Tyne and Wear	2,375	4,500	40,115

Source: CLES (1990b) and personal communications with the UDCs.

(BDC), and Leeds (LDC) with the extension of the Black Country UDC into Wolverhampton. In 1988, a further UDC was announced for Sheffield (SDC) followed by the most recent designation in Birmingham Heartlands (March 1992), and Plymouth (announced, but not formally designated as yet).

The UDCs are primarily located in inner city localities, yet, as Table 1.1 shows, there is great variation between the UDC areas (Urban Development Areas, UDAs) in terms of size and character. The UDAs range from Teesside with a massive 4,858 hectares to Central Manchester with just 187 hectares. Moreover, contrary to government assertions that UDCs were declared in areas that were essentially derelict, Table 1.1 clearly illustrates that the majority of UDAs contain a significant industrial and employment base. Indeed, as CLES (1990b) notes, one can make a further distinction between UDAs which contain parts of the city centres, like Bristol, Merseyside, and Manchester, and those which primarily comprise off-centre industrial land, like Sheffield's Lower Don Valley, Trafford Park and Teesside. The new Plymouth UDC, once formally designated, is likely to consist of three sites in a single ownership, as opposed to Bristol where, as Oatley points out in Chapter 9, part of the case for designating the UDC was the alleged fragmentation of land ownership.

As Batley (1989), and others note, there are, nevertheless, a number of features common to all the UDCs. In particular, central government, through the Secretary of State for the Department of the Environment (or the Welsh Office in the Welsh context), controls key elements of the UDCs' organization. The Secretary of State, utilizing the advice of consultants and other sources, defines the UDA and appoints a Board with responsibilities for appointing staff, devising strategy, and administering finance and resources. All UDCs, with the exception of Cardiff Bay, have planning control powers, with powers to operate outside of their immediate boundaries if they consider such actions to be beneficial to their regeneration plans, while their funding is gained through a mixture of three sources: an annual budget from central government;

finance borrowed from the national loan fund; and the utilization of receipts from land sales.

The UDCs also have the power to purchase land by agreement, to 'vest' it from public sector bodies, and/or to compulsorily purchase it from private sector landowners. As Coulson (1990) notes, UDCs are dedicated bodies with the specific remit to secure land and property development, and, in this sense, they typify the property-led approach to urban regeneration which characterizes the central element of urban policy in Britain. Indeed, 'development' is the key term characterizing the UDCs, yet its definitional basis is restricted to 'bringing derelict and/or vacant land back into productive use'. As Healey (1991) notes, the objectives of the UDCs are to achieve local economic growth by providing the physical infrastructures and locales appropriate for the new industrial and commercial sectors. In particular, the UDCs have the remit of 'unblocking' supply-side constraints on the development potential of land and property, to assemble land parcels, develop infrastructure, and pump-prime land values in the inner cities as a means of attracting private sector investment.

As Lawless (1989) and others have stated, it was always intended that UDCs operate as catalysts by providing a framework for private sector development interests, not as developers themselves. The UDCs are not the plan-making authority, and their development proposals must, in theory, take account of local authority planning frameworks. Yet, as Lawless (1989), CLES (1992) and the case studies in this book indicate, the UDCs have never been effectively bound by local planning frameworks, although the majority try to operate within agreed strategies with the local authorities. Indeed, a number of UDCs, including Trafford Park, Tyne and Wear, and Sheffield, have drawn up agency agreements enabling the respective local authorities to process planning applications on their behalf. Yet, as Byrne (1992) concludes, if UDCs want to, then they can effectively ignore the statutory planning process, and this has certainly occurred in a number of the UDAs.

Healey (1991) also recognizes the importance of the marketing of UDC strategies and a significant proportion of UDC expenditure is spent on 'marketing regeneration', pursuing campaigns to publicize sites, premises, and investment opportunities. Indeed, an important feature of the UDCs' remit is the utilization of 'place-marketing', promoting and advertising the opportunities for private development, as one of the keys to levering private sector invest-ment. As Healey (1991) comments, the imagery and rhetoric of regeneration is seen as important, 'not just as political publicity, but to regenerate confidence in the property development possibilities of older industrial cities' (p. 100). To such ends, the UDCs collectively spent £14.6 million, or 2.5% of total grant-in-aid received, on advertising and marketing in 1990–91, with the LDDC alone spending £2 million, or 0.6% of its allocated budget for that financial year. Since 1981, the LDDC has spent £20 million on promotion and publicity (CLES, 1992).

The financing of urban policy is, of course, a key area of debate. In particular, the funding of the UDCs, and the extent to which it involves a diversion of resources from other areas of urban policy expenditure, has been of paramount concern. As Figure 1.2 shows, there has indeed been a shift in the balance of expenditure on the urban programme and the UDCs. What is clear is the

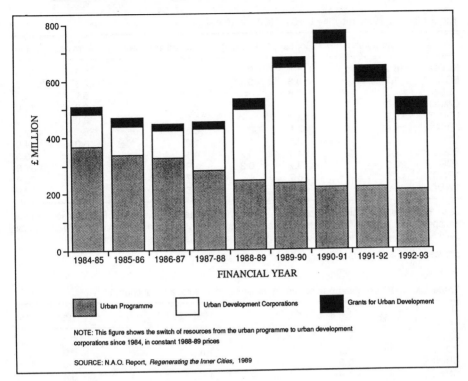

Figure 1.2   Switch of resources from urban programmes to UDCs.

Table 1.2   UDC grant-in-aid 1989–92 (£ million)

	1989–90	1990–91	1991–92
BCDC	31	32	33
BDC	5	10	7
CBDC	29	31	34
CMDC	11	14	16
LDC	8	14	8
LDDC	256	332	225
MDC	23	24	25
SDC	10	19	13
TDC	36	38	36
TPDC	17	29	30
TWDC	36	38	36

Source: Department of the Environment (1990) and Cardiff Bay Development Corporation, Annual Report (1991–92).

marked switch of resources from the former to the latter, especially in the mid 1980s. Indeed, the resource base of the UDCs is quite staggering when placed beside total government expenditure on urban policy. As Figure 1.2 indicates, total UDC funding from 1981 to 1990 was £1.8 billion and over the 1980s the

Table 1.3   Expenditure by the UDCs, 1990–91 (£ million)

	Land purchase	Roads	Housing	Private assistance	Admin.	Total
BCDC	16.7	1.4	0.7	3.8	5.2	27.8
BDC	6.7	0.6	0.1	–	2.3	9.7
CBDC	–	3.6	–	–	5.7	24.9
CMDC	7.6	–	0.6	3.5	2.3	14.0
LDC	5.7	4.7	–	1.6	2.0	14.0
LDDC	25.0	244.0	38.0	0.3	25.2	332.5
MDC	14.3	2.3	1.1	1.3	5.0	24.0
SDC	7.7	4.1	0.2	4.1	2.9	19.0
TDC	20.6	9.7	0.3	1.9	5.3	37.8
TPDC	13.1	6.7	0.1	5.7	3.4	29.0
TWDC	25.0	1.0	0.3	6.6	4.9	37.8

Land Purchase also includes reclamation and environmental improvements; Roads also includes transport and other infrastructure; Private Assistance includes assistance for private sector development; Administration includes marketing, promotions, and estate management.

Source: CLES (1990b) p. 38.

Table 1.4   UDC spending on community projects (% of total annual spend)

	1988–89 (%)	1989–90 (%)	1990–91 (%)
BCDC	1.3	1.8	2.7
BDC	0.0	1.0	0.0
CBDC	0.6	0.9	1.0
CMDC	1.4	1.6	3.4
LDC	0.9	0.1	0.2
LDDC	3.3	6.5	5.3
MDC	4.5	3.1	4.2
SDC	0.4	0.7	1.0
TDC	2.4	0.3	0.2
TPDC	0.1	0.3	0.4
TWDC	0.3	0.9	1.3
ALL	1.38	1.56	3.7

Source: Hansard (1989) and Annual Reports and Accounts of the UDCs (1990–91).

UDCs became the priority funding initiative of the government, receiving, in total, considerably more than the total grant for all 57 Urban Programme Districts in England (CLES, 1990b). In particular, Table 1.2 indicates the privileged status of the LDDC compared to the other UDCs, in terms of receipt of grant-in-aid. As CLES (1990b) notes, between 1989 and 1992, the LDDC had an allocation from the DOE of £813 million while all the other UDCs together received £600 million (p. 34).

The expenditures of the UDCs reflect their property-led, leverage role with the overwhelming proportion of UDC expenditure directed to subsidizing the development of land, particularly through land acquisition, reclamation, and road building. The DOE (1990) has estimated that of total expenditure of the UDCs (excluding the LDDC) in 1990–91, 56% went on land purchase and assembly (see Table 1.3). As Table 1.4 shows, UDC spending on community projects is small when set against expenditures on physical infrastructure. CLES (1992) comments that projects that have a social or community content are seen as a 'poor investment' by UDC Chief Executives, primarily because their remit is to invest in schemes which bring in the largest amount of private investment at the lowest direct public subsidy. Nevertheless, such projects can be significant for local communities and for the relationship between local communities and the UDC.

As Lewis (1992) notes, the UDCs, especially the LDDC, have 'levered' large sums of private finance. In 1989, the Public Accounts Committee noted that the LDDC had received over £2 billion, while the TWDC claimed that £250 million had been committed by the private sector in its first two years of operation. An important source of revenue for the UDCs has also been land sales, and prior to the property crash in 1989, the UDCs, especially the LDDC, were making significant profits on land purchase and sales deals. For instance, land sales by the LDDC raised £10 million in 1985–86, rising to £115 million in 1988–89. However, since 1989, sales have fallen dramatically and many UDCs have incurred debts on land purchase deals. For example, CBDC only generated £84,000 from land sales in 1989–90 while spending £1 million on land reclamation and £16.8 million on land acquisition. As Table 1.5 shows, many of the UDCs are incurring liabilities at a time of falling land values, while committed to capital projects with few capital receipts to offset their costs.

CLES (1990b) notes that the implications for many UDCs are serious and, as Table 1.5 illustrates, while the TWDC, for example, spent £16 million on land purchase in 1988–89, the value of its sales over the same period was only £2 million. It was not alone in facing this predicament. A recent analysis of government answers to questions posed in the House of Commons shows six of the UDCs losing out on land purchases and sales since their creation. For instance, the Black Country, which received £46.2 million in grant aid for 1991–92, shows a loss on property deals, based on March 1992 values, of £26.5 million. In 1991, Bristol, Central Manchester, Leeds, Trafford Park, and Tyne and Wear, received grants of, respectively, £19.1 million, £16 million, £13.6 million, £28.1 million, and £40.5 million, yet their losses on land transactions were, respectively, £12.9 million, £8.3 million, £3.4 million, £10 million, and £6.3 million.

Table 1.5   Selected UDCs' losses on land deals

UDC	Amount spent on land transactions (£ millions)	Amount received from land transactions (£ millions)	Value of land 31 March 1992 (£ millions)	Loss (£ millions)
BCDC	68.0	3.7	38.8	26.5
BDC	24.4	nil	11.5	12.9
CMDC	12.3	nil	4.0	8.3
LDC	17.5	1.8	12.3	3.4
TPDC	41.6	9.3	22.3	10.0
TWDC	42.4	5.8	30.3	6.3

Source: *Independent* 13 July 1992.

The limitations of the UDCs general approach has intensified the fiscal pressures on their expenditure programmes. The collapse in property markets meant that by 1991 UDCs became even more dependent on government grants and public sector schemes to ensure that the momentum of regeneration was maintained (CLES, 1992). By the early 1990s, the UDCs were unable to dispose of land they had bought during the boom period of the mid- to late 1980s, and the underlying ethos of the UDCs, rapid development, was under severe threat. Indeed, as CLES (1992) has documented, a number of flagship projects were delayed and suspended, budgets and corporate plans were revised, while the collapse of Olympia and York in London Docklands stands as a symbol to the vicissitudes of property-based regeneration. As Wynn Davies (1992) has noted, these revaluations could speed the demise of some of the existing UDCs, particularly those which have already been told to devise 'exit strategies', though the recent designation of new UDCs suggests that the Conservative government is far from disillusioned with the concept.

There is also a clear recognition that progress can be easier with the cooperation of local actors, agencies and the wider range of community interests. This conclusion was reached by the LDDC after eight years of protracted conflict with the local authorities, though, as Brownill points out in Chapter 3, the increased sensitivity to community and local authority interests was born of expediency, not altruism, and was reversed when political conditions changed. In addition, the London experience of almost total exclusion of local authorities from the regeneration process seems to have cautioned most local authorities against too critical a stance in relation to UDCs in their areas. As a result, the House of Commons Employment Committee (1988) reported that the newer UDCs had 'the full cooperation of the local authorities'.

Indeed, since the first phase designations, subsequent UDCs have developed a softer, more conciliatory, approach to local consultation by devising closer links with a range of community and local organizations. The second wave of UDCs coincided with a reappraisal of the nature of UDC strategy and policy with a number of influential bodies criticizing their focus purely on physical regeneration. In 1988, for instance, the House of Commons Public Accounts Committee, while acknowledging the physical achievements of the LDDC, noted that 'UDCs should seek from the start to strike a reasonable balance between the physical development of their areas, and the social and other needs of those living there'. Echoing this, the House of Commons Employment Committee concluded that the UDCs should adopt a more precise definition of regeneration, including employment and unemployment objectives. The Committee noted that UDCs 'should be charged with greater responsibility for ensuring that communities directly affected by them, and in their neighbouring areas, benefited from regeneration'. It was concluded that, 'UDCs cannot be regarded as a success if buildings and land are regenerated but the local community are bypassed and do not benefit from regeneration'.

These comments reflected an amalgam of community and political pressures on the UDC programmes to widen their scope, yet, only in very few of the UDCs did community and social issues feature as an integral component of their strategies at the outset (CLES, 1990a,b). For instance, the Black Country, Tyne and Wear, Sheffield and Central Manchester UDCs, all appointed community liaison officers, while Tyne and Wear appeared to be one of the more progressive in preparing a Community Development Strategy while recognizing the need to obtain community gain from the property developers. As Robinson and Shaw (1991) note, the more sensitive second and third generation UDCs have undoubtedly paid 'lip service' to the community, while falling far short of a genuine democratization of urban policy.

This criticism reflects a wide range of negative opinions which have been held of the UDCs since their inception. Indeed, the UDCs have been criticized by all sides of the political spectrum, by the left for circumventing local democracy and asserting the primacy of market goals over social and community objectives, and by the right for running projects and programmes seen as 'wasteful expenditure', replicating much of the bureaucracy they were supposedly put in place to overturn. Indeed, one of the main concerns has been job creation, yet reviews of the UDCs suggest that their strategies have been less than successful in translating investment into jobs (National Audit Office (NAO), 1988). As the NAO (1988) commented, on the Merseyside DC, 'their job creation programmes have only had marginal impact' (p. 4), yet, as one Chief Executive of a UDC has argued, 'we were not given a brief to create employment'. Indeed, the DOE have reinforced this view, most recently to the House of Commons Select Committee in 1988, in that, 'we do not see UDCs as being primarily or immediately concerned with employment; they are about regeneration, and indeed the physical regeneration of their areas'.

Yet, even in physical terms, the success of the UDCs has been questioned, and many consider that what has been built in the UDAs would have been constructed anyway; that the designation of the UDCs has made only marginal difference to the investment climate (Turok, 1991). While this is a contestable statement, the property crash since 1989 has fuelled political debate concerning the status of property-led regeneration, and, as CLES (1990a,b) indicates, the majority of UDCs have been slow to show any results. The property-led approach of the UDCs has also led to the charge that there is a lack of concern for the strategic implications of UDC activity (Imrie and Thomas, 1992). CLES (1990b) argues that, in spite of UDC rhetoric about strategy, the view of local authorities is that UDC policies and programmes are not strategic in looking at city or community-wide implications. A concern for a comprehensive strategy within its boundaries – as in the case of CBDC – does not imply a great concern for implications outside the boundaries (though, in CBDC's case, it has been put under pressure to jointly fund studies on the implications of its policies for public transport links to the city centre, and city centre retailing).

All of this suggests that the seemingly 'single-mindedness' of the UDCs, much lauded by Heseltine in 1979, has failed to deliver the expected returns. Indeed, it was this single-minded approach, the evasion of local government bureaucracy, which was held up as the key to UDC success. Yet, one of the ironies of the whole programme are the bureaucratic and legal ties on UDC operations emanating from central government, and, as the following chapters will show, UDCs are far from the *laissez-faire*, debureaucratized organizations that they were purported to be under the 1980 Act. For instance, DOE guidelines prevent UDCs from making payments in excess of £1,000 without prior government consent. Moreover, all land purchases by the UDCs must gain prior approval by central government, and, as CBDC have commented, 'while we want to buy up land at the market rates central government won't let us . . . they want it on the cheap' (Imrie, 1993).

This paradox is hardly reflected in writings on the UDCs, while academic literature still has a tendency to characterize them as institutions 'standing outside' of their localities, autonomous islands of development, with few, if any, institutional linkages with local politicians and community groups. But, as CLES (1990b), and others, indicate, a wide range of institutional linkages characterize UDC–local authority relations, from joint forums, projects, and budgets, to a wide range of informal meetings at member and officer level (CLES, 1990b, p. 29). These linkages suggest, that while UDCs share a range of similar powers, their actual practices, strategies and approaches to regeneration may well vary considerably. Some of the more obvious continuities and differences in the successive generations of the UDCs have been discussed by Stoker (1989). In particular, Stoker notes how the second generation has been less conflict-ridden than the first, partly because of the transformed political climate of the mid- to late 1980s where pragmatism, or what Stoker refers to as a 'watchful cooperation', became a defining feature of UDC–local authority relationships.

Moreover, contrasts between the different styles and policies of each of the UDCs is illuminating in highlighting the diverse approaches underpinning strategies of property-based regeneration. While many accounts portray the UDCs as invariant institutions, Stoker (1989, 1991) and others note how the specificity of local politics and the diverse material conditions in the designated areas have led to significant contrasts in the strategies and policies of the UDCs. For instance, in the field of equal opportunities, SDC is unique in monitoring the ethnic background of applicants who submit planning applications, largely because of the agency agreement it has with the city council in relation to development control. Moreover, BDC has signed a 'Concordat' with the city's Race Equality Council on the necessity to secure gains for black and ethnic minorities in the city, while the CBDC operates training initiatives and work schemes for locally unemployed people. In Chapter 9, Oatley casts doubt on the value of the Bristol Concordat, but concedes that the BDC has had to make some moves to forge links with local groups and agencies.

Indeed, the range of institutional networks, between the UDCs and local actors and agencies, are much greater than is supposed, while it is increasingly clear that the property-led objectives of the UDCs do not remain unaffected by alternative, competing policy goals which emanate from local sources (Clavel and Kleniewski, 1990). This is certainly one of the observations by CLES (1990b), yet there is still an issue of how far, and in what ways, a pluralist policy system is able to emerge and operate under conditions largely set by the central state, an issue which the contributors to this book address in some detail.

Urban Policy, Locality, and the UDCs

Despite the considerable volume of academic research and reporting on the UDCs, relatively few attempts have been made to document and assess the range of UDC policies and practices. The UDCs have been submerged under stereotypical conceptions which variously portray them as 'executives' of the central state, 'puppets' for global corporate capital, and mechanisms for overriding local democratic institutions. Yet, as the chapters in this book will go some way to illustrating, no single UDC rigidly conforms to the contours outlined above, while it is clear that there are significant variations in their modes of operation. In particular, it is increasingly clear that there is imperfect understanding of the localized development and delivery of national urban policy, or of how its wider development objectives are sustained, modified, or contradicted, by local sociopolitical milieux.

Thus, the starting point, common to all contributors, is the likelihood of significant variation in the delivery and implementation of urban policy, its unevenness, whatever the stated objectives of national government. In particular, this perspective, a need to acknowledge contingent relations, layers of local, or sub-national, political and institutional autonomy, also seemed self evident given the very different socio-economic and political histories of the UDC localities, legacies which have been fundamental in shaping the precise configuration of (local) policy content and implementation. In making the commitment towards a more sophisticated view of the UDCs, the contributions in this book signal a discontent with policy studies literature which takes agencies and institutions out of the analysis, while reading off urban development as, in particular, a part of a uniform (economic) global logic. The totalizing nature of such conceptions tends to ignore the general point that all social phenomena have causal powers at whatever spatial scale they are identifiable. Indeed, the UDC initiative, far from emasculating local political autonomy and responsibility, has been part of a wider process of institutional changes which have redefined the roles of local authorities inside the state.

Yet, there are a number of senses in which the themes of the book also go beyond the local in discussing some of the major structural influences on the content and scope of local actions. Echoing Logan and Swanstrom (1990), any contextual understanding of the UDCs, and urban policy as a whole, necessitates some discussion of how local actions are fashioned by wider structural opportunities and constraints. In particular, the book identifies a number of powerful structural forces which influence the content of contemporary urban policy. Foremost is the embeddedness of cities in central state structures which clearly define the limits of local government autonomy, and the policies of the central state are a major player in the content of local policy formation and implementation. In particular, the poll tax fiasco highlighted the authoritarian centralism of the British state, while legislation, like the 1989 Local Government and Housing Act, has only served to dilute once taken-for-granted local government powers.

Moreover, Sassen (1991) and others stress the importance of international, global, economic and political forces in determining the trajectory of urban development. Indeed, the globalization of financial services, coupled with new technological capabilities, has only served to speed up flows of capital into, and out of, the world's cities. As Amin and Robins (1991) note, if we are to consider 'that this global arena is shaped and informed by formidable relations of power, then the scope for local autonomy becomes considerably narrow' (p. 28). However, the book also tries to challenge the idea of a purely economic imperative underpinning strategies of UDC policy. While conservative ideologues call for increased competition between cities, adapting to the imperatives of economic restructuring and the market, the contributions in this book echo Logan and Swanstrom (1990) in questioning the view that there is a market logic to capitalism to which urban policy (including the UDCs) at all levels must submit. In this, we concur with Walton (1990b) who notes that both neo-liberal and neo-conservative theory have produced erroneous theoretical accounts of urban change, comprising a reification of markets or structures, a neglect of agency, and a failure to recognize or explain variation in the patterns of urban policy and performance, whilst, simultaneously, legitimizing growth policies over social redistributive, or welfare, goals.

In developing some of these conceptual points, the original remit of the book was the concern with the delivery, development, and implementation, of UDC strategies and policies. In particular, we collectively identified three significant issues which have provided the focal points for the case study chapters in Part Two of the book:

(1) How do UDCs develop and formulate policies and programmes in relation to the opportunities and constraints of their locales? UDCs are not passive institutions that impose solutions or remain unaffected by their localized operational environment. Much of the theoretical literature is increasingly sensitive to how external pressures are mediated by individual agents (Goodwin, 1991). More recently, Healey and Barrett (1990) have identified the need to give more attention to the way individual firms and agents interrelate in the negotiations of particular development projects and how, through these transactions, land and property markets are constituted and built environments made. In particular, the renewal of many UDAs rejects a commonly held view that UDCs seek, as a deliberate aim of policy, to exclude both local government and local interests from its legitimate functions. Such crude instrumentalism is questioned by the range of chapters in this volume which reveal the development of a more flexible approach towards policy formulation and delivery, one which is encouraging pro-active inter-agency involvement. This reveals the limitations of theoretical positions which exclude the possibilities of 'local modifications' of national urban policy (Healey and Barrett, 1990).

(2) What is the nature, extent, and influence of institutional innovation, interaction, and collaboration, between the UDCs and local participants in development? The actions of UDCs represent the implementation of a strand of modified national urban policy. The factors which are influencing its impact undoubtedly include the local institutional milieux, local political systems, and the interactions between local and national actors. In this sense, the evolving strategy is a 'hybrid', or amalgam of interests, characterized by new institutional forms and relations to those which traditionally deliver and formulate urban policy. This perspective contrasts with those who present the UDCs as institutions which remain largely unaffected by their local operating contexts, almost, at will, able to impose national policy guidelines and strategies. Yet, as the chapters in this book document, many of the UDCs are actively involved in complex inter-institutional relations at the local level, depicting a breakdown in some of the real barriers of (perceived) prejudice between the private, public, and voluntary sectors.

(3) Transferable practices and learning: the development of 'best practice' urban policy. One of the undercurrent themes of the book's chapters is the

sustainability of the UDCs in their present form, and the likelihood of the continued primacy of property-led urban regeneration. Clearly the two are interlinked although evidence from a range of UDC localities suggests that very few UDCs solely pursue a 'bricks and building' approach to urban policy. However, City Challenge, the collapse in property markets, and the increasing costs of UDC infrastructure, and other programmes, suggest a wider, political, dissatisfaction with the approach and a recognition, even tacit government acknowledgement, of its structural limitations. As Part Three of this book suggests, the transferability of the practices of UDCs is hardly an issue at this time.

Coulson opens in Chapter 2 by considering the role and significance of non-elected local government in urban regeneration. In particular, he develops the idea that the UDCs are increasingly involved in a form of urban governance which is characterized by political patronage. If this thesis is accurate, of course, then one implication could well be that UDCs become more integrated into local institutional networks: patronage is a relationship which involves the building-up of expectations and links on both sides. In particular, Coulson recognizes the case for dedicated local bodies, with specialized expertise, which can act quickly and commercially, and which are not necessarily held back by entrenched local opinion. This is a moot point because it raises the wider issue of the probable incompatibility between democracy and capitalism and/or free markets, a notion underpinning the UDCs. And, if we accept the general incompatibility thesis, then the case for UDCs might not seem so problematical.

Part Two of the book comprises eight studies of the policies, programmes, and operations of the British UDCs. Taken together, they provide a fascinating account of the implementation, to date, of this major part of urban policy. In Chapter 3, Brownill considers the significance of the regeneration of London Docklands as a politically contested area, by detailing how and why the LDDC modified its strategies and policies in the light of a variety of (local) socio-political, and community, pressures. Meegan's account of the Merseyside DC in Chapter 4 questions the rationale of the UDCs in pressurizing localities to go down the route of urban entrepreneurialism, or a form of inter-urban or regional competition characterized by an abandonment of the traditional economic and cultural roots of the cities. As Meegan notes, it is difficult to see how cities like Liverpool can revive themselves by utilizing introspective, self-referential strategies, ones which create an illusion that the city is able to control its own economic and political destinies.

In Chapter 5, Thomas and Imrie show how Cardiff Bay DC gained local political and community acceptance by its incorporation into a pre-existing political consensus revolving around the idea of modernization. By grafting itself into the locale, extending and reworking many of the widely held, and local, convictions concerning spatial development, CBDC has diffused much opposition while assuming a powerful role in determining the spatial trajectory of the city. In contrast, Byrne, in Chapter 6, develops the theme of how the material, cultural, and symbolic significances of places are being overturned by the seemingly crude, instrumentalist policies and approaches of the UDCs. In the case of the Tyne and Wear DC, Byrne compares it with a form of 'colonial administration', an organization wholly inappropriate to the task of maintaining the industrial and maritime heritage of the locality. Here, apparently, is an analysis which sees little evidence of the Development Corporation embedding itself into its locality. Nevin, in Chapter 7, provides a pessimistic picture of the Black Country DC, noting that a myopic concentration of resources on the UDA, as if it were an independent, autonomous, spatial unit, has created a mechanism for a transfer of dereliction within the conurbation.

Dabinett and Ramsden, in Chapter 8, provide an evaluative framework of the Sheffield DC, lamenting the general absence of 'people-centred' planning. They extend their analysis in prescribing an urban policy, in a new 'Europe of Regions', that should resist strong mayors or concepts of city regions, but, instead, ensure a networking of community groups with common objectives and problems. These, according to Dabinett and Ramsden, should include four ingredients for coherent city revitalization: the strengthening of local participative democracy; placing distributive issues on the political agenda; an end to a property-led urban policy; and the drawing up of a 'quality of life' agenda. In Chapter 9 Oatley outlines the case of the Bristol DC, developing the argument that its designation was always an inappropriate response to the social and economic problems of the city, not the least of which was in undermining the entrepreneurial activities of the City Council in advancing city-wide commercial developments. As Oatley notes, Bristol appeared to receive a UDC less for reasons of economic and social regeneration, but more to advance central government's political and ideological thinking. In contrast, Roberts and Whitney's account of urban policy in Leeds (Chapter 10) indicates that a crucial contribution made by the local UDC was in galvanizing the City Council in resurrecting its almost moribund development company, and in constructing a leadership forum for partnerships in the city. In particular, Roberts and Whitney's account shows how the Leeds DC has defined a niche for its activities by operating within a predefined policy context, slotting into an already existing local corporatism in the city.

All the studies in Part Two of the book portray the UDCs as having to recognize, to some degree or another, the socio-economic, political and institutional context within which they have found themselves, though the extent to which there is an accommodation varies considerably. The Bristol experience, as described by Oatley, might tempt one to generalize that sensitivity (or lack of it) is, to quite an extent, a result of the history of the UDC. If there was strong local authority and/or community resistance and resentment (as in London and Bristol) then it might be portrayed as natural that the UDC keep its distance from the locality. However, the Cardiff Bay and, perhaps, the Tyne and Wear experience (to cite only two) suggest otherwise. For instance, in Cardiff, where the County Council invited the setting-up of a UDC, it is nevertheless generally perceived (and not unreasonably) as somewhat aloof from the local community, whereas in Tyne and Wear where there was no great desire for a UDC, Byrne suggests a complex relationship, with at least some degree of common ground at times between Newcastle City Council and the development corporation.

As Brownill points out, in her chapter on London Docklands, relationships vary over time, and her account is valuable in sketching how both local and extra-local forces and circumstances can affect relationships. In London, early bullishness about development prospects seems to have been a major factor in underpinning the brash line of the LDDC; we could surmise that, in general, local property market conditions are an important determinant of the extent to which UDCs, as property-led regeneration agencies, are prepared to consider the sensitive task of building up meaningful local relationships. Thus, for example, in Cardiff, a promising property market in the late 1980s seems to have encouraged the view that CBDC did not need local alliances, a point we develop in Chapter 5. Moreover, local pressure, from councils, community groups and business associations has also encouraged, or forced, some development corporations into more or less significant attempts to sensitize policies to local circumstances. Some of these, such as BDC's Concordat with the Bristol Race Equality Council, are dismissed as tokenistic, but there is evidence of some significant initiatives in addressing local employment difficulties (see the Cardiff case, Chapter 5).

There is also evidence (e.g. Tyne and Wear DC) of a ruthless ability to ignore representations by local interests (both business and community) which appear to be incompatible with the trajectory of the area desired by the development corporations (Imrie and Thomas, 1992). Moreover, community/social expenditure will always be marginal within development corporations' budgets and it seems that the depression in the development industry (with its knock-on effects on corporations' incomes) will force the UDCs to reappraise the necessity of such expenditure. We surmise that they may follow a policy of selectively developing relationships with local institutions/bodies which can assist in their primary task of facilitating development with only tokenistic expenditures targeted at disadvantaged communities within their areas.

The variety in the nature and extent of relationships with other agencies, which UDCs have already developed, is a striking feature of the case studies which follow. In neither Leeds, Sheffield, or Bristol, was a development corporation sought, yet in Leeds the UDC has been absorbed into an inter-agency network which is a model of cooperation. In contrast, the BDC stands alienated from the local authorities, while in Sheffield a *modus vivendi* has been established between the UDC and a local council increasingly focusing on flagship projects. In Newcastle, TWDC has supported the Newcastle Initiative, yet, in Cardiff, joint 'place-marketing' has been strictly limited in scope as the County Council and UDC look after their own interests. All of this suggests that local political cultures and circumstances may well be significant in explaining some of the variations. For instance, local corporatism was already an established feature of Leeds, pre-UDC, and has undoubtedly underpinned LDC's incorporation into the political culture of the city.

In contrast, the long-standing interest of the Welsh Office in Cardiff's development seems to have resulted in the creation of a corporation closely monitored by central government. In Liverpool, by way of contrast, the political control of the City Council by Militant sympathizers was such that the MDC could do little in the way of finding common ground, even if it had wished to do so. However, as Meegan makes clear, the corporation still followed broad policy objectives and analyses enshrined in established structure plans. Meegan points out that, in part, this reflected the fact that

MDC's workforce contained many refugees from the abolished Metropolitan County. This is very different from Cardiff where local professionals have been noticeably absent from the CBDC's payroll.

In Part Three of the book, the chapters reflect on UDC policies and programmes and examine the transferability of their approaches and the likelihood of their survival as an element of future urban policy. In Chapter 11, Colenutt questions the longevity of the UDCs by talking about a new policy culture for the 1990s, one in which the UDCs are 'out' and partnerships are 'in'. In particular, Colenutt highlights the references by UDCs to 'community involvement' and even the LDDC are providing a community line in recognizing that 'lasting regeneration will only be achieved by improving the quality of life for everyone who lives and works in Docklands' (LDDC, 1989b, p. 4). Yet, while central government is now espousing a softer line on 'community involvement' in urban policy, Colenutt argues that it remains akin to American-style growth coalitions, bringing together partnerships which solely comprise development elites. In this sense, Colenutt is pessimistic about the future of local authority involvement in urban regeneration, predicting their retention of a facilitative role but with little or no control over the regeneration process.

In the concluding chapter, Burton and O'Toole examine the continuities and discontinuities in current urban policy, questioning how the role of the UDCs has changed over time. In particular, most of the authors in the volume concur with Burton and O'Toole in seeing fatal flaws in a property-led regeneration strategy of the kind pursued by the UDCs. For instance, the dependence of UDCs on a cyclical, sometimes volatile, property market is seen as a strait-jacket within which options for improving the social welfare of existing residents within or close to UDAs are inevitably limited. Indeed, as the cases show, without any property market the whole approach is redundant. Moreover, the intense insularity of the kind of competitive place-marketing which is characteristic of UDC operations is considered wasteful, often inappropriate, a hit and miss approach. Meegan, Byrne, and Brownill, sketch alternative strategies for the areas they write about, all of which depend upon sensitive analyses of the role, current and potential, of that place, and its industries and people, in national and international networks and markets. Finally, most of the case studies echo reservations made by a number of commentators about the lack of effective democratic accountability of the UDCs. Nowhere are the councillors on the Boards of UDCs seen as significant mechanisms for ensuring a democratic input into its activities. A few corporations have moved towards open meetings (e.g. LDC, LDDC) but the overall judgement remains a caustic one. Overall, the transferability of the practices, policies and values of the UDCs to the wider broadcloth of urban policy is seen by the contributors as neither possible, probable nor desirable.

2

URBAN DEVELOPMENT CORPORATIONS, LOCAL AUTHORITIES AND PATRONAGE IN URBAN POLICY

Andrew Coulson

Introduction

Gerry Stoker's textbook *The Politics of Local Government* (1991) gave prominence to 'non-elected local government':[1]

> *The range and depth of the interventions undertaken by the organisations of non-elected local government make it plain that if we are to fully understand the world of local government politics we cannot neglect these non-elected bodies. . . . Local authorities have increasingly had to work through, alongside, or in consultation with a range of non-elected organisations.*
>
> (1991, p. 87)

This chapter is an explanation and development of this theme, with particular reference to Urban Development Corporations (UDCs). It starts by defining non-elected local government, and its importance in British urban policy in the 1980s.[2] UDCs are examples of non-elected local government. In order to understand why they developed as they did, three themes are identified that characterized urban policy at the start of the 1980s: a commitment to free enterprise and away from land-use planning; corporatism or partnership with local authorities and the private sector; and, patronage whereby central government exerts its influence through the arbitrary dispensation of resources. By the end of the 1980s policies based on patronage were in the ascendant.

By the 1990s the limitations of the UDC model had also become apparent, and, as outlined in Chapter 1, the government was looking for ways of limiting its financial commitments to UDCs. In the meantime, a new form, the City Challenge Company, with yet more explicit use of patronage, but also partnership between government, private business and local authorities, was becoming one of the more prominent institutional responses to multiple deprivation on inner city estates.[3]

But, staying with UDCs, this chapter examines their relationships with local authorities, another patron–client relationship, since the UDCs had money and the local authorities plenty of ideas as to how it could be spent.

Non-elected Local Government

One only has to follow Stoker (1991) and list some of the main institutions of non-elected local administration to realize how prevalent and significant they are. Non-elected local administration may be defined as publicly funded administration with local discretion exercised by individuals or groups of individuals (e.g. boards of directors) appointed by central government. It does not refer to the private sector, or independent non-statutory (or 'voluntary') agencies, even though these may be funded by central or local government. There must be local discretion, or else it is no more than part of central administration.

But those who exercise the (decentralized) power are appointed by central government, which thereby exercises indirect control. There are some grey areas: governing councils of polytechnics, universities, institutes of higher education, boards of governors of opted-out schools (elected by those parents who happen to have children in the school at that time but funded by central government); police and fire joint boards in metropolitan counties (indirectly elected – i.e. comprising councillors from several districts, plus magistrates in the case of the police joint boards but in practice dominated by Home Office circulars and policy).

A dramatic illustration of the use of non-elected local administration – only a glint in the government's eye when Stoker wrote his first edition – is provided by the 82 Training and Enterprise Councils (TECs) in England and Wales and 22 Local Enterprise Companies (LECs) in Scotland which have taken responsibility for the programmes of vocational training and enterprise support previously run by the Training Agency (and before that by the Manpower Services Commission, (MSC)), spending some £3 million of government money annually. These were created, at central government instigation, by groups of private sector chief executives who proposed their own boundaries. The boundaries, and individual board members, had to be approved by central government before expenditure could be authorized.

Non-elected local administration is, of course, nothing new in Britain. It can be traced back to the poor law commissioners, justices of the peace, and boards responsible for schools, drainage, roads and many other functions in nineteenth-century cities. The majority (but not all) of these were taken under local government control during its 'heyday' around the turn of the century, once a system of local government had been established whereby central government set down the rules, so that local councils could only do what they were permitted under central government legislation.

But, by the Second World War, central government had already taken back direct control of 'national assistance' (i.e. unemployment benefit), and of electricity. After the War, local authorities were given two major tasks, of implementing a national system of education under the 1944 Education Act, and of providing housing to replace war-damaged and slum housing. However, in both education ('a national service locally administered') and housing, central government had great influence: it is no coincidence that tower blocks and systems building were adopted by the majority of urban local authorities in the 1960s (in the process creating the worst housing problems of the 1990s) (Dunleavy, 1981). Other responsibilities were deliberately kept out of local government hands. The most important was the National Health Service, where the budget was controlled nationally, and administration carried out by regional, area and district health authorities.

Another example was the New Town Development Corporations, of which there were eventually 17 in England. They were run by non-elected boards precisely because the elected local authorities in the counties and market towns where they were established would not have welcomed, nor been equipped to handle, large influxes of urban population. In England nine regional water authorities were, according to Holland and Fallon (1978, p. 11) 'designed deliberately by central government as a means of avoiding local government control'. It is a paradox that Conservative governments, which in 1979 were committed to reducing the number and increasing the power of non-elected quangos, should instead have built on the precedents of earlier years and made ever-increasing use of them at the local level.

Non-elected local government has always been controversial, for obvious reasons. Elected local authorities lose powers. There is a tendency for boards of directors to act arbitrarily, and to regard consultation as a luxury. They may 'go native' and lose the confidence of their paymasters – without necessarily gaining that of local people. There is a risk of wasteful duplication of services. There are also issues presented by any boundary within which investment has privileges – the boundary is inevitably perceived to be unfair by those just outside it, and it encourages uneconomic behaviour, e.g. moving inside the boundary simply to gain the benefit of incentives.

On the other hand, arm's-length bodies, with an active chief executive or Chair, may be able to gain the confidence of the private sector in a way that is not possible for local authorities. They may also enter into joint ventures in ways that local authorities would find much more difficult. There is no way in which it can be proven that an arm's-length body can do things that could not be done without it (because others will always claim that they could have done what the arm's-length body has done), but circumstantial evidence does suggest that dedicated arm's-length bodies do provide effective means of getting things done.

It would be instructive to compare elected and non-elected local government in expenditure terms. Stoker did not attempt this and it has not been possible to do so in this chapter. There are some obvious problems of definition. But in order of magnitude they are probably similar – with non-elected local government possibly spending more than local government if primary and secondary education is removed from the latter.

Three Approaches to Urban Policy

The government's urban policies of the 1980s were founded on three contrasting philosophies or approaches:[4]

(a) non-interventionalist free enterprise policies that denied or minimized the role of the public sector. Enterprise zones, freeports, and simplified planning zones are obvious examples; also, the abandonment of the regional planning councils and the end of non-discretionary regional investment grants.

(b)   policies based on partnership or corporatism, such as the Urban Programme (partnerships between local and central government) and the schemes of the MSC (tripartite between employers, trades unions and educational interests in both the Commission and its Area Manpower Boards).

(c)   a patronage model where central government resources are channelled to local intermediaries in return for policy initiatives. Most non-elected local government is of this form. New town development corporations, UDCs, urban development grant (now city grant) and TECs are relevant. The recent City Challenge competition (decided personally by ministers) and proposals to allocate Housing Investment Programmes on a similar basis take the principle a step further.

There was an element of confusion (or, with hindsight, overkill) between UDCs and Enterprise Zones. Parts of four UDCs were also designated as Enterprise Zones. Thus the Isle of Dogs, an important part of the London Docklands UDA, became an Enterprise Zone in 1981. Many of the problems relating to Canary Wharf, and, in particular, the failure to coordinate transport infrastructure with office developments, were in part a consequence of this (Brownill, 1990, pp. 133–45; Docklands Consultative Committee, 1992). Most of the office developments in the Trafford Park UDA (as well as Salford Quays just outside), the Newcastle Business Park, and smaller commercial developments in Middlesbrough have taken off in parts of the UDAs which were also in the enterprise zones.

By the 1990s, the government's pure free enterprise policies had largely been discredited. Enterprise Zones were seen to have failed economically, with cost per job created exceeding £30,000 (PA Cambridge Economic Consultants, 1987). They had also failed precisely because of a lack of planning – most publicly in the case of Canary Wharf and other projects in the Isle of Dogs which were constructed without transport infrastructure that could cope with the large numbers of people involved. Other Enterprise Zones, such as Dudley and Gateshead, had become locations for huge out-of-town shopping centres and office complexes which benefited from Enterprise Zone tax concessions.[5]

The corporatist policies had become victims of the government's distrust of trade unions and local authorities. Thus while the MSC was allowed to expand rapidly to provide a response to youth and adult unemployment in the slump of 1981–86, its end was signalled during the 1987 election campaign, and eventually it was replaced by the 82 TECs in which local authority influence was minimized and trade unions excluded altogether. The Urban Programme was allowed to wither on the vine – with resources held roughly constant in cash terms but declining in real terms. Urban Development Grant, with local authority involvement, was replaced by City Grant, negotiated directly by the government with private developers.

Patronage was flavour of the day, whether in land and property oriented programmes such as UDCs or City Grant, or in training (through the TECs and colleges removed from local authority control, or schools that opted out). City Challenge was patronage on a grand scale, in that the choice of receiving areas was based on 'beauty contests' with winners and losers selected by ministers. But it also involved local authorities as partners and hence recipients of patronage.

We may conclude that by the early 1990s the Conservative government had resolved to use its national democratic mandate to ensure that policies were implemented locally in accordance with its priorities; that this was achieved by use of discretionary spending, i.e. patronage; that the private sector was to be involved in partnership arrangements, not just left to its own devices; and that increasingly local government was drawn into patronage arrangement, e.g. through City Challenge.

UDCs, the lead institution in the second half of the 1980s, had, by this time, been left behind. Docklands was becoming an embarrassment, overtly so when Canary Wharf went into receivership in July 1992. There had been relatively little progress on other flagship sites, such as the site of the 1983 Liverpool Garden Festival, Trafford Park 'village', the Cardiff Bay barrage, East Quayside or Royal Quays in Tyneside, or Patent Shaft in the Black Country. The costs of road building and derelict land clearance in UDAs were in danger of escalating out of control. DOE ministers had started talking of 'exit' and in July 1992 hinted that UDCs should give up 'developed' parts of the areas and hand over projects and sites to local authorities.

Before proceeding to specific considerations of UDCs, we need to draw out a little more of what is involved in patronage, or patron–client, relationships. This is the purpose of the next section of this chapter.

Patron–Client Relationships

In ancient Rome freed slaves had little alternative but to attach themselves to a strong 'patron', who offered protection in exchange for services. Anthropologists and historians (see for example Runciman, 1989, p. 200) explored the resulting relationships; the clients generally acting in a subservient fashion, but with a degree of freedom and independence, and in the last resort the right to leave the patron; and the patron liable to be presumptuous and arrogant, but losing the clients if they were too much taken for granted. Similar relationships have been studied by anthropologists in many tribal societies (e.g. Clapham, 1982; Eisenstadt and Lemarchand, 1981, which also includes a bibliography; Gellner and Waterman, 1977). It became clear that the relationships were often complex, and clients not as subservient as appeared superficially.

The ideas were applied to local government in inter-war Chicago, where powerful bosses dispensed favours to selected clients who depended on them for employment or contracts. It has been used as a tool to understand politics in Italy (Caciagli and Belloni (in Eisenstadt and Lemarchand, 1981)) and the USA (Toinet and Glenn (in Clapham, 1982)). But writers on contemporary British local government have hesitated to use this analysis.[6]

The essence of a patron–client relationship is that the patron holds power – in the form of resources, money, protection (through control of arms, the police, etc.) which can be used in an arbitrary, unaccountable way. The client needs these resources (money, protection, etc.) and manoeuvres to get them, by flattering the patron, promising to do what the patron wants, and demonstrating loyalty in practice whenever required. But the resulting politics is more complex than it seems. The patron is too busy to supervise all clients – and so some become favourites entrusted with special responsibilities. Meanwhile the clients will do as little as they can for the patron. So by no means all that is promised is fulfilled. The relationship is potentially fraught and dishonest, backed by power in the last resort and largely or wholly outside a legal framework where either party if aggrieved can seek redress through independent arbitration or courts.

The relationship between central government and a UDC fits this pattern. Central government had the power through its control of taxes and the opportunity to legislate in Parliament. The UDC board has a nominal independence, but in practice must perform in line with what the government wants. Yet the relationship may not be smooth. In order to justify establishment of the UDC, ambitious claims will have been made about what is possible, and these may become difficult to achieve (especially in the depths of a recession). Costs increase (or are greatly underestimated) and so UDCs may become seen as voracious users of capital. The client may use its autonomy and 'go native' – i.e. enter into agreements and contracts that go beyond the patron's approval (as clearly happened in Docklands during the early days). In this case the patron may intervene and take more and more of the power directly – for example, placing experienced civil servants in key positions. In the last resort the patron may live off the client or some clients, and want to be out of the relationship as quickly as possible. It may, however, not be so easy to disengage, as the client may have the power to expose the patron, or just to stop work, leaving messy unfinished business open to public scrutiny.

The relationships between UDCs and local authorities may be studied in a similar framework. Then the UDC becomes the patron, with the resources. The local authority is the client with the ability to develop and implement projects, if finance is available. So the local authority adopts a collaborative, partnership relationship with the UDC in its areas, seeking in this way to get the UDC to implement projects it has conceived. This may fail if the resources are small, or not wanted, as in the case of Bristol, where the council had no strong commitment to any of the flagship projects of the UDC, or Royal Quays in North Tyneside where the Tyne and Wear Development Corporation's (TWDC) proposals are fundamentally at odds with the Council's; or if the UDC decides not to implement major projects in the area (e.g. Middlesbrough as compared with Stockton or Hartlepool); or if the UDC is unable to deliver major projects, such as the Black Country Spine Road or development of the Royal Docks in the east of London Docklands.

It is instructive to use this framework to compare UDCs with City Challenge. City Challenge is more overt patronage, as the decisions over which bids to fund are taken by ministers following presentations ('beauty contests') by local authorities. The criteria for rewarding some bids but not others are inevitably subjective. However, it becomes clear that the patron (the government) has certain requirements which score very highly – for example preparedness to demolish tower blocks and systems-built housing and to replace them with some other tenure – usually housing association – involving higher rent. There are tendencies to produce glossy proposals, to minimize difficulties or negative aspects of proposals, and (no doubt) to overestimate private sector commitments, underestimate costs, and to exaggerate what can be achieved in a short time. A major difference is that City Challenge boundaries include large populations whereas most UDA boundaries largely excluded resident populations. Thus consultations and tenants'/residents' involvement is central to City Challenge. If the programmes fail, or throw up significant dissatisfactions, there will be a much higher political price to pay than for UDCs.

Local Government Responses to UDCs

The local authorities in London Docklands and Merseyside, where the first UDCs were created, did not welcome them. The new bodies took away their sites and opportunities for development, as well as their town-planning powers, and would not be slow to claim credit for any development that took place. This was particularly the case in London. In Liverpool the City Council had less interest in the land involved and, broadly speaking, stood back and allowed the Merseyside Development Corporation (MDC) to run the Garden Festival and refurbish the Albert Dock warehouses at Government expense.[7]

The second wave of UDCs were not opposed by local government so directly.[8] Their boundaries were announced after the 1987 general election, at a time when there was no possibility of the Conservative Government giving the necessary resources to local authorities to revive these areas. The UDCs had the money. The way to get this money was to work with them. So they restrained their criticisms and pointed the UDCs to their own proposals for the sites in question, in many cases persuading UDCs to adopt them. Some councils welcomed UDCs in their areas: Trafford, Hartlepool and Sandwell, respectively, welcomed Trafford Park, the development of Hartlepool Marina and the large out-of-town shopping and leisure development on the site of Patent Shaft, renamed Sandwell 2000. By this time the London local authorities had realized the London Docklands Development Corporation (LDDC) was here to stay, and Newham negotiated a Memorandum of Agreement under which the LDDC agreed to try and build 15,000 units of social housing and a range of community facilities.

Opposition that did occur was often on technical grounds. For example, local authorities questioned the need to relocate existing businesses in long-established Industrial Improvement Areas in Cardiff Bay; various technical aspects of proposed barrages in Cardiff Bay and on the Tees; proposals based on luxury housing in North Tyneside; and the effects of retail developments at Stockton Racecourse on the existing shopping centres in Stockton and Middlesbrough districts. Even when opposing views were being stated in public, most of the local authorities managed to maintain working relationships with the UDCs at officer level.

When the third generation of UDCs was announced, the councils in Sheffield and Bristol gave notice that they would petition against their imposition. The sums of money were much less. The third generation of UDCs were specifically announced as short-life institutions, and were at first intended to have no central government budget at all, and then only very modest budgets (since revised upwards, but still small compared with the first and second generation).

As Dabinett and Ramsden outline in Chapter 8, in the case of Sheffield, the Government decided to negotiate, and the Council and the Development Corporation agreed a code of practice under which the UDC agreed to hold quarterly open forums, to hold open meetings of its sub-committees on planning matters, to provide a short summary note of its activities to the Council each month, to attend Council meetings as required, to make minutes publicly available, and to allow councillors on the UDC board to freely discuss its activities with council colleagues.

As Oatley, in Chapter 9, shows, Bristol argued that the proposed area of land near the city centre would regenerate without a UDC. The outcome was a reduced UDC area and a nine-month delay in designation. The council in Bristol feared that the UDC would cost jobs in manufacturing and was lukewarm about more jobs being created in offices, and in any case the proposed UDC budget was minimal. The council sustained its opposition – alongside that of the LDDC London boroughs who funded the Docklands Consultative Committee. Newham had particular cause for anger once it became clear that the LDDC could not meet its commitments under the Memorandum of Agreement and there was little sign of development in the Royal Docks.

Conclusions

UDCs illustrate a patronage approach to regeneration, i.e. the channelling of resources to non-elected local arm's-length agencies. There is economic logic behind this to the extent that all these areas need substantial central government funding if derelict land is to be brought back into productive use. There is also a case for dedicated local bodies, with specialized expertise, which can act quickly and commercially, and which are not necessarily held back by entrenched local opinion.[9] There are similar arguments for arm's-length enterprise boards (or local authority-owned investment companies) and it is interesting that Brayshaw (1990) should report a convergence between UDCs and enterprise boards: UDCs were started as commercial organizations but forced after 1988 to respond to community pressure, while enterprise boards were started to act for local communities but had to become commercial to survive.

Thus, in return for its patronage, the Conservative government wanted:

- private sector forms of urban regeneration;
- visible quick activity on the ground, publicity, locally and nationally;

and, if possible, also:

- employment creation;
- good relationships with local communities.

The UDCs meanwhile had to deliver, and quickly, to satisfy the government. An easy way forward was to take over local authority plans and projects. Thus many 'successful' projects have had local authority support. Many were conceived by local authorities, or had local authority involvement: for example, the Calthorpe Hotel in Newcastle; the Meadowhall Shopping Centre outside Sheffield, and the road and light rapid transit proposals between there and the city centre; the refurbishment of the Albert Dock in Liverpool and Hamilton Square in Birkenhead; projects around G-Mex in Central Manchester; Sandwell Civic Centre, and a number of smaller housing developments.

But many other projects have been more expensive than planned, and much slower. The case studies in this book – from Docklands and Merseyside to

Newcastle and Bristol – show that regeneration is not quick, or cheap. Costs have been underestimated, consistently. The time taken to assemble land, conduct compulsory purchase orders, remove dereliction and chemical pollution, to install new infrastructure and services, and then to get complex projects on site, has also frequently been underestimated. Moreover, the development corporations were affected by the down-cycle in the property market from 1988 – the third generation particularly, since they were buying land that was often priced unreasonably high.

As a result of all this, using the most modest estimates of 'success' (i.e. whether regeneration is visible on site), the success of UDCs is not proven.[10] The position would improve if there was an upturn in the British economy. But, at present, in-depth research that took account of job losses as well as gains, and compared UDCs with other models of regeneration, could be expected to show that UDCs, like Enterprise Zones, are extremely expensive in terms of the cost for each job that can definitely be associated with the public sector investment.[11]

With the failure to achieve targets, the reputations of UDCs suffered in the eyes of central government, and tensions increased. Much of the Board and top management of the LDDC was replaced. Flagship projects such as the Black Country Spine Road were downgraded. The need to prepare 'exit strategies' was re-emphasized (Stewart, 1991). The patron was beginning to lose faith with at least some of its clients.

The debate about whether arm's-length bodies are needed remains open. Successful development at Salford Quays, the Southampton and Hull docksides, the Metrocentre in Gateshead, G-Mex in Manchester, as well as major projects in many other cities, show that local authorities working closely with the private sector, and with access to government grants and schemes, can manage complex large-scale regeneration projects. The case for dedicated bodies remains, however, especially where there are extensive areas of land available for redevelopment. The issue is who should control them, and sit on boards of directors. Anecdotal evidence suggests that they work best when they build on pre-existing local plans and knowledge, and develop working relations with local authorities and their local private sectors.

In terms of our discussion of patronage, the relationships function best when both client and patron benefit: when the patron sees redevelopment on the ground, and the client is broadly satisfied with this development, is consulted about the detail, and has some involvement in it. This is easier, but by no means inevitable, when there is plenty of money around. The relationship can easily be soured if there are unexpected delays, cost overruns, or a blatant disregard of plans that have been worked out in detail and shared with the local community. The case studies which follow provide many illustrations.

This chapter began with discussions of non-elected local government and of patronage. It concludes by showing that non-elected local governments can easily be in tension, if not outright conflict, with their sponsors. Local government whether elected or not, will represent local interests, and these may not coincide with national priorities. Patronage assumes that in return for assistance the client will be able to deliver. A short-term political dividend from UDCs has already been received. Their problem is that the long-term dividend is fast fading. Meanwhile regeneration is expensive, and UDCs (especially Docklands) appear as potentially limitless drains on the public purse. That is why they are vulnerable to proposals to wind them up, even while it is apparent that many of their flagship projects are far from being signed and sealed.

Acknowledgements

The author would like to acknowledge the contributions of the local authority officers and members of the INLOGOV UDC Workshop who made possible his research on UDCs, and of Rob Imrie and Huw Thomas, whose comments assisted in the restructuring and focusing of this chapter.

Notes

1. He was not the first to do so. See, for example, Elcock (1986) Chapter 11.

2. This is not to say that non-elected local government was not important in earlier years. A Conservative Party research report (Holland and Fallon, 1978) provides a comprehensive classification and listing of quangos, including a category of 'local bodies', showing how the numbers of these bodies had grown with 'a lack of accountability', and describing 'the abuse of patronage'. It then proposed that these quangos should be brought under direct parliamentary accountability, or wound up.

3. This is a very significant difference between UDCs and City Challenge areas. The latter typically include difficult post-war housing estates, and it is inevitable that many of the projects to be undertaken are people-oriented.

4. Compare Goldsmith (1992, pp. 401–2) who suggests that 'the first half of the 1980s was a period in which the Thatcher government lacked a consistent programme'.

5. See Anderson (1983) for discussions of small area regeneration programmes in general and Enterprise Zones in particular.

6. For example Michael Goldsmith refers to a 'clientelistic/patronage model' in his *Urban Studies* article (1992, p. 395) and in his chapter in King and Pierre (1990), but in such a way as to rule out use of this ideal type in discussions of contemporary British and US local government. He prefers instead to talk of a 'new corporatism' of public/private partnerships in major cities; but this is a much weaker theoretical concept. Richards (1963) is concerned with patronage in the particular sense of appointment to public office.

7. See National Audit Office (1988) for trenchant criticism of these UDCs. The LDDC was particularly criticized for not involving local communities in its activities.

8. The relationships between UDCs and local authorities is further discussed in Coulson (1990).

9. The countercase can also be made, as it was by Sheffield City Council in the early 1980s, i.e. that dedicated bodies are not needed, because a local authority, if it so determines, can act quickly and maintain confidentiality. Indeed there is a risk of an arm's-length body taking on a life of its own, and not being accountable to anybody.

10. On this basis, the most successful UDC is probably the Teesside Development Corporation. It was able to concentrate on a small number of key flagships, some very easy, others very expensive, and to use other public sector investment as well as private (e.g. a new university campus). See Cleveland County Council *et al* (1992).

11. This author is not aware that any such research has been commissioned by the Department of the Environment, or is being undertaken systematically by any other body. An incomplete statistical exercise (INLOGOV UDC Workshop, 1991) suggested that figures claimed by UDCs for jobs created in their areas were often exaggerated.

PART TWO

The British Urban Development Corporations: Policies and Practices

3

THE DOCKLANDS EXPERIENCE: LOCALITY AND COMMUNITY IN LONDON

Sue Brownill

Introduction

There has been increasing interest over recent years, of which this collection is evidence, in how the 'locality effect' can contribute to variations in policy. But what is also interesting, yet often ignored, is how the relationship between the locality and policy can change over time as well as over space. The main aim of this chapter is to show that what happens in particular localities is not static but subject to change, influence and renegotiation. This will be illustrated by exploring the changing relationship between urban policy, as represented by the London Docklands Development Corporation (LDDC), and the local area over the lifetime of the LDDC. In this way differences *within* localities can be seen to be as important as differences *between* them.

Through looking at these temporal variations in Docklands a related theme which emerges is the importance of seeing locality as a politically contested area. Not only do different approaches and interests promote differing definitions and policy prescriptions in regard to locality but also policies themselves are constantly restructuring in response to a variety of factors. In particular the issue of who should benefit from urban policy and what strategies should be adopted in respect of this are central to the relationship between localities and urban policy in Docklands as elsewhere. These issues will be explored throughout the chapter and will be returned to in the final section which discusses possible alternative approaches to the relationship between urban policy and locality.

The LDDC and the Locality

London Docklands (see Figure 3.1) is often taken to be the flagship of the UDC experiment, despite the fact that the flagship may well have run aground in the property recession of the early 1990s. Since 1981, if the publicity accompanying the tenth anniversary of the LDDC in 1991 is to be believed, £8.4 billion of private investment, over £1 billion in LDDC spending alone, a further £3.5 billion in transport expenditure, 27 million sq ft of commercial floorspace, 600 ha of reclaimed land, 15,000 new dwellings, and 41,000 jobs

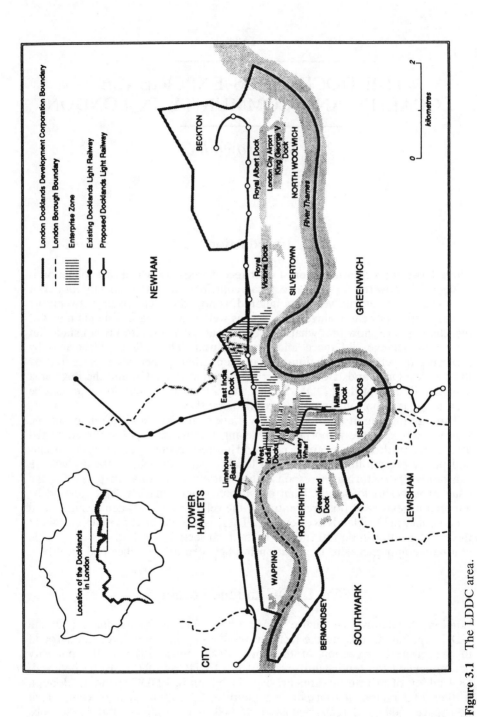

Figure 3.1 The LDDC area.

with estimates of up to 200,000 bear witness to the activities of the LDDC. The impact on the ground has been immense.

At first sight this could be interpreted as what Smith (1986) has labelled 'space fixing' whereby a locality is given over to service the spatial and locational requirements of the particular elements of economic activity expanding at the time. As Docklands was initially shaped by the speculative scramble to develop the docks themselves so it has been transformed by the expanding financial services, print, residential and retail markets and the operations of speculative property development. The strategy adopted, that of facilitating and subsidizing private sector activity and excluding local interests from the decision-making processes, only acted to support and increase such trends.

Canary Wharf could be seen as the most extreme example of this process. It is likened to Venice and New York, is designed by architects from all over the world, its street names have a distinctly cosmopolitan feel and it did not even need planning permission, let alone strategic assessment. According to such a thesis the locality would have little redress and little involvement in the area's transformation. But in reality the story is more complicated and it is important to look beyond the physical changes that have taken place, for at least two reasons.

Firstly, as later sections will show, local factors have had no small part to play in the Docklands experience. Secondly, the LDDC's strategy has been far from monolithic. It is possible to distinguish three phases in LDDC activity and strategy each of which has had different implications for the locality (see Table 3.1). From an initial belief in the 'trickle-down' effect and a dismissal of local interests, the LDDC briefly shifted to a championing of 'social regeneration' and partnership only to move back to market primacy in later years. Underlying

Table 3.1 Phases of LDDC activity

1. *Priming the pump 1981–85*	
Land acquisition & disposal	Private housing
Publicity and marketing	Docklands Light Railway
Infrastructure provision	London Bridge City
Area frameworks	STOLport
Targeting of high tech	*Daily Telegraph* and other EZ developments

2. *The second wave 1985–89*	
Large scale developments	Canary Wharf
Targeting of financial services	Royal Docks – three schemes
Land and house price boom	Docklands Highway
Infrastructure problems begin	DLR extensions
Planning gain agreements and 'social regeneration'	Surrey Quays
Personnel changes	Print industry

3. *Slump and crisis 1989–*	
Stock market crash	Royals schemes founder
Property market slump	Kentish Homes collapses
Critical parliamentary reports	Tobacco Dock collapses
Government/LDDC conflict	7,000 empty dwellings
Land and house prices slump	42% office space unlet
Budget crisis	Canary Wharf in crisis
Transport chaos	Jubilee Line

these trends was the LDDC's market-oriented approach. The Docklands area
went from being a boom town in the mid- to late 1980s to a victim of slump in
the early 1990s with projects and firms being taken into receivership, acres of
unlet space and falling prices. In the following sections I want to look at these
three phases concentrating on two major issues; how the policies and strategies
have developed, and the fluctuations in relationships with local participants and
interests.

But first there are a number of definitional and conceptual issues which need
briefly clarifying. The first relates to the concept of locality and its context in
London's Docklands. 'Locality' has become an increasingly popular concept in
recent years, over which there have been various debates about definition and
usage (Cooke, 1989b, Duncan et al, 1988). While there is no space to go into
this issue in detail here it is important to clarify that the definition adopted in
this chapter considers a wider set of relationships than that of the economic or
journey-to-work area. A consideration of cultural factors, relations of gender
and race – in short 'local social relations' (Duncan et al, 1988) – are all
important in understanding what has happened in Docklands.

There is also an issue of whether or not it is possible to speak of the
Docklands locality. Docklands has only ever been a line on a planner's map
and does not correspond to any shared definition of space or administrative
boundaries beyond planning agencies. Not only are there three local authorities
operating in the area, the Boroughs of Newham, Tower Hamlets and Southwark,
but also there are distinct communities such as Wapping, Limehouse, the
Isle of Dogs and North Woolwich. In addition the population is far from
homogeneous. For example, 16% of the area's population are black or from
ethnic minorities and house-building activity in the area has also led to real
as well as imagined splits between the existing population and newcomers.
Therefore although the term 'locality' will be used in this chapter to refer to
the three boroughs, it should also be borne in mind that within this area there
are other geographical, cultural and racial localities.

Phase One: Priming the Pump. A Greenfield Site? (1981–85)

Policies and Strategies

The details of UDCs have been well rehearsed elsewhere and I do not intend
to repeat them here. One point, however, that is worth making, is the failure
of the legislation to define regeneration and the enabling of UDCs to 'carry on
any business or undertaking in or for the purposes of achieving its objectives'
(Local Government (Planning and Land) Act 1980). Given the looseness of the
legislation it was up to the LDDC to define its own regeneration strategy and
this definition has changed over time.

The initial phase of the LDDC concentrated on the 'pump-priming' of
private investment through public activity and investment, belying the rhetoric
that Docklands' redevelopment has been 'demand-led'. Substantial public
spending on land acquisition, infrastructure and marketing the potential of
Docklands was therefore the priority. During this time LDDC doubled its
landholdings to become the largest landowner in the area. This was the time

when LDDC was trying to massage the market's perception of Docklands as an investment location. As a result little attention was paid to anything other than getting development going. Regeneration was seen in terms of private money invested, floorspace built and value added to land and property.

Coupled with the anti-planning stance of UDCs which saw planning as part of the cause of inner city decline and the 'socio-political plans' of Labour local authorities as turning away developers, this strategy had the effect of enabling the processes of restructuring. Moreover certain trends were heightened by the encouragement of speculative property development through planning and financial incentives. In effect LDDCs approach led to the oversupply of space and poor coordination of land use and transportation, thus boosting the tendencies towards boom and slump in the property development process.

What the market was providing at the time consisted largely of sectors of the economy which were themselves restructuring, and residential development (Church, 1988). By 1987 most of the major national newspapers had relocated their printing presses to Docklands as part of their programme of introducing technological change and shedding labour. Retailing and leisure were other locating (or more accurately re-locating) activities, despite the fact that the LDDC was targeting the higher-status and higher-value 'hi-tech' sector.

Strategies designed to meet local needs were seen as old-fashioned and constraining on the activities of capital. For example, in response to calls to match new jobs to the skills of local people LDDC answered in 1982, 'This represents a very limited horizon which would constrain the marketing strategy and the new Docklands economy that is required to provide a secure future for the area' (LDDC, 1982: 11). The market would provide and local benefits would occur as a result of what Massey (1991) has referred to as the 'horrible metaphor' – trickle-down. Therefore no major action was needed to direct resources to rented housing, community investment or supporting local businesses.

The role of the locality was reduced to one of providing a value-enhancing backdrop to investment activity. Two things were seized upon by the LDDC – the location close to the City and the waterfrontage of the docks and river. Thus Docklands became the emerging City and the waterfrontage was seen as the important difference between Docklands and other large scale development locations in London. It was this that was aggressively marketed by the LDDC. Burgess and Wood (1988) showed how aspects of Docklands culture were turned around to market it as a development location. The same can be seen in some architectural features, the mock ships' prows and portholes in the Cascades development and the use of cranes as landscape furniture.

LDDC also recognized that the area was not homogeneous, but again its recognition of locality was in property market terms. The Docklands area was divided initially into five localities – Wapping, Limehouse, Surrey Docks, the Enterprise Zone and the Royals. For each area an Area Framework was drawn up, not as a local plan (although the LDDC admitted they were in all but name) but as a marketing strategy based on the market potential of each area. Thus Wapping was seen as closest to the City and would provide high-value residential development plus offices round St Katherine's Dock, and the Isle of Dogs had the Enterprise Zone. However social differences, such as those of race and gender were not acknowledged.

Local resources were ignored or seen as being in the way. References to a greenfield site were made despite the fact 40,000 people lived in the LDDC area and numerous firms were located there. The approach was to deny local resources and any strategy based on these and instead to bring in a new community and a new economy. Locality for the LDDC at this time was defined through the perspective of the market and a political and policy framework designed to promote private sector activity. No wonder residents began to feel they were being developed into oblivion.

Relations with Local Agencies

In this early phase relationships between the LDDC and local authorities and local groups could at best be described as strained. The setting up of the LDDC was accompanied by a storm of protest and a 52-day hearing in the House of Lords where all the local authorities and many local groups opposed the proposals. Their argument was that given the resources and powers of a UDC they could do the job just as well.

The decision-making structure of UDCs enabled the LDDC to insulate itself from local pressure and influence. Not only was planning to be swept away but also the time-consuming consultation, public scrutiny and basically democratic mechanisms that had preceded it. These were 'a relic of the local authority days' according to first Chief Executive, Reg Ward. Thus one of the important links between the locality and policy was broken.

Local government is characterized by its local democratic and representational role. Duncan and Goodwin (1988) cite this as being one of the essential mechanisms for local resources and relations to be translated into policy. UDC boards are made up of government appointees. These appointees can include local councillors. In the case of the LDDC the three leaders of the local authorities were originally appointed on a *personal* basis. When two of them ceased to be leaders or even councillors they remained on the board.

Despite being required by law to draw up a Code of Consultation with local authorities this took the LDDC ten years to complete with the result that many decisions were made on planning applications and other issues without the boroughs' views being canvassed. The relationship between local organizations and residents and the LDDC was again distant. LDDC had one community liaison officer at this time. In the House of Lords Committee report the LDDC was called on to 'always let the Docklands Forum (a Docklands-wide consultative group) know what it is thinking of doing', but in reality never did. This high-handed approach led to significant local opposition.

Added to this was the failure of economic and social benefits to 'trickle-down' to the local area in any substantial amount (see also Association of London Authorities (ALA), 1991; Brownill, 1990). Instead the inequalities on which the market is based were increased to produce a growing polarization between those that have and those that have not. For example, in 1984 while 40% of residents in the new housing developments earned over £15,000 per year, over 75% of existing residents earned less than this amount. 30% of buyers were in the professional and managerial socio-economic group (SEG) while only 7% of Newham and 13% of Southwark residents fell into that category. 93% of purchasers were white compared with 85% for the two boroughs as a whole. Despite the claims put forward for numbers of jobs attracted to the area, unemployment levels in 1992 were higher than in 1981. Similarly over 80% of the housing built in Docklands has been for sale but at the same time homelessness in the three Docklands' boroughs increased by 200% compared with 60% for London as a whole. The physical juxtaposition of new and existing housing is often taken to be one of the starkest indicators of the 'two nations' in Docklands. A survey into population change in Wapping and Limehouse carried out by Queen Mary College stated 'rarely have social distances so vast been matched by physical distances so minimal' (Crilley et al, 1990).

Another feature of polarization has been the way in which it has interacted with social and economic divisions, particularly those of gender and race. For example, a recent household survey showed that Bangladeshi men constituted 6% of the total population of the LDDC area, 14% of the unemployed and only 2% of the working population. Increases in service sector employment have meant increased employment opportunities for women but this is often of a poorly paid or insecure nature (Docklands Forum, 1990: 48). Due to the lower economic power of women, black people and members of ethnic minorities they are less likely to gain from a market-based strategy despite the fact that due to their greater needs they have most to gain from regeneration.

One effect of this strategy was local opposition to developments and the production of alternative proposals. Despite the LDDC having the lion's share of power and resources the boroughs continued to draw up local plans for the area (which the DOE subsequently refused to adopt); local campaigns were formed, for example to oppose luxury housing development at Cherry Garden Pier in Rotherhithe and alternatives were put forward, for example the People's Plan for the Royals, the Limehouse Petition, and the Docklands Childcare Project's calls to integrate childcare into the planning of Docklands. The publicity aroused by this activity and the growing criticisms of the LDDC were to have a major effect in the next phase of LDDC activity.

The Second Wave (1985–89)

A number of factors came together in this period to produce certain modifications to LDDC's strategy and a new direction in its approach to the locality. More attention to local needs, resources and participation in the regeneration strategy was therefore attempted. This could have been done by adopting an approach which aimed to put the locality at the centre of the agenda or by making minor adjustments to the market-led approach to meet certain limited social and community needs. The LDDC chose the latter strategy in its second wave. Returning to the idea of locality being politically contested, the LDDC sought to link local benefits to the market. Instead of its previous lack of attention to the locality and seeing it as a hindrance to regeneration, the emphasis was on incorporation of local energies into a marginally redefined regeneration brief.

As well as the highlighting of the unequal benefits by effective local campaigns creating an image problem for the LDDC, the property market in Docklands took off, with the most dramatic development being Canary Wharf. Three major schemes proposed for the Royal Docks indicated that LDDC might be succeeding in its task of filling up Docklands. LDDC was targeting other sectors in the economy, notably the financial sector which was buoyed by the Big Bang of financial deregulation. Land and property prices began to rise at phenomenal rates as the LDDC capitalized on the South East housing boom and a mini-boom in the economy. For example in Gun Wharf, a luxury residential development in Wapping, the prices of flats rose 195% between 1984 and 1988. Land which was priced in 1981 at below half a million pounds an acre was selling for nearly £5 million. This created opportunities for creaming off some of the increased value.

Personnel changes in the LDDC included the replacement in 1985 of Nigel Broackes, the first Chair, by Christopher Benson who appeared to have more of a social conscience, and, in 1988, of Reg Ward, the original Chief Executive, by Michael Honey who had a local authority background. Political changes prompted the local authorities to adopt a different stance to the LDDC. Local elections in 1986 brought a change in political control in Tower Hamlets from Labour to Liberal. The general election in 1987 removed any hope by the other Dockland's councils for a Labour government and led Thatcher to exhort private business to do something about those inner cities.

Significantly, calls for a different strategy were not confined to the local population. The House of Commons Employment Committee in a highly critical report on UDCs stated that 'UDCs cannot be regarded as a success if buildings and land are regenerated but the local community are bypassed and do not benefit from regeneration' (House of Commons, 1989). Recommendations included a widening of the definition of regeneration to include community benefit. And then there was the private sector. In evidence to the Employment Committee David Dickenson from Stanhope properties (which at that time was planning two major developments in the area) voiced concern among investors about the quality of the local workforce. 'Unless they can see a concerted and cohesive programme they may well be dissuaded from risking a transfer of activity', and he added; 'In my opinion the LDDC have not been particularly successful in winning the hearts and minds of the people to support their policies'.

It was at this time that many of the second round UDCs were set up and it shows the very different national context from the first round. From the vantage point of Docklands it was very interesting to hear and read them say 'We're not going to be like the LDDC'.

However this change was not universally shared. Senior civil servants and advisers to Nicholas Ridley, at that time the Secretary of State for the Environment, in their response to the Employment Committee's report argued vigorously for a physically based regeneration strategy. 'We do not see the Corporations as being primarily concerned with employment. They are about regeneration, and indeed about physical regeneration' (Docklands Forum, July 1988). It was LDDC's financial independence from central government through its income from land sales that allowed it some relative autonomy to pursue its own programmes.

Policies and Strategies

As a result of these factors some apparently major policy and organizational shifts occurred. LDDC began to assert that 'social regeneration – meeting

Table 3.2 Planning gain agreements

Canary Wharf: Olympia and York, and London Borough of Tower Hamlets (LBTH)
    2,000 local jobs.
    £2.5 million over eight years for training.
    LBTH to withdraw objections to Docklands Highway.

The Royals: London Borough of Newham (LBN) and LDDC
    Target of 1,500 social housing units.
    Training facilities.
    £60 million Social Development Programme over lifetime of development.
    25% of employment for local residents.
    Protection of local shopping centres and industrial sites.
    Consultative group to be established; members LBN, LDDC, community and developers.
    LBN to withdraw objections to Highway and not proceed with South Docklands Local Plan.

Docklands Highway: London Borough of Tower Hamlets
    Replacement of 450 demolished tenancies through Housing Associations. £96,000 to LBTH for
      every tenant rehoused by borough.
    £30 million of social, economic and community schemes.
    LBTH to carry out traffic management and play role in ensuring road built on time.
    Implementation committee between LBTH and LDDC.

---

people's needs – is more important than physically building the fabric' (LDDC, 1987: 2). Just a year later the LDDC was to claim that 'it has always recognised that regeneration was not purely about the physical provision of buildings'. The LDDC's publicity video was changed to include pictures of smiling residents and list the LDDC's investment in the community. Alongside this was an improved effort in communication and joint working with local councils and organizations. The locality was to be included in a partnership – albeit on unequal terms.

The two most visible manifestations of this redirection were firstly, the signing of three major planning gain agreements between the LDDC, local authorities and developers. These were aimed at linking public investment to major private sector schemes and redirecting some of the surplus and capital investment associated with them to the community. The developments concerned were Canary Wharf; the Royal Docks where three consortia were lined up to redevelop the entire area; and the Docklands Highway, a dual carriageway road running the length of the Docklands area but involving widespread demolition in Tower Hamlets. The details of the schemes are included in Table 3.2 which shows that in all they included plans for 2,000 social housing units, £100 million of community spending and consultation mechanisms.

The second change was the establishment of a Community Services Division (CSD) as a department within the LDDC. The objectives of the CSD were as follows: that local people secure advantage from regeneration; that balanced communities are fostered; that services are delivered to meet the needs of those who live, work and employ in the LDDC area, and that decent housing is provided at a price which local residents can afford to buy or rent (LDDC, 1989b). This division had a budget in 1989–90 of £51 million to invest in education, community development, social housing and training. The highest spending area was to be housing. A social housing strategy was drawn up to provide 2,000 units and refurbish existing estates at a cost of £50 million over three years.

Training schemes were another area highlighted, the aim being to minimize the mismatch between incoming jobs and local residents' skills. In 1990–91 LDDC allocated £14 million for training (a large part of this was capital costs for a tertiary college in Tower Hamlets). LDDC also began to recognize the need to highlight certain sections of the community through promoting, for example, childcare initiatives and ethnic minority training schemes. Funding for this strategy came from a variety of sources. However LDDC's income from land sales and the money it could hope to lever out of central government through the expectation of future sales was vital. Support within the government was also forthcoming for social spending at that time. For example Michael Trippier, Junior Environment Minister, asked LDDC in September 1988 to concentrate on local housing problems as part of 'the Minister's wider encouragement for LDDC to extend its role in the sphere of social provision and community infrastructure' (Docklands Consultative Committee (DCC), 1989).

Relations with Local Agencies

'The biggest change is that they talk to us now'. This was one Newham planning officer's summing up of the second wave. Partnership, as elsewhere, became the buzzword during this time – a partnership that included the LDDC, the private sector, local government and other government bodies, housing associations and community organizations.

An earlier change had been the establishment of area offices, one aim of which was to build up closer relationships with their local communities through the employment of their own community development officers. At this time previous critics of the Corporation went to work for it and Olympia and York (O&Y) employed one of the leaders of the Association of Island Communities as a community liaison officer. In the Royals Docks, a four-way consultative group was established between the LDDC, community groups, Newham council and developers.

LDDC thus attempted to change its uncaring image by listening to and working with organizations within the Docklands area. But this was not a direct input into decision making. For example the LDDC's planning committee was open to the public from 1986 onwards – but people attending had no speaking rights. Local representation on the board was increased when Tower Hamlets appointed a member in 1986 but Newham and Southwark still refused to appoint members on the grounds that Board meetings were closed and members were not allowed to consult their councils on issues prior to meetings.

Residents and community organizations were similarly consulted on some issues, but not major issues of strategy and direction. The drawing up of the planning gain agreements illustrates the limitations to involvement. The Canary Wharf agreement was finalized between the Mayor and Leader of Tower Hamlets and the Canary Wharf consortium only. No other councillors, officers or community representatives were involved. The Newham agreement was slightly more open in that community groups pushed the council for meetings and reports back from negotiations, but these negotiations were still closed to the public. Consultation was allowed on the implementation of the programme, but not its formulation.

Despite the fact that UDCs have in some ways been seen as extensions of central government in a local area this phase of LDDC activity shows how lax monitoring, ministerial changes and LDDC's autonomy through its own income led to more local influence than imagined. By engaging with the local area LDDC opened itself up to the influence of local social relations and therefore some limited policy changes. However, LDDC's strategy was still based largely on bringing in new investment from outside the area rather than building on local strengths and on relying on private sector initiative with some channelling of resources to the community. There was no fundamental shift from the restructuring approach to policy. Therefore while representation and collaboration had increased it was still an unequal partnership between the LDDC and the locality. The limitations inherent in trying to tack on more socially oriented elements to a market-oriented strategy were also apparent (see also ALA, 1991; Brownill, 1990). These limitations were to become even more obvious as moves into the third stage of LDDC policy took place.

Phase Three: Slump and Retrenchment (1989–   )

We are now in a new phase in the ongoing story of the redevelopment of Docklands and the relationship between the LDDC and the locality has been reconstituted yet again. The area, always seen as marginal to the market, has been hit hard by the recession in the UK property market. As early as Black Monday in 1987 the residential market began to decline with Kentish Properties eventually collapsing in 1989. Since then residential property prices have fallen by 20–30% and there are at least 1,400 empty flats and houses (ALA, 1991). 50% of office space is unlet and rents have fallen to as low as £8 per square foot. Other firms and schemes have followed Kentish: Tobacco Dock, the London Arena, South Quay Plaza, Docklands Minibus.

Yet the most dramatic signal of the move from boom to slump in Docklands came in May 1992 when Canary Wharf was placed in the hands of administrators. In 1987, when O&Y took over the scheme, rents in the City were £60 per sq ft as opposed to the £25–£30 at Canary Wharf. But by 1992 oversupply in the City had cancelled that difference and Canary Wharf was only 60% let with many tenants having rent-free periods or having been given expensive incentives to move in. As a result O&Y could not keep up the interest payments and the banks refused more loans.

It would be wrong to see the collapse of Canary Wharf and other projects as solely a result of recession. It was also a direct result of LDDC's restructuring strategy. The fact that no strategic assessment of developments was carried out, the massive public subsidies to the schemes in the form of cheap land, EZ incentives and up to £3 billion in transport infrastructure and the failure to integrate land use and transportation all had their part to play. The inherent tendency of LDDC's approach to heighten the boom/slump cycle became all too evident.

The impact on the LDDC's policies and finances has been severe. LDDC's income from land sales has plummeted from £115 million in 1988–89 to £24 million in 1989–90 causing a budget crisis and a £4 million operational deficit in the year 1990–91. The result has been that central government is once again in control of LDDC spending. In response to the collapse of the Docklands' property market, and the severe criticisms about lack of infrastructure provision, expenditure was redirected to transport; in particular the £600 million Docklands Highway, the upgrading of the DLR and the proposed Jubilee Line extension. LDDC was also forced to make 20% cuts in staffing levels for each of the years 1991–92 and 1992–93.

Policies and Strategies

One of the first casualties of this situation has been the social programme. The physical definition of regeneration has reasserted itself as the market has changed and the locality has once again receded into the background. Table 3.3 shows how progress to date on the planning gain agreements has been slow. The Tower Hamlets Accord was enshrined in a legal document and has therefore been able to retain its budget. The Newham agreement has suffered as the development schemes have all foundered and there are no legal agreements to secure the fulfilment of the memorandum. The future of the Canary Wharf agreement must also be in doubt given the collapse of O&Y.

The CSD has now been reorganized into an 'Emerging City' directorate which also deals with estate management and transport planning and the head of the unit has left along with most of the other CSD officers. The budget for community spending has been cut from £43.5 million or 17% of total LDDC spending in 1989–90 to £19 million or just 7% in 1990–91. Grants to voluntary groups have been cut by 20% between 1990–91 and 1991–92. The Social

Table 3.3 Progress on agreements

Canary Wharf
  Monitoring of local employment unsatisfactory.
  1988; Olympia and York (O&Y) admit to House of Commons Committee that majority of jobs will be transfers.
  Money for training being paid but insufficient for major initiative.
  Separate construction training scheme closed in 1990.
  1992; O&Y under administrators. Redundancies. Future of agreement in doubt.

The Royals
  All three development consortia pulled out by 1990.
  Scheme for 470 social housing units built but without developer contribution. Other 1,000 units remain to be achieved.
  Training centre.
  Royal Docks Consultative Group set up in 1989.
  Instead of £10 million of community investment 1987–89 only £1.8 million committed. 1990–91 £3 million and 1991–92 £3 million.

Tower Hamlets accord
  Timber Wharves bought by LDDC from Comden homes for £142,000 per unit for rehousing along with other sites and estates.
  Legal agreement signed between LDDC and LBTH has ensured instalments of £30 million social fund.
  LBTH successfully taken LDDC to court over environmental pollution caused by road building.
  SPLASH tenants propose further legal action.

Housing Strategy has been more than halved to £21.7 million and the priority has been shifted from new build to refurbishment.

Michael Honey, the Chief Executive most closely associated with the 'social regeneration' phase, has been replaced by Eric Sorensen, an ex-DOE mandarin. The new regime is busy trying to pass the buck back to the local authorities as evidenced by Sorensen;

UDCs quite deliberately were set up as temporary or short-life organisations with a remit to promote development as fast as is reasonably possible. It is not consistent with that objective to also require UDCs to engage in a wide range of investment and social provision programmes. If that were the case, there would be long delays as the speed of change in the area went at the pace of the slowest development.

(*Docklands News*, May 1991)

Such a view is made easier by the fact that the government has indicated that it wishes to see the LDDC wind up its activities by the mid-1990s. Ministerial changes helped swing the balance back to the floorspace approach to regeneration. Michael Portillo had main responsibility for Docklands until the election in 1992 and he was undoubtedly a floorspace man, stating 'The LDDC is about economic growth, it is not a social or welfare programme'.

Relations with Local Agencies

The failure of LDDC to implement the social programmes, particularly in Newham, has inevitably led to tension between the LDDC and the Docklands' boroughs. In addition the winding down announcement has also led to representations to the DOE asking for the LDDC to go and to let the local authorities get on with the job. Community organizations are being cut and have less influence. Many of those who went to work for the LDDC hoping to represent community views have left or are finding their work more constrained. However local opposition continues as incorporation recedes. The policy changes have left the community feeling that once again they will have to bear the disbenefits of development without seeing any of the benefits. One example of this anger is a potentially historic court case between LDDC and SPLASH, a group of local organizations in the Limehouse and Poplar area most affected by the construction of Canary Wharf and the Highway. They are suing LDDC on environmental and health grounds.

What this shows is the failure of the 'social regeneration' strategy to have any lasting significance for the locality. Firstly, the dangers of financially linking community investment to the market is clear. In a downturn it disappears. As Boyle (1987) has stated, and the Docklands experience would appear to bear out, such partnerships are basically unequal. The needs of the private sector become paramount and the power of local councils and people to secure the benefits is limited. Such deals can be seen in terms as 'an anaesthetic for social needs' (Alterman, 1988) and a covering up of the withdrawal of public investment. They are seen as substitutes for planned and democratically agreed programmes for change and therefore provide a legitimation for the redirection of public policy and finances to support private profitability.

The 'people'-based LDDC regeneration has in effect been a minor modification to an unchanged programme. What is most significant is that this has left the processes of restructuring untouched. Major private sector developments still proceed, as do their inherent impacts on the local community, but with some additional optional extras. The unequal benefits remain as the partnerships are fundamentally unequal in the first place. The unequal and divisive results of restructuring will continue – the two nations in Docklands have not been brought significantly closer together by LDDC's flawed attempts to merge social and physical regeneration.

Community-Led Alternatives

The political and policy context of the LDDC's approach to and definition of locality was therefore one of linking local benefits to private sector investment and widening the local to include 'those who live, work, employ and visit in the area'. Attention to local detail was more an attempt to make private sector led regeneration work better than a genuine attempt at equalizing regeneration benefits. Yet other initiatives in Docklands have shown that there are some fundamentally different approaches to the locality possible within urban policy.

Again detailed accounts of these exist elsewhere (Brownill, 1988; Thompson, 1990; Brindley et al, 1989) and space does not permit a major description here. What is important to stress is that such examples as the People's Plan for the Royal Docks, the Courage Brewery Site and, just outside the Docklands area, Coin Street, take as their starting points the needs and resources within an area and are based on a bottom-up rather than a top-down process. They see regeneration as being participatory and are based on strategies which include the meeting of local needs as a priority. These approaches Thompson (1990) has termed regeneration as opposed to the restructuring of UDCs. For example the People's Plan, drawn up as an alternative to London City Airport in the Royal Docks, was based on extensive consultation with local residents during which they were asked to put forward their own ideas for their area's future. Proposals were based on investing in the existing economic base and on linking different areas – home and work, meeting needs and making jobs – in an effort to break down spatial and social divisions. Public investment was to be accountable and directed towards the implementation of an agreed strategy rather than geared towards the private sector.

The political definition of locality informing the Plan and its translation into policy were different from the LDDC's. Instead of a local area being a back-drop to development, the participation of local agencies and interests, the existence of local skills and resources and meeting local needs was seen as vital to policy. Achievement of the Plan's goals was to be brought about in essence by intervention in the process of restructuring rather than through the unequal partnerships of social regeneration. However, even this approach still leaves questions unanswered. It is doubtful whether such approaches could be implemented without recourse to the private sector. There is also the perennial problem of community-based initiatives that the local is not enough. Forces and processes outside the locality and the scope of policy are to a large extent influencing events. Plus the issues of democracy, equalities and power still remain even within 'alternatives' (Brownill, 1988).

Talk of alternatives and best practice thus raises as many questions as it answers. However, as the UDC approach to regeneration sinks alongside its flagship Canary Wharf, the time is right for some fundamental reassessment of policies towards the inner city. By way of conclusion I want to draw out some issues which the Docklands experience raises in relation to locality and urban policy.

How to Link the Local and the Global: Restructuring or Regeneration?

What is happening in areas such as Docklands cannot be seen in isolation from the processes of restructuring occurring on national and international levels or the national policy context. But at the same time this chapter has shown that the Docklands locality has had a major influence on events and outcomes and we have to look wider than external forces and events for the full picture. This presents some interesting paradoxes and challenges when thinking about policy. On the one hand it is important that we are alive to the particular social, economic and political relationships in localities. This means thinking how policies and processes are going to impact differently in different areas, how the local response will be different and how needs are different. In particular there can be no one policy blueprint that is appropriate to every area, only guiding principles that can be adapted to local circumstances.

Yet, on the other hand as we saw with the People's Plan, the local is not enough either. Without some purchase over economic, social and political trends happening outside local areas, policies and strategies are severely limited. It could be all too easy for locality, like community before it, to be uncritically adopted as the proverbial 'good thing'. Building links and recognizing the common processes operating within and between localities is therefore important, especially when thinking about collective forces for change.

One lesson to be learnt from the UDC experience is how an approach which aims to facilitate restructuring (the global) can make an area a hostage to the fortunes of the property market as well as working to the detriment and exclusion of the locality. The calls for regeneration through intervention in the market as opposed to restructuring are important in this context (Thompson, 1990). Yet, how can we draw up strategies for redevelopment in particular localities which can intervene in these wider forces in a positive way? In some senses the People's Plan is a good example here. The cargo-handling proposals would make use of local skills and resources, they would be part of regional and national transport and economic policy and they would fit in with European and world trade developments.

Who Makes Up the Locality?

Issues of equality need serious consideration in urban policy. On a new public housing estate in Southwark Docklands, built as a result of community campaigns against luxury residential development, security guards had to be employed to protect black tenants who had been allocated houses on the basis of their housing need, rather than on the basis that they lived in the local area. This goes to show that there are negative as well as positive forces in the locality which call for some strategic intervention and policy guidelines. It is too easy to forget that the local population is not homogeneous. Issues to do with equalities have to be central to any approach. The development of the urban environment can repeat and reinforce existing relationships of inequality unless this is recognized and challenged.

Where Does Power Lie, and Issues of Democracy?

UDCs are obvious examples of the process whereby power is removed from the locality and shifted towards the centre and the private sector. But partnerships and other agencies do little to alter these basically unequal structures. Even alternatives can still be centralized – as was the role of the Greater London Council in the People's Plan. A traditional model of local democracy or of planning expertise which repeats rather than challenges existing power divisions is maybe not what is wanted in any move back towards more local control.

This implies more attention to the carrying out of policy. The aims of achieving greater local accountability and sensitivity to local needs along with increasing equality in the policy process are highly dependent on having a process which is compatible with such aims. Docklands has also proved to be false the rhetoric that the private sector alone can revitalize the inner city. The massive public intervention and expenditure in Docklands points to the need for the democratization of this public sector activity.

Strategies not Structures

The Docklands experience has shown the limitations of the UDC approach through, among other things, the resulting boom/slump cycle, the dangers of relying on the market for community benefit and the realization of the results of discarding planning. Despite this, proposals for future inner city policy tend to centre around structures and agencies – for example, partnerships and Development Agencies – rather than strategies. This tends to reflect a growing consensus around the approach which favours minor modifications of the market. The infrastructure may well be put in first now, but the basic strategy remains unchanged. This implies that the shifts in policy identified as benefiting localities, for example intervention in restructuring and greater democratization, remain excluded from the agenda.

The Politics of Locality

The dynamism in the locality/policy relationship in Docklands has been shown to be the result of a number of factors. However, the shifting and competing claims over the place of the local area and its population in regeneration that have occurred in Docklands over just ten years have to be seen within the context of political and theoretical debates about the nature of policy and the nature of locality. The role of the locality has been variously defined as part of a marketing strategy based on waterfront locations by the new right, as an unequal partner with the private sector by the post-Thatcher right and as the focus for urban policy by the left. Moreover, the process of implementing policies within localities itself raises many political issues.

The essentially political nature of the choices over the relationship between locality and urban policy has to be made clear in order that discussion does not get trapped in categories which limit debate and reinforce inequalities. This is especially important to bear in mind at the moment as urban policy in the UK is at something of a crossroads fuelled in part by the crisis in Docklands. Only by charting and discussing the changes in and conflict both within and between different approaches will it be possible to maximize the potential and minimize the limitations associated with paying more attention to the locality in urban policy.

4

URBAN DEVELOPMENT CORPORATIONS, URBAN ENTREPRENEURIALISM AND LOCALITY

Richard Meegan

Introduction

Along with the London Docklands Development Corporation (LDDC), the Merseyside Development Corporation (MDC) formed the first generation of urban development corporations in the UK. In the eleven years of its operation it has experienced somewhat volatile public criticism. The National Audit Office in 1988, for example, compared it relatively unfavourably with the LDDC and argued that there was a *prima facie* case for its abolition. Before this report was published, however, the government went ahead and significantly expanded the Development Corporation's boundaries (an almost 3-fold increase in its size) and guaranteed further funding. Since this rebirth, the Corporation has garnered relatively more favourable public reviews and particularly so in relation to its pioneering contemporary in London (see, for example, Dalby, 1990).

This chapter will not attempt a detailed, formal evaluation of the MDC in terms of its relative success in achieving its stated goals. This has been effectively attempted elsewhere (Dawson and Parkinson, 1990; Hayes, 1987; National Audit Office, 1988; Parkinson and Evans, 1988, 1989). The aim rather will be to extend these attempts by relating the activities of the MDC to current debates in the social sciences and particularly human geography. The first of these debates surrounds the significance of local spatial variation in the operation of socio-spatial economic processes (often referred to, albeit controversially in shorthand, as the 'locality debate'). The second addresses the alleged shift in urban governance in advanced capitalist countries from 'managerialism' to 'entrepreneurialism'. The chapter concludes with a discussion of the broader lessons that can be drawn from the experience of the MDC for urban policy.

The Merseyside Development Corporation Through the Filter of 'Locality'

The 'Locality Debate'

There has been a resurgence of interest in the spatiality of socio-economic, political and cultural development in the social sciences (see, for example, Agnew and Duncan, 1989; Gregory and Urry, 1985). In human geography an inspirational force has been Massey's (1984) work on spatial divisions of labour with its focus on the spatial organization and reorganization of the social relations of production. Central to the approach is the notion of waves or rounds of investment in the social and economic landscape which recondition both the physical and social aspects of place. The approach recognizes that, while places are interdependent, they are also unique, representing at any given time a synthesis of political, cultural, social and economic histories and characteristics. These locally based, historically produced characteristics have a dialectical relationship with wider social processes. 'Geography' does not simply reflect social relationships but actively helps to mould them: space is a social construct but social relations are themselves constructed over space (Massey, 1985).

The 'spatial divisions of labour' approach informed a recent Economic and Social Research Council (ESRC)-funded research initiative, 'The Changing Urban and Regional System (or 'CURS') Research Programme' which has provoked a wide-ranging, at times exasperating and, at others stimulating, political debate. Initial criticism was marked by a degree of misunderstanding (with for example, Smith (1987) – as Cooke (1987b) points out – confusing the empirical research of CURS with an empiricist approach). The debate has also been characterized at times by a rather unconstructive degree of acrimony (see, for example, the exchange between Duncan and Savage (1989) and Cooke (1989a), and between Harvey (1987) and just about everyone else; and, for a calming antidote, Walker (1989) and Duncan and Savage's (1991) edited collection). Nor has it been helped by being sucked into the quicksand of 'post-modernism' (see, for example, Harvey (1989a) and Soja (1989); and Massey's critique (1991b) and by being exposed to the often opaque realms of realist philosophy (see Lovering (1989) on Graham (1988) and, for an overview of the salient misconceptions in this aspect of the debate, Sayer (1991)).

Where the debate surrounding locality has been particularly effective, however, has been in reinforcing the basic argument of Massey and Allen's influential (1984) edited collection that 'geography matters'. By illustrating the ways in which actual patterns of spatial uneven development have unfolded over time, and the degree to which present and future spatial trajectories are conditioned by historical events, it has undoubtedly helped the project to reinstate space and spatial variation into the analysis of social processes. In terms of the subject of this book, the debate has also been important in demonstrating the interaction between locality and policy. Policies are mediated through, to refer back to the earlier discussion, the particular socio-economic, political and cultural characteristics of place. Given that these characteristics are historically contingent and vary between places, policies can potentially operate with very different effects in different areas.

Indeed the interactive relationships may not just produce different impacts but may also act to modify the goals and operation of the policies themselves. Thus, for example, it has been argued that the current government's housing policies have not necessarily achieved the desired results on Merseyside's outer estates precisely because of such 'locality effects'. The development, for example, of housing cooperatives in these areas through the government's 'Estates Action' Programme, far from encouraging the development of some privatized and individualistic break from a 'dependency culture' has instead tapped on, and in so doing, further strengthened the development of a local collectivist ethos (Meegan, 1990). It would not seem unreasonable, therefore, to expect the operations of development corporations to differ from place to place.

The Merseyside Development Corporation and 'Locality'

As already argued, any evaluation of the MDC has to appreciate the complex social, economic, political and cultural make-up of the area into which it has been inserted. Dominating this mix is the recent devastating scale and pace of economic decline. 1966 marked the peak of post-war employment growth on Merseyside. Between then and the establishment of the MDC in 1981, something like 183,000 jobs were lost in the county as a whole, a decline of one-quarter. Particularly significant was the fact that 72% of the job loss was in manufacturing, the sector that had been targeted by politicians and planners as the saviour of the local economy and necessary compensation for the long-term decline of the port. A milestone in this latter decline (and to be a significant factor in the operations of the future MDC) was the closure in 1972 of the three-mile dock system south of the Pier Head, as the then Merseyside Docks and Harbour Board finally caved in to mounting financial difficulties and embarked on a central government-assisted restructuring.

Unemployment returned to the political agenda with a vengeance. 121,260 people were registered as unemployed in Merseyside County in June 1981 representing an unemployment rate of 16.9%, over one and a half times the national rate. Population decline had begun in the 1930s and been further encouraged by the decentralization policies of the 1950s and 1960s but by the end of the 1970s emigration in search of work took a hold that has still to be loosened (with population declining by about 9% in each of the two decades since 1971 and distinguishing Merseyside County as the fastest declining conurbation in England and Wales). This highly pressurized period of social and economic decline (with a particularly intense phase in the 1978–81 recession) was finally punctuated by the outbreak of rioting in 1981 giving the area the further unwelcome distinction of containing the first city in mainland Britain to experience the use by police of CS gas to quell civil disturbance.

Social and economic degeneration was accompanied by serious environmental degradation with economic restructuring leaving a legacy of industrial dereliction and environmental despoliation. This environmental degradation was particularly severe in the core of the county, and especially so in the sites along the riverside previously housing chemical works and refuse disposal activities and in the non-operational docks where the river system had been allowed to re-establish itself, leaving deposits of silt and mud (sometimes topped up by sewage) nearly 30 feet deep in places and overlooked by rows of warehouses in various stages of dilapidation. 80% of the land initially designated for the MDC was derelict and unused, a significantly higher proportion than was the case in the LDDC (where the figure was 45%) or in all of the subsequently created development corporations (see Dalby, 1990).

The MDC has made much of this environmental legacy with, for example, John Ritchie, the then Chief Executive, using it to fend off criticisms of the Corporation's relatively unfavourable balance between public and private investment (with the former far exceeding the latter) at the end of the first five years of its operations. He pointed to the extraordinary scale of the reclamation work that it had faced and stressed that over 50% of its public investment thus far had gone 'straight into the ground' (*Financial Times*, 1986). This theme has been frequently rehearsed by other development corporations, perhaps most bluntly of late by the Chairman of the Black Country Development Corporation, Sir William Francis, who has argued that, 'Developers need the abnormal cost removed before they will build' (quoted in Dalby, 1990). The precise status of these 'abnormal costs' is something to which we will return in a later section.

The goal of levering private investment (after successive rounds of private disinvestment) and of employment generation as set out in the MDC's Initial Development Strategy (MDC, 1981) was therefore clearly going to be severely tested in such an economically and environmentally distressed locality. And sure enough, little private investment has been forthcoming, most significantly for industrial development. Strategy had to be rethought and the resultant shifts in policy were quickly reflected in changes to the original planned land-uses. Key sites zoned for industrial or mixed housing and industrial development have been re-zoned for housing or retail land uses (Hayes, 1987) as the MDC gradually adopted the property-led development style that has come to typify the activities of the UDCs as a whole (CLES, 1990b).

The unwillingness of the private sector to invest in the MDC schemes, however, has not simply been a reflection of the depressed state of the local economy and/or the scale of what it perceives as 'abnormal costs'. Local politics – that other important ingredient in the making of 'locality' – has also played a key role. On balance, the MDC was given a relatively free ride in its first years from local politicians. The three local authorities directly affected by the MDC (Liverpool, Sefton and Knowsley) made no formal objections to the Corporation's establishment. The most sustained objections came from the Merseyside County Council and these were quickly undercut (first, subtly, by the appointment of its leader, Sir Kenneth Thompson, as the first Vice Chairman of the Corporation and then, more crudely, with its abolition in 1986).

The debate in Parliament, of the Bill establishing the MDC, clearly reveals – and for this reader at least, with hindsight, rather surprisingly – the enthusiasm of local MPs for the proposed Corporation. This enthusiasm covered the political spectrum encompassing not just the lone Tory (Anthony Steen) or the right-wing Labour MPs that were later to defect to the SDP (James Dunn, Richard Crawshaw and Eric Ogden) but also the two redoubtable left-wingers (the late Eric Heffer and Alan Roberts). For the Labour MPs, a particularly welcome feature of the proposed Corporation (and again somewhat discon-certingly given subsequent furore over development corporations' lack of local political accountability) was its bypassing of local authority powers. Alan Roberts was particularly scathing about the 'Scrooge-like' Sefton District

Council in his constituency (Hansard, 1981). At the time, of course, the local authorities were controlled by either Tory or Liberal–Tory administrations.

The MDC, unlike its London counterpart, was thus initially received with relatively little local political opposition. The situation was changed somewhat in 1983 with the election of a radical, Labour administration in Liverpool, an administration effectively led by members (or 'supporters' to use the preferred terminology) of the far-left 'Militant Tendency' (for an interesting discussion of the influence of 'Militant' in the Labour Party both nationally and in Liverpool, see Crick, 1986). The City Council was certainly critical of the MDC (see for example the comments of Tony Byrnes, Chairman of the powerful Finance Committee in the *Financial Times*, 1986). This critical stance, however, had little direct impact on the Corporation's activities as the Council became increasingly embroiled in other political battles both with central government over rate setting and policy direction and eventually with sections of the local community (Meegan, 1990). With their energies focused elsewhere, the Council's politicians simply ignored the MDC. Between 1983 and 1989 no one from Liverpool City Council took up the available seat (albeit as a representative in a personal capacity) on the MDC Board (although officers did maintain the working links established by the already agreed Code of Consultation).

What did reverberate on the MDC's activities, however, were the more indirect effects of the City Council's policies. The Council's 'municipal socialism', resolutely based on an 'Urban Regeneration Strategy' involving municipal house building and environmental and leisure development not only jarred with the public–private approach of the MDC but also actively undermined it by alienating potential private sector investment (see, for example, *Financial Times*, 1986; Parkinson, 1990). MDC policy thus shifted even further towards public sector-led infrastructural work and development activities for which some private sector involvement was forthcoming such as tourism and leisure and building on the success of the International Garden Festival and Tall Ships Race in attracting visitors to the city. The steadily growing numbers of visitors to the refurbished Albert Dock complex further reinforced this policy shift. Although even here private sector involvement was far from secure. Thus, for example, the private developer to which the MDC had handed over the Garden Festival site (against the advice of both the DOE and Liverpool City Council and for which it came in for particularly severe criticism from the National Audit Office (1988)) quickly went bankrupt. So too did one of the developers of the first housing units on the Garden Festival site leaving the scheme in question incomplete.

On balance, however, the MDC has not seen any failures on any comparable scale to that of Olympia and York's Canary Wharf débâcle in the LDDC area. Nor has it presented the Exchequer with escalating demands for public infrastructure investment to service its property development as has its counterpart in the capital city. These factors largely explain the relatively good press that the MDC has received of late (see, for example, Dalby, 1990). Of course, the fact that Merseyside was barely affected by the essentially southern property boom of the late 1980s and experienced none of the development pressures experienced in the capital city goes a long way towards explaining the MDC's relatively prudent development programme. An indication of the very different property markets' pressures is indicated in the figures for land transactions by the two development corporations. In June 1992 the MDC still held some 87% of the land that it had acquired (333 out of 382 hectares) and had a negative balance on land transactions (of nearly £18 million with expenditure of £29 million and receipts of £11.2 million). The LDDC, in contrast, held only 68% of its land acquisitions (594 out of 870 hectares) and had been able to make a surplus on its land transactions (with a spend of £161 million and receipts of £302 million giving a positive balance of £141 million) (Hansard, 1992a). Thus, while local economic circumstances did steer the MDC away from industrial towards property development, the slackness of the local property market did not allow any of the speculative excesses that have characterized development in the LDDC area.

The MDC's strategic objectives were thus reoriented by the feedback from the interaction of the local economy and the local political situation. Another interaction was also significant in this context, this time between local politics and local culture. The designated area of the MDC initially had a population of only 450 people. Extension of the area in 1988 increased the population to 7,000. While this figure was relatively small (it was, for example, less than a fifth of LDDC's 40,000 population), it did include some of the oldest and most tightly knit working class neighbourhoods. The people living there had a long history of adversity (in both employment and housing) and a strong sense of place – inner-city Liverpool. This sense of, and commitment to, place had a direct bearing on the MDC's development. Indeed it played a key role in the very redefinition of the Corporation's boundaries.

One of the most active neighbourhood groups was in the Vauxhall area in north Liverpool, historically dominated by dock work and a dominant employer (Tate and Lyle, which closed its factory in 1980). A group of residents, the 'Eldonians', formed a housing cooperative to resist dispersal to outer council housing estates. This approach brought them eventually and inevitably into bitter confrontation with the City Council and its municipal-housing preference and resulted in some intense battles within the local Labour Party (Meegan, 1990). Central government, already at odds with the City Council, certainly made the most of this conflict by financially supporting the Eldonians through the Housing Corporation. But the Eldonians also felt the need to lobby for an extension of the MDC's boundaries into their patch to allow them to escape (with a degree of reluctance given their support for, and indeed in many cases membership of, the Labour Party) from what they saw as malicious local authority control. When the MDC's boundaries were altered these alterations neatly took in the Eldonian community.

The larger population created by the extension of the MDC's boundaries did, of course, mean that its policies now had to accommodate new political pressures. These pressures have seen their reflection, for example, in the MDC's strategy for the Vauxhall area which recognizes the importance of housing cooperatives and the provision of low-cost housing. This emphasis is also visible in other 'Area Strategies' (with, for example, the support of local authority housing schemes in Bootle, in the North Docks area). Indeed the fact that the MDC has defined separate 'Area Strategies' only reinforces the broader argument that policy has to be sensitive to spatial variation (in this case at neighbourhood level within the Development Corporation's overall designated area).

This is not to argue, however, that the relationship between the MDC and local community groups has always been smooth sailing. The MDC, for example, commissioned a skills audit for the Vauxhall area by a London-based consultancy in preference to a competing proposal from the Eldonians in collaboration with researchers at Liverpool Polytechnic. But in general, community groups do appear to have been reasonably successful in influencing MDC thinking and bending MDC spending in their direction. As CLES (1990b) show, the MDC comes out relatively well in the ranking of UDCs by community spending (coming first in 1988–89 and second in 1989–90) and this in a Development Corporation with, as already argued, particularly severe pressures on its spending from a markedly low 'leverage' of private investment.

The shift in strategy was also influenced to some degree by the fact that the MDC had from the outset a more public interventionist, planning orientation than had the LDDC, for example. Key appointments were made from the public and planning sectors, thus, its first Chief Executive and second Chairman were recruited from New Town Development Corporations (Northampton and Warrington respectively) and many of the professional staff came from the local authorities (with the Merseyside County Council, initially the major critic of the MDC, being a major recruitment source). The orientation was clearly reflected in the Corporation's Initial Development Strategy (MDC, 1981) which drew heavily on former planning policies of both the Merseyside County Council and the Liverpool City Council and on the Merseyside Structure Plan. The Development Corporation was also quick to establish the statutorily required Code of Consultation with the local authorities. The MDC's strong planning predilection helps to explain why, as Hayes (1987) and Parkinson and Evans (1989) point out, there have been relatively few planning disagreements between it and its surrounding local authorities.

Urban Entrepreneurialism and Development Corporations

The shift from 'urban managerialism' to 'urban entrepreneurialism'

Harvey, building on his previous pioneering work on the urban process under capitalism (Harvey, 1989b), detects an evolution in urban governance from 'urban managerialism' to 'urban entrepreneurialism'. He links this transformation to a paradigmatic shift in capital accumulation from the rigid mass production and Keynesian regulation of 'Fordism' to the flexible accumulation of 'post-Fordism' (Harvey, 1989c). It is not necessary, however, to accept uncritically the idea of the post-Fordist transformation to agree that there has indeed been a pronounced shift to a more entrepreneurial form of urban governance – not least in the UK context where development corporations have played a leading role (Lawless, 1991; Pacione, 1990; Parkinson, 1989).

Harvey (1989c) identifies four key competitive strategies pursued by the class-alliances and coalitions engaged in urban entrepreneurialism and all of these can be detected, with different emphases, in the operations of the UDCs. The strategies entail competition over: first, the international division of labour (attracting mobile investment and employment); second, the spatial division of consumption (tourism and consumerism – 'attracting the consumer dollar'); third, the acquisition of control and command functions (securing high-status activities – corporate headquarters, media and financial decision makers – in the hierarchial division of labour); and, finally, the redistribution of surpluses by central government (transfer payments, defence expenditure, etc.).

The MDC and 'urban entrepreneurialism'

The MDC has certainly attempted the urban entrepreneurialism strategies that Harvey identifies, although it has been somewhat reluctant, until recently, for example, to engage seriously in 'place marketing' for major inward manufacturing investment (with the recently retired Chief Executive, John Ritchie, arguing that it was too expensive; see *Financial Times*, 1986). A new administration has seen a reassessment of this view and recently sponsored a 'place-marketing' promotional tour of the eastern seaboard (with the Liverpool Philharmonic Orchestra in tow). But its principal competitive strategy to date has undoubtedly been over what Harvey terms the 'spatial division of consumption', most notably with the Albert Dock development (now claiming to be the second largest tourist attraction in the United Kingdom with 6 million visitors last year) and the promotion of various 'spectacles' (for example, the Garden Festival, the Tall Ships Race, the Mersey River Festivals and the Paul McCartney concert). It has also been involved in competition over the attraction of control and command functions having helped to persuade the Customs and Excise Department to move a headquarters' activity to the South Docks while the attraction of Granada TV News Centre to the Albert Dock was undoubtedly a major factor in the latter's development. And the MDC's very existence, of course, is a testimony to the redistribution of surpluses by central government (via 'grant-in-aid').

What is significant, however, is the fact that the MDC's efforts in this direction have thus far been relatively isolated. The development of 'urban entrepreneurialism' has undoubtedly been constrained by 'locality'. A broad-based class alliance that full-blown urban entrepreneurialism requires has not developed. This is largely because the conditions for building such an alliance have not been propitious. As Harvey (1989b) persuasively argues, urban politics is not an autonomous phenomenon but closely related to the process of capital accumulation, being spawned by the tendency inherent in the social and economic structures of urban regions towards a 'structured coherence'. This coherence reflects a distinctive mode of production and consumption, social relationships and physical and social infrastructures in individual urban regions.

Merseyside, and especially its inner core, last experienced anything approaching a genuine 'structured coherence' in the heyday of its port-based industrial economy. Since then the story has been one of incoherence and dysfunction as mismatches between production and consumption possibilities, antagonistic class relations and deteriorating physical and social infrastructures have testified to the area's difficulties in adjusting to a new position in new international and national divisions of labour. One expression of this has been a deeply polarized space-economy. Within what might be described as the Greater Merseyside sub-regional economy (as defined in terms of input–output relationships – see, Regional Science Research Group, 1991), there are major social and economic

Figure 4.1 The Greater Merseyside area by local authority districts (source: CRED Research Unit, Department of Geography, University of Liverpool).

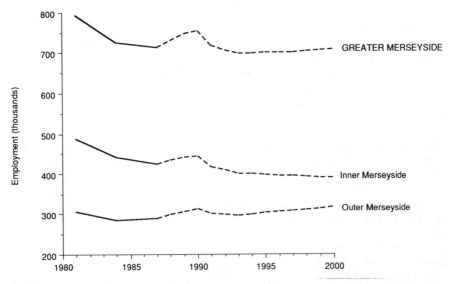

Figure 4.2 Projected total employment, Greater, Inner and Outer Merseyside, 1987–2000 (source: CRED Research Unit, Department of Geography, University of Liverpool; estimated figures based on county-level projections supplied by NIERC/Cambridge Econometrics).

differences between the constituent 'Inner' and 'Outer' areas (Figure 4.1). It is the former, broadly conforming to the Merseyside County, in which employment decline has been concentrated. It is significant, for example, that the Inner Area continued to lose employment during the national economic recovery of the late 1980s – and that decline is forecast to continue into the next century (Figure 4.2). In direct contrast is the continuing growth of the 'Outer Merseyside' area (with the key growth points of Chester and Warrington).

It is the Inner Area, containing Liverpool's inner city and the outer estates of Liverpool, Knowsley and Wirral, which has the most severe problems of social disadvantage and unemployment (Knowsley Metropolitan Borough Council, 1989; Liverpool City Council, 1991; Meegan, 1989). While unemployment in the Inner Area has fallen in absolute numbers in the years since the MDC was established, it is a depressing indication of the intractability of the problem that the area's unemployment rate has remained stubbornly at about one and a half times the national rate. This performance fits in with the broader findings of the Policy Studies Institute's overview of trends in social and economic conditions in Britain's most disadvantaged urban areas throughout the 1980s (Willmott and Hutchinson, 1992). This overview demonstrated that, despite the plethora of urban policy initiatives (including UDCs) the gap between deprived urban areas and other areas has remained just as wide as it was when urban policy was first introduced at the end of the 1970s and, indeed, in a number of key respects the gap has widened. Merseyside's representatives in the survey – Liverpool and Knowsley from its inner core – were no exceptions to this general, depressing rule. Moreover there are signs of a degree of polarization between the depressed areas in the inner core with, for example, the growth being encouraged along the riverside by MDC developments in Liverpool contrasting with the continuing decline of the outer industrial estates in both Liverpool and Knowsley.

This incoherent, polarized, development has helped to produce a fragmented urban politics and a barren soil for the development of class alliances and political coalitions. One element in this phenomenon has been a private sector dominated by large multinational capital with no attachment to place mirroring, indeed helping to create a relatively weak entrepreneurial base in the form of small-firm development (Parkinson, 1990). Another has been local government responses in the form of an introverted 'municipal socialism'. This response not only alienated the private sector but also other local authorities both inside and outside the metropolitan region. The failure to develop an effective institutional framework for local authority collaboration either between the authorities in the 'Inner' and 'Outer' areas or those within the two areas (especially in the case of the 'Inner Area' since the abolition of the Merseyside County Council) has also been important. The very different conditions of economic growth throughout the urban region have made the definition of common interests very difficult. And the insertion of the MDC into this political situation has not made things any easier.

The local authority districts have had to contend with steadily diminishing financial resources while central government money has been diverted into funding the MDC's activities. This resentment was expressed by Michael Reddington, the then Chief Executive of Liverpool City Council in 1987 in an interview in the *Municipal Journal* which was subsequently quoted in the Parliamentary debate on UDCs (Hansard, 1987). In a telling comparison, Mr Reddington showed how the City Council's spending allocation would have been nearly doubled if it had access to the MDC's expenditure on capital works. The MDC was spending some £30 million on 27 acres of Liverpool land while the City Council had just £37 million to spend on the remaining 236,973 acres. And this financial imbalance has not been ameliorated as the figures in written answers to Parliamentary questions reveal (Hansard, 1992b,c). While grant-in-aid to the MDC has increased by 61% in the five financial years following Mr Reddington's complaint, Liverpool has seen its urban and housing investment programmes cut by 18 and 41% respectively. A degree of resentment on the part of local authorities in these circumstances is not difficult to understand.

This is not to argue that attempts at coalition formation have not been made. They have, in Inner Merseyside at least, but these have been limited and unstable in the past and it remains to be seen whether the latest attempts can overcome the inherent pressures for division and fragmentation. These attempts include, for example, the formation of a private sector lobbying group to 'market' the area ('BOOM': Business Opportunities on Merseyside), although it is limited in terms of both resources and political 'clout'. The most significant initiatives are emerging from the public sector with the close involvement of the MDC. Thus, in Liverpool, for example, an Officer Steering Group has been formed comprising officials from central government agencies (Merseyside Task Force, City Action Team, Granby-Toxteth Task Force, Departments of Trade and Industry and Employment), the MDC, Housing Corporation and

Merseyside TEC and the City Council. The group meets to consider the individual strategies and programmes of the constituent agencies and to explore how these relate to each other. The Group is currently considering, for example, Liverpool City Council's Economic Development Plan. The five Merseyside County local authorities have also agreed to work together on a 'Merseyside Image Campaign'.

Liverpool City Council's recently awarded 'City Challenge' financial package involves the establishment of a 'Partnership Forum' and 'Executive' which draw together representatives from the public, private and voluntary sectors. Collaboration between these has also been encouraged by the European Commission's 'Merseyside Integrated Development Operation' (1989–91). This conduit for EC funding required a Directing Committee comprising the major central government departments and agencies, the five local authorities in Merseyside County, the MDC, the Merseyside Chamber of Commerce, the Merseyside Tourism Board, Merseytravel, the North West Water Authority, voluntary sector representatives and European Commission representatives. MIDO represents an important initiative because it brings in the international level which, as will be argued below, must be a key element in any progressive approach to urban regeneration.

While avoiding the limitations of urban development being driven by a single-purpose, territorially-constrained body like the development corporations, such initiatives, as with all coalitions, still have to contend with the danger of slipping into the kind of competitive 'boosterism' on which 'urban entrepreneurialism' is fundamentally based (Harvey, 1989c). The picture, however, is surely not as starkly black and white as Harvey makes out. Implicit in all the policies are tensions between out-and-out entrepreneurialism of the 'place marketing' kind and the pursuit of policies responding to issues of social need which, if not addressed, will result in there being ultimately no 'marketable place'. Thus the MDC is pulled toward community issues like social housing or training (the latter through its sponsorship of the training organization, METEL). Likewise, while participating in the Merseyside Image Campaign, Liverpool City Council is also developing a 'Poverty Strategy' and exploring positive discrimination policies like its Vocational Training Initiative (aimed at unemployed black youth) and the funding of the Women's Technology Centre (Liverpool City Council, 1991).

What is important is politics, and the politics in question is one that can decisively weight policies towards the long-term development of democratically decided and sustainable welfare-based development. Given the instability engendered by the still parlous local economic situation, the development of such a politics is charged with difficulty. The current Labour administration of Liverpool City Council, for example, is beset by factional infighting as it attempts to get to grips with its serious financial difficulties. The danger is that this division will encourage an even more inward-looking politics.

To break out, on the one hand, of introspection and political inertia and, on the other, of the 'urban entrepreneurial treadmill', a coalition politics that builds on the strengths of 'locality' but transcends 'localism' is necessary. Again this will not be easy to secure. Relationships between the Liverpool City Council and other similarly placed metropolitan authorities have been soured by the tactics of the confrontational years of the 1983–87 administration.

Financial pressures have also meant that the City Council has been further isolated since then, having had to rescind its membership, for example, of the Centre for Local Economic Strategies (CLES), the local-authority funded organization for coordinating and exchanging local government experience of local economic development. Only Knowsley, of the five Merseyside County local authorities, is currently a CLES member. International links are even weaker. Yet without such links Merseyside is likely to be forced into entering the global 'urban entrepreneurial' competition with potentially crippling handicaps (an unfavourable image and a divided voice).

Broader Lessons

Perhaps the most important and obvious lesson from the experience of the MDC surrounds the scale of resources that is required to begin to regenerate the urban cores of older industrial regions. The MDC has spent £247 million since it was established in 1981 in a tightly delimited area in Merseyside's inner core. And the bulk of this money has had to come from public sources. There is no question that the public sector must continue to take the lead in urban regeneration.

Another related lesson is that single-purpose agencies like development corporations have to be linked to broader planning frameworks and strategies if their activities are to contribute to the social and economic regeneration of the wider metropolitan regions in which they operate. Between 1981, when the MDC was established, and 1989, the last available date for comparable official statistics, Merseyside County had a net loss of something like 70,000 jobs. Liverpool accounted for just over 64,000 of these net job losses. The MDC's own figures for the net gain of permanent jobs created in its area (to March 1992) was 2,000 (Hansard, 1992d). This figure could be doubled by the eventual move of Customs and Excise activities to new purpose-built offices to the south of the Albert Dock complex in Queen's Dock. This emphatically emphasizes the point made earlier about the key role that the public sector has to play in urban regeneration. One Civil Service move will match, in terms of net permanent job creation, 11 years of job creation. But even so the figures still pale into insignificance given the severity of job loss in the surrounding areas.

The MDC has long-since recognized that the success of its schemes depends crucially on their being integrated with the plans of surrounding areas. The classic example here is the need to link the Albert Dock complex into Liverpool City Council's plans for the city centre to avoid it being simply a relatively isolated tourist attraction. Merseytravel's plans are also crucial here. The City Council sponsored Officer Steering Group and the Merseyside Integrated Development Operation also testify to the need for the MDC to operate in a broader planning framework. The question thus arises as to whether it makes sense for the planning framework for urban regions to compose the voluntaristic network of local authorities, central government agencies and other interested bodies. There once was a planning authority that was able to operate at the level of the metropolitan region – in Merseyside's case, the Merseyside County Council. But this tier of government has been removed while an agency to plan a selective slice of the remit of the lower tier of local government (district councils) has been inserted and preferentially funded – the UDC.

This leads on to the question of accountability. The much-publicized resignation from the MDC Board two years ago by the Liverpool University Professor of Economics, Patrick Minford, brought this question into sharp focus. What was at issue was the proposed siting of a coal-fired power station and deep-water jetty in Birkenhead which Professor Minford supported on the grounds of the semi-skilled and unskilled manual work that it would provide in an area suffering from a chronic deficiency of such employment. The Board disagreed, arguing that there would be greater employment multipliers generated by competing plans for office and light-industrial development (although the 'image' of the power station was undoubtedly another factor in the decision). The debates over the proposals were, of course, carried out behind closed doors and were only made public in the wake of Professor Minford's resignation. Such decisions require wider public consultation and political debate. While the power station might well have been inappropriate for the site in question (or, for that matter, any other within the MDC's territory) there were surely sites elsewhere in the sub-region that could accommodate it. It is the *Merseyside* Development Corporation after all. The debate should not be confined to one favoured territory – which accounts for just 1.5, 0.5 and 7.4% respectively of the land area, population and employment of Merseyside County – but to the area as a whole.

The broader planning framework itself needs to be built upon a comprehensive strategy for social and economic regeneration. As I have argued, the MDC has found its own policies inexorably tugged in the direction of social rather than market evaluations (in, for example, recognition of the need for social housing). Darwin (1990) captures the essence of the argument in his idea of an 'ESCHER' strategy, namely one which combines policies for economic, social, cultural, health and ecological regeneration. A strictly market approach will only address narrowly defined economic issues. The MDC's experience of environmental reclamation is perhaps instructive in this context.

The MDC, in line with other development corporations, has argued strongly that its public-funded physical reclamation work is essential to remove the 'abnormal costs' deterring private sector investment. But where did those abnormal costs originate? From the private sector and the public sector using private market calculations. Take, for example, the MDC's reclamation of the 250 acre site for the International Garden Festival. Nearly £11 million was spent on what at the time was the largest single reclamation project in Europe. What was being reclaimed? The private sector donated derelict oil tank farms (previously operated by Esso and Texaco) and a graveyard of disused petrol-storage tanks (courtesy of BNOC). The public sector chipped in an unstable, methane-generating refuse tip, while the public–private restructuring of the South Docks bequeathed the silted-up Herculaeneum Dock. (The future costs of the reclamation of the Albert Dock complex were also, of course, crucially affected by the decision in 1972 not to meet the expense of securing and maintaining the South Dock system.)

What this all adds up to, of course, is a local manifestation of the broader failure of economic policy to address seriously, to use the title of Kapp's sadly neglected classic, the 'social costs of business enterprise' (Kapp, 1978) or the complex issue of 'sustainable development' (Redclift, 1987; World Commission on Environment and Development, 1987). To insert 'local' into the latter clearly requires national and international public policy intervention. The international scale is also important in terms of developing alternative strategies to urban entrepreneurialism. Darwin (1990) and CLES (1990b) are surely correct in arguing that the public sector and, in particular, local government should take the lead in regeneration strategies given their responsibility for taking into account the public good. What then has to be avoided is a lapse into urban entrepreneurial 'boosterism'. Some elements of this may indeed be positive – such as the development of a sense of place upon which local confidence can be built – but these have to be carefully handled (whose images? whose sense of place?).

An introspective, self-referential strategy (if the supporting coalition can be sustained) will only reinforce the pressures on localities to go down the urban entrepreneurial route. If Murray (1991) is correct and we are now entering into a new European regionalism – a 'Europe of Regions' rather than nationally-defined economic blocs – then it needs to be a regionalism based upon the principles of mutual cooperation rather than competition if the problems of older industrial regions and their metropolitan cores are to be seriously addressed (see, for example, CLES, 1990a). A framework for such cooperation for

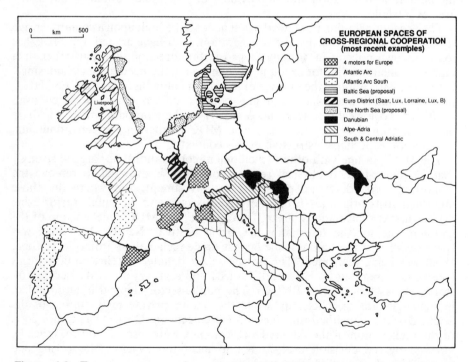

Figure 4.3 European spaces of cross-regional cooperation; most recent examples (source: CRED Research Unit, Department of Geography, University of Liverpool; based on a map from the FAST Research Programme, Commission of the European Communities, Brussels).

Merseyside, for example, is offered by the European Commission's recently designated group of 'Atlantic Arc' regions on the Western seaboard of Europe (Figure 4.3). The aim is to encourage these regions to develop economic, cultural and political collaboration to enable them to act as a counter-axis to the cumulative growth of the regions forming, in DATAR's unforgettable terminology, the 'Blue Banana'. Collaboration between the latter and the 'Atlantic Arc' would be the next step to produce, to retain the somewhat bizarre imagery, a new geometry and a more fruitful trajectory of urban and regional development. (As a postcript in this context, it is interesting to note that, at the time of writing, the five District Councils on Merseyside have established a Merseyside Liaison Unit and are advertising for a Merseyside European Liaison Officer – not before time.)

5

CARDIFF BAY AND THE PROJECT OF MODERNIZATION

Huw Thomas and Rob Imrie

Introduction

Cardiff Bay Development Corporation (CBDC) was set up on 1 April 1987 charged with the task of establishing 'Cardiff internationally as a superlative maritime city, which will stand comparison with any similar city in the world, enhancing the image and economic well-being of Cardiff and of Wales as a whole' (CBDC, 1988, p. 2). This definition of its task makes it plain that more than inner city regeneration (however that may be construed) is envisaged. Physical, social and economic restructuring and revitalization there will be, but the goals of the Corporation are established from national, indeed international, perspectives. It is a central thesis of this chapter that the apparent vanity, even absurdity, of a provincial city of under 300,000 population seeking comparison with maritime cities worldwide (with, perhaps, Boston, Sydney, Buenos Aires, even Venice) can only be understood against the distinctive political background of South Wales and what this has meant in terms of postwar state intervention at central and local level to physically restructure Cardiff. The city's development has assumed totemic significance in a project to modernize a regional economy which has been diagnosed as outdated and in decline.

Indeed, CBDC's proclamation, of grasping 'a unique opportunity for Cardiff and for Wales', reflects the power of modernity in a locale which has expanded with the assistance of over thirty years of very active state-sponsored development (CBDC, 1990; Imrie and Thomas, 1993b; Thomas, 1992b). Far from CBDC simply representing an imposed central government solution to the problems of Cardiff docks, the Corporation is clearly wedded to some of the more widely held political values within the regional politics of South Wales, and, as we shall show, the terms of CBDC's engagement has, in part, facilitated some continuation of local authority involvement in the redevelopment of the city. All of this might suggest that a form of corporatist planning has emerged in the city, yet the actions of CBDC are also linked to a 'capital logic', creating the 'right' type of physical environment for private investors, a logic which has created tensions in Cardiff, particularly with groups seeking to promote social and community regeneration. In this sense, CBDC is indicative of the wider context of urban policy in pursuing strategies which seem to represent segmented interests, yet claiming to be planning the city of the future for all.

In considering these themes, we begin by placing the origins of CBDC within the particular political ethos of urban modernization, modernity, and local corporatism. We then look at the role of CBDC in the future of the dockside community indicating its partial involvement in developing wide-ranging links with local community organizations. This section provides background for our subsequent discussion of the institutional linkages between CBDC and local actors and agencies. Here we highlight the role of political incorporation and consensus building as the basis for the political and community acquiescence to the wider development objectives of CBDC. We conclude the discussion by considering the future for the evolving institutional frameworks in Cardiff and generalize our findings to the wider context of urban policy in Britain.

Regeneration as Modernization

CBDC's responsibilities cover an area of 2,700 acres, within which there are about 5,000 residents and around 1,000 enterprises employing 15,000 people (Figure 5.1). It is one of the larger Urban Development Corporations (UDCs),

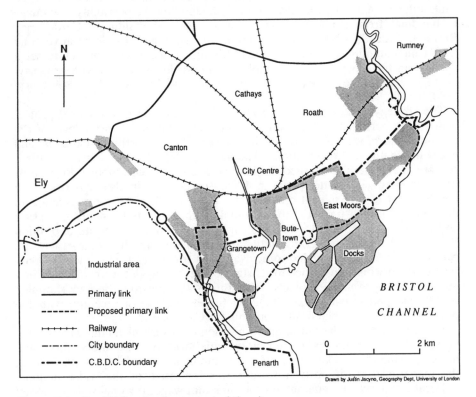

Figure 5.1 Cardiff Bay in the context of the city.

with annual grant-in-aid in 1991–92, for example, of £29.5 million. To date it has published a *Regeneration Strategy*, an ambitious document which foresees a physical and socio-economic transformation of Cardiff Bay with the creation of 3–4 million square feet (and perhaps more) of offices, 5–6 million square feet of industrial space (including 'high tech' and 'modern business'), 6,000 houses (25% social housing), and a range of tourist and leisure facilities (CBDC, 1988). The strategy is to be flexible and market responsive. One unintended consequence is that to date very little development has actually taken place, as the 1990s' recession bites. However, the direction of change which CBDC seeks to promote is very clear, the creation of a strategy 'to enable Cardiff City to take on the mantle of one of Europe's finest maritime communities' (CBDC, 1990, p. 2).

Yet, as previous research suggests, the regeneration strategy for Cardiff Bay cannot plausibly be presented as a concerted attempt to address the stubborn social and economic problems of inner Cardiff (Imrie and Thomas, 1992). The city has its poor people, and has the social inequality and segregation found in all British cities of its size (Cardiff City Council, 1984). But even if there are areas of particular deprivation – and social stigma – in Cardiff's docklands, there are also areas of great disadvantage in inner areas and peripheral housing estates which are outside the urban development area (UDA). Some of these have seen civil disorder, with an apparently racist dimension, in the 1990s, while others are among the areas most threatened by the possibility of damage to buildings from rising groundwater as a result of building a Cardiff Bay Barrage. Indeed, while CBDC presents its strategies as 'integrative' and 'balancing community needs', there is little difference in its approach to set it apart from the (socially) divisive policy frameworks associated with property-led regeneration elsewhere (Healey, 1992; Imrie and Thomas, 1993b; Solesbury, 1990; Turok, 1992).

The strategy makes more sense as the latest episode in a political project which has, periodically, gripped the state at local and central level – the creation of a modern Cardiff which is a capital city worthy of national, and even international, recognition (Thomas, 1992a). In the early twentieth century, a commercial bourgeoisie, finding its political feet, lobbied for Cardiff to be granted city status (and, in 1905, succeeded); it also undertook the development of a civic centre at Cathays Park which strove for grandeur and dignity, and ended up with strong colonial echoes in its formality, materials and design. In 1955 Cardiff became capital city of Wales, despite opposition from elsewhere in the Principality, and from around that time, the state centrally and locally struggled to devise a plan for the restructuring of the city centre which would do justice to its status. These struggles were reflected in a number of modernizing projects, from the 1960s onwards, the new shopping centre, the pedestrianization of Queen Street, and, most recently, with the centre complete, the blueprint proposals for Cardiff Bay.

All of this reflects the era of modernization of British planning, what Cooke (1988) refers to as the 'perceived moral superiority of state intervention over market domination in key areas of social and economic life' (p. 482). Indeed, the modernization of postwar Cardiff was indicative of the wider national political economy, the guarantee of a minimum wage, regional policies aimed at redressing social inequalities, and a significant central government commitment to ensuring the minimum conditions of social reproduction. As we show elsewhere, the processes of city modernization largely followed the ethos of the wider political economy, yet the regional dimensions were clear, a new civic order, an expression of the power of the local polity, and the ideals of a collective state apparatus (Imrie and Thomas, 1993b). In all these senses, postwar planning in Cardiff reflected what Cooke (1988a) terms a particular socio-spatial paradigm, suburban expansion, the grand schemes for city centre reconstruction, and economic development spreading out to the new social locales on the city periphery.

Of course, the massive city centre redevelopment proposals of the 1960s and 1970s (Cooke, 1980; Imrie and Thomas, 1993b) reflected, and depended upon, flows of capital searching for profitable investment on a national, perhaps international, stage. But the particular forms which the proposals took, and justifications which they received, the close involvement of central government in supporting and guiding the nature of the city centre development, these factors reflected what has been referred to as a regional spatial coalition (Pickvance, 1985), a broadly supported view of the desirable trajectory for the South Wales economy, and Cardiff's role in it (Rees and Lambert, 1981). In brief, a broad consensus, a form of local corporatism, has existed for decades among the major political parties, at central and local tiers of government and in business circles, that the South Wales economy, to be modernized, needs to shed its dependence on declining heavy industry and embrace the employment of the future (whatever that may be). Cardiff is to spearhead this transformation as a city of national, perhaps even international, significance.

The Cardiff Bay regeneration strategy, with its rhetoric about creating a 'superlative maritime city' and its sweeping away of allegedly redundant or under-used industrial space to allow for offices, leisure and other consumption-related uses, is a contemporary restatement of the modernizing theme of the 1960s, 1970s, and 1980s. Moreover, its proposal for a grandiose ceremonial mall, connecting the city centre to the waterfront, has clear architectural echoes of the early twentieth century civic centre (now an Outstanding Conservation Area), of bourgeois order and dignity becoming focal points for the appreciative gaze of the populace at large. Indeed, the vigorous place-marketing of CBDC reflects what Wilkinson (1992) terms an increasing consumerist style of urbanization, emphasizing new lifestyles, and the pleasure to be had from the self-conscious city landscapes. These linkages are evident in CBDC's brochure 'Building a Quality Environment' (1990b) where its corporate objectives play on consumption ideals in restating the need to 'promote development which provides a superb environment in which people will want to live, work and play' (p. 14).

Yet, there are senses in which the modernization ethos is running counter to some of the more deeply held spatial development convictions in the city. The spatial restructuring, promoted by CBDC, is perceived by some city councillors as diverting investment from the city centre to a peripheral part of Cardiff, thus contradicting a cornerstone of the postwar consensus concerning 'the integrity of the city centre', the maintenance of its place and dominance as the commercial and financial core. CBDC has sought to diffuse such criticisms by playing-up the theme of spatial integration, of wholeness and balance, by stating how 'the development of Cardiff Bay will unite the former commercial heart of Cardiff with its City Centre and give back to the city its waterfront'. Such powerful (physical) imagery, the idea of organic synthesis, seeks to reassure and placate, although, as we shall see, the underlying tensions remain important undercurrents in the evolving strategies for Cardiff Bay.

Yet CBDC's co-option of the modernization theme is most identifiable as an ideological coup, in as much that the new development processes being unleashed by the development corporation run counter to many of the institutional linkages, political, and community goals, which held together the postwar regional coalition. The principles underpinning CBDC are, in fact, contrary to key elements of the modernization ethos in the city, the utilization of the market as the primary mechanism of economic development, the reduction in welfare and social programmes in property-led development, and the primacy of the private sector over the public in social and cultural provision (Cooke, 1988a). In as much as the institutions and politics of modernization have been eclipsed, CBDC's project is less modern than post-modern. This is crystallized in the evolving institutional and political linkages which, in the CBDC case, are characterized by the emergence of new socio-spatial inequalities in the city, new consumption elites, and an increasingly marginalized stratum of social groups in and beyond the UDA. We now consider some of the dimensions of CBDC's project of 'modernization'.

Cardiff Bay and Local Social Relations

In the background of local public and political attitudes towards CBDC is the complex role of Butetown – the 2,000 strong community geographically and symbolically the centre of the Bay – in the city's history and politics. Modern Cardiff owes its existence to the astonishing growth of its docks in the late nineteenth and early twentieth centuries (Daunton, 1977). By 1913 it was the premier coal exporting port in the world, with all that this entailed, an international coal exchange, a sophisticated financial and service infrastructure, and a cosmopolitan dockland community unique in Wales. As the port declined in the interwar years, so the city's commercial centre of gravity shifted to coincide with its civic centre, around the castle and main shopping streets. Butetown was left, 'down below the bridge', an area still socially and economically distinct from the city, and with little political clout as the economic significance of the docks declined and residential and commercial expansion was concentrated in the city centre and its northern periphery (Evans *et al*, 1984). Memories of the institutionalized and personal racism which has isolated the dockland community throughout the twentieth century remain vivid (Sherwood, 1991). In the postwar period Butetown was the subject of municipal redevelopment, but otherwise the area's concerns appear to have been overshadowed by major peripheral development for private and public sector housing.

Meanwhile, the industrial areas around Butetown barely featured in local authority policy making, as planners concentrated on city centre redevelopment (Cooke, 1980; Imrie and Thomas, 1993b). As late as the early 1980s, many significant industrial access roads in the docks were in private ownership with all that this implied for poor coordination and maintenance. The closure of the

East Moors steelworks in 1978, with the direct loss of around 4,000 jobs, increased the political profile of the industrial enclave in the docks, and a great deal of public investment followed in land reclamation and highway improvement (Thomas and Imrie, 1989). However, the area was still conceived, in policy and political circles, as having an industrial future and, to that extent, it remained a place socially and economically distinct from the rest of a commercial city.

CBDC's strategy and rhetoric challenges these relationships, while seeking to establish a continuity between its activities and a particular reading of Cardiff's history. Its very name highlights tensions between these objectives. 'Cardiff Bay' is redolent of the city's maritime past, as are the names of new developments such as 'Atlantic Wharf' and 'Windsor Quay'. But until CBDC's formation, there *was* no Cardiff Bay. The provenance of the term lies in public relations not cartography or history, and a similar tale might be told of the other names which are gracing developments in 'Cardiff Bay'. The name marks a new beginning, a fresh start, as much as maritime continuity. Indeed, CBDC's approach rejects the apparent failures of modernization while espousing post-modern pretensions to a new future, the appeal of the market, the abandonment of the industrial heritage, and the power of the individual, the private sector, in spatial development planning.

We are told that Cardiff Bay, unlike Cardiff Docks, is going to be at the heart of a vibrant, internationally acclaimed maritime city (Pickup, 1988); a city which has turned its back on the waterfront is now to embrace it. In the absence of a local revolution in social attitudes, the 'respectable' citizens of Cardiff might not be expected to embrace easily the socially isolated, multi-racial Butetown, or the scrap-merchants, gypsy sites and heavy engineering of the docks. So it is the character of Cardiff Bay which will need to change if it is to become familiar territory to most inhabitants of the city, let alone a scene of superlative maritime developments. If the ambitious plans to create tourist and leisure attractions of national significance in the Bay area are realized, then, of course, local social stigma and reserve will break down. However, five years after designation of CBDC, this kind of wholesale physical transformation remains on the horizon, and continuing effort goes into events which might influence local social perceptions of the 'docks' even if they do not have a wider impact. In recent summers a series of 'Bay Days' have been held – low or no cost festival-type events targeted at a city-wide audience. Rock concerts, bicycle races, and carnivals have featured among the attractions on offer. The County Council, a major supporter of mixed development in the Bay, has held open days and other 'fun' events at its new dockland HQ, which have also aimed to pull people from the remainder of the city to the unfamiliar territory of the docks.

But if generally held perceptions (and prejudices) about Butetown and the docks, as a place to visit, are being attacked by CBDC, fundamental aspects of social relations are left untouched. The corporation's current small community development team replaced its original appointment of a retired policeman as a community liaison officer (an appointment hardly designed to challenge local social and economic inequalities), and funding for 'community support projects' has increased from £169,000 in 1988–89 to £368,000 in 1991–92. The current team liaises with community and residents groups on a variety of topics – for example keeping them informed of CBDC's policy stances, suggesting small scale projects which might qualify for grant (CBDC funds 'homework clubs' for local children, and advisory services for Somalis, for example). Its difficulty is that painstaking work can be undermined by tensions arising from the inevitable dislocation involved in redevelopment. Thus, a long running dispute has developed between CBDC and local residents over the fate of the Mount Stuart Primary School, in Butetown.

In this episode, much needed County Council funded repairs were postponed some years ago on the advice of CBDC, which has plans to relocate the school, and build a car park on its site. Unfortunately, the Corporation seems to have been over-optimistic about the funding which the Welsh Office would sanction for the relocation. It has not been undertaken, and the school is in a worse state of repair than ever. Resident morale was not helped by the discovery that the original relocation site was too contaminated to be developed economically as a school; after a frantic search, CBDC has suggested an alternative site in a nearby industrial area. The reaction of the increasingly frustrated residents to this proposal is awaited. The episode reveals CBDC as not so much malign as somewhat inept – in having raised local expectations, which it could not then fulfil – and hamstrung by Welsh Office controls. The result, however, is tension with local authorities and the local populace. In the example of the primary school, the County Council, as education authority, has found itself having to explain decisions, and a lack of action, with which, at the very least, it had little sympathy.

No systematic and detailed total evaluation of CBDC's community development activity has appeared, but its marginal position in the organization expenditure, and anecdotal evidence, suggests that its role is to present a human, and very local, face for an organization whose main thrust and purpose is, quite clearly, to create a physical and socio-economic transformation which is likely to have limited benefits in the short term for local people. In interview, one major local property owner and developer was candid about the fact that for the current generation of 'Bay' residents, CBDC's strategy held out, at best, the prospect of a greater supply of low-grade service sector jobs. But, he argued, the children of the cleaners, caretakers, and cooks might aspire to, and challenge for, the high grade service sector jobs which will also be located in the area. Butetown and other parts of 'the Bay' have their share of 'success stories' – the doctors, professors, television presenters – of humble local origins. But the realities of educational inequality and social stratification make mass social mobility unlikely, particularly for communities which have a history of racial prejudice (which, as far as we know, is not being addressed, or acknowledged, directly by CBDC). 'Trickle-down', here as elsewhere, is the unexamined hope of those who have no well-grounded social policy.

Nevertheless, it is argued by local supporters of the Bay initiative that after decades of neglect by the state at all levels, it at least offers some hopes of benefits for local people; its training and employment strategy, for example, has tried to involve all those agencies operating locally who have an interest in training, in putting in place mechanisms which at least encourage new employers to recruit locally. A Cardiff Bay Construction Training Charter, launched in the spring of 1992, urges employers to recruit locally and invest in training. Major construction contractors have been anxious to be seen to be supporting the Charter's aims (Anon, 1992). In addition, CBDC encourage all developers to allocate 1% of capital expenditure to provide outstanding public art, while the independent Cardiff Bay Art Trust has been established to encourage and advise developers on the integrated use of art within the UDA. However, these apparently philanthropic activities of CBDC reflect a wider, structural, tension in the locality between property-led goals, underpinned by voluntaristic social, employment and community programmes, and a generally unresponsive private sector which is failing to deliver in every way. But, despite local reservations and disappointments, CBDC are not the focus of widespread and persistent criticism. Our next section examines in more detail its institutional relationships.

Institutional Context and Attitudes

There are certainly some good reasons for expecting CBDC to have bedded itself particularly well into local institutional networks. By the time it began operating, the principle of large mixed use redevelopment of hitherto industrial land in the docks had been pioneered by Tarmac's 100 acre Atlantic Wharf development, planned and promoted in the early 1980s (Thomas and Imrie, 1989). Not only did that redevelopment change local political and planning ideas about the future (and commercial potential) of the largely industrial southside of Cardiff, it also established regular dialogue between the two local authorities for the area, central government (the Welsh Office), the major local landowner (Associated British Ports), and industrial employer (Allied Steel and Wire) (Thomas, 1992a). These agencies set up a network of joint working groups involving officers and (on occasion) councillors to plan and manage the implementation of the Atlantic Wharf redevelopment, networks which have been extended into the regeneration of Cardiff Bay.

Atlantic Wharf was the result of opportunism on the part of developers and South Glamorgan County Council (SGCC), and the Welsh Office who sponsored it for Urban Development Grant (UDG) of £9 million. A commercial opportunity for a profitable mixed use development coincided with a political will to see radical changes in the spatial structure of South Cardiff. Atlantic Wharf was largely vacant, so the chance was taken to redevelop it. A corollary of opportunism is a lack of strategic planning, and we have argued elsewhere that one consequence of a lack of strategic vision was disadvantage to some sectors of the local economy (Imrie and Thomas, 1992; Thomas and Imrie, 1989). But the muted public responses to Atlantic Wharf also made it clear that those adversely affected had little political clout or expertise, and were not being offered a platform in the local press, which was consistently supportive of high value uses being introduced into the area (Thomas and Imrie, 1993; Thomas, 1992b).

This ostensibly consensual approach to dockland redevelopment was typified by the September 1986 County Council submission to the Welsh Office which proposed that a UDC be established to 'have charge of the regeneration of South Cardiff' (SGCC, 1986 p. 6). The County Council claimed to have the necessary expertise to take on the job itself but recognized that 'a local authority led initiative may not be universally acceptable' (p. 6). A UDC was proposed as an alternative solution, particularly if local authority representatives had places on the corporation's board, and control of development and building and strategic planning remained in local authority hands. By December 1986 the Secretary of State was ordering the setting up of a UDC which bore noticeable similarities to the County Council's proposals (Edwards, 1986). There were fewer local authority members than the County had suggested (and they were not *representatives* of local authorities) but, uniquely, the new development corporation was not granted planning powers – local and strategic planning and development control remained in local authority hands.

It is natural that the County Council might congratulate itself on having exercised such apparently compelling and swift influence over the Welsh Office, but it is, perhaps, more plausible to suggest that its submission reflected its understanding of the way Welsh Office thinking was developing. It certainly seems to be the case that years earlier the Secretary of State for Wales was thinking of dockland regeneration on a major scale in Cardiff. Reeves (1987) has suggested that the whole Cardiff Bay idea originated in a trip to the area by Nicholas Edwards in the early 1980s. By 1983 he was speaking of 'the sharp contrast between the condition of the city south of the railway and that of the commercial and civic centres to the north'. He looked forward to 'the rebirth and rapid growth of South Cardiff' (Edwards, 1983). Whatever the direction of influence there can be no doubting, by 1986, the desire, on the part of both the County Council and the Welsh Office, to have no major public policy differences over South Cardiff's regeneration. This very positive relationship appears to have continued.

SGCC also volunteered to provide a parliamentary bill to allow a 1.2 km barrage to be built across the estuaries of the Taff and Ely, two of the rivers which flow through Cardiff. This contentious, and increasingly expensive, project was conceived and publicized by the Welsh Office prior to its setting up of CBDC, and political commitment to it seems solid. However, it has encountered vociferous opposition, principally from two sources. A conservation lobby, including the Royal Society for the Protection of Birds (RSPB), is concerned about birds (including a Site of Special Scientific Interest) when tidal mudflats are permanently covered in an impounded lake (RSPB, 1989). Meanwhile, residents in lower lying areas of the city are concerned about the consequences of a rise in groundwater levels which will be one result of the barrage. A vocal group of Labour city councillors and a local Labour MP have harried CBDC for years, refusing to be convinced by CBDC's scientific advisers, or by its scheme of compensation. There have been intermittent successes in delaying the Bill's parliamentary progress, but government support for it is set to ensure its eventual passage. Nevertheless, the campaign seems to have influenced local opinion – a MORI poll of local residents conducted on behalf of the RSPB in early 1992 found that of those who felt they knew enough about the barrage to form an opinion (some 35% of the sample), one-third felt it was a good way to regenerate Cardiff Bay, but one-fifth felt it was not (RSPB, 1992).

Certainly, the barrage – and, more particularly, the influence of those councillors with reservations about it – has been a major factor in the markedly more cautious relationship which has developed between the City Council and CBDC, compared to the County Council's relationship with it. Both local authorities are Labour controlled (though from 1988–92 the city was hung, with Labour as the largest single group). Among the County Labour councillors the strongest grouping is a knot of long-standing male councillors, most to the right of centre, from South Cardiff, including past leaders of the group, and current chairs of Finance and Economic Development Committees. Their primary motivation for ensuring virtually no public disagreements between the County Council and the development corporation seems to be a combination of wanting more investment, whatever its nature, in South Cardiff (and there being no obvious alternative to CBDC in their view). But another significant motivation is a desire to re-establish the south of the city as a vital component of the modern, international capital city, the creation of which has been a focus for urban policy at local and central government level for over thirty years. It is probably the case that this project currently has a firmer grip on the Labour group of the County Council than it does on the City Council's Labour group.

In the city, each political party has seen the emergence of a new generation of councillors during the 1980s, but the significance for Labour has, perhaps, been most profound. While it would be an exaggeration to talk of a 'New Urban Left' having established itself, it is certainly the case that there has been greater concern about the distributive consequences of local authority policy, and a sporadic concern to increase public involvement in policy making. Among newly senior Labour members there appears to be a deep reservation about the undemocratic and market-responsive approach of development corporations. However, with the exception of the issue of the barrage, the city council has stopped far short of opposing the CBDC. Indeed, it has undertaken two of the less sensitive planning briefs for CBDC, on a consultancy basis. Its strongest reservations, or advice on improving practice, have related to the plight of small dockland firms forced, or encouraged, to relocate to make way for CBDC's 'new look' Cardiff Bay. It has consistently, and for some years, voiced concern about the lack of suitable sites within Cardiff, and adequate financial packages to smooth the disruption of relocation (especially the almost inevitable increase in rentals). For its part, of late the development corporation has appeared to respond to this concern (which has been shared, and voiced by, other local agencies), while claiming that it would do more but for central government constraints.

However, it would be misleading to suggest that the city council's official reservations about the Cardiff Bay initiative are the product of a fraction of the Labour group. For there were reservations among councillors of all parties, and among city council officers, to the earlier dockland redevelopment at Atlantic Wharf (Thomas, 1992a). It is a paradox that the reasons for these reservations are also the basis for the ostensible local consensus in support of Cardiff Bay's regeneration. The city council has, in large measure, managed the redevelopment of the city centre over the last twenty years, with all-party support, and the cooperation of the County Council and Welsh Office (Imrie and Thomas, 1993b). The redevelopment has been a central component of the city's modernization, of its becoming a true capital city in a region which is, supposedly, undertaking the restructuring of its economy (Rees and Lambert, 1981). The political resonance of this project has already been discussed, and for the moment it is enough to note that there have been deep and genuine anxieties among politicians and officers in the city council that the modern city centre, for which it has assumed stewardship, will be undermined by diversion of investment to Cardiff Bay (Cardiff City Council, 1988). The City Council has pressed, successfully, for jointly funded studies of transport and retailing to assess the potential impact on the city centre of the redevelopment envisaged for the Bay, though it is difficult to point to any concrete change of direction which has resulted.

Indeed, it is difficult to find many significant episodes where CBDC has clearly responded to the influence of local agencies – be they private or public sector. Consultation exercises in relation to the regeneration strategy and subsequent area planning briefs are extensive, but, at most, result in minor changes. The development control powers retained by the city council, which have been identified as potentially significant (Cooke, 1988b), are a source of unofficial irritation to CBDC, but have yet to result in major disruption to its activity. A dispute resolution procedure involving the Secretary of State for Wales has yet to be invoked, and some very senior local authority officers will admit privately that to date CBDC has had its way on every major planning issue. A recent example of the complexities involved in planning the Bay was a planning application by CBDC itself to dump hundreds of thousands of tons of spoil from a major highway currently under construction, onto some tidal salt-marshes adjacent to housing and a small hospital (City Council Application No 91/498R). The original idea was to raise the level of the land and create sites for a large park, two relocated schools (including the ill-fated primary school referred to earlier) and new housing. Despite the obvious advantages in having a spoil tip close to the construction site, thereby minimizing lorry journeys through residential areas elsewhere, the proposal aroused strong opposition from a range of groups and institutions.

A local residents' group was worried about the scale of the tipping, and eventually gave grudging support to a scaled down proposal (still allowing over 250,000 tons of spoil to be tipped), which would include a guarantee of an early start on the park. The County Council, generally sympathetic to the proposal, was concerned about the proximity of the tipped soil to a new bridge it was constructing; the Area Health Authority objected to the park and the school as uses incompatible with a hospital which might be open for another nine years; the RSPB and Countryside Council for Wales (CCW) objected strongly to the loss of salt-marshes and other feeding and roosting areas within a designated Site of Special Scientific Interest. The City Council appears to have been particularly influenced by these latter objections, and deferred formal consideration of the application for over seven months while haggling continued over details. The local Labour MP was an enthusiastic supporter of the application. By late November, a revised proposal had been agreed, with a reduced tipping area (excluding any site for future housing) and a range of devices for mitigating the impact of habitat disruption on birds. The RSPB remained in opposition, but all other groups were willing to accept the revised proposals. We have here an example of CBDC giving ground, of the City Council using perhaps its most potent weapon – that of delay – but ultimately, the opposition to the *principles* of what was being proposed (e.g. from the RSPB) failing.

So CBDC is not entirely impervious to influence and we should not overlook the significance of the daily and weekly contact at officer level between local authorities, major private interests and the development corporation. Clearly, such links, sometimes involving discussion of minutiae of operations, can result in useful changes in working practices or the details of implementation. But the overall impression gained through interviews remains one of a distance between CBDC and local agencies. Of course, local influence need not be exercised entirely through conflicts over individual decisions (Lukes, 1974), and CBDC's commitment to, and action on, social housing is likely to be an example of its pre-empting the possibility of criticism. The regeneration strategy includes a target of 25% of new housing being social housing, thereby deflecting damaging allegations that regeneration had nothing to offer the resident population of one of the poorer parts of Cardiff. Implementation has continued apace, with a number of local housing associations undertaking schemes with assistance of various forms (including donations of land) from CBDC. It is true that the sites which have been allocated are at the periphery of the Bay, but then it could be argued that these sites are the ones which relate best to existing settlements.

It also appears as if a remoteness has been felt by local small firms. CBDC's regeneration strategy acknowledges the existence of almost 1,000 small firms in the docklands area, and also the fact that since the late 1970s a central thrust of local authority economic development policy has involved giving assistance to such firms (Thomas and Imrie, 1989). The strategy refers to the need to protect and nurture existing industries in the Bay, and as early as 1988 CBDC had asked Cardiff and Vale Enterprise (CAVE), the local well-established enterprise agency, to liaise on its behalf with indigenous firms, and to act as a conduit of information in both directions. Indeed, CAVE has been an important agency in influencing CBDC's ideas and strategy towards the local indigenous business community, and its actions illustrate the possibilities of (local) agency involvement in the evolution of UDC strategy formulation.

For instance, since 1990, CAVE has been contracted by CBDC to advise local businesses on CBDC's plans and to provide them with legal and financial assistance to help them relocate and to take advantage of various compensation packages being made available by the development corporation. Until CAVE was appointed, the general approach of CBDC towards the local business community was poor, characterized by minimal communications, a reluctance to negotiate, and a general prevarication in settling any terms of compensation. Yet CAVE, in combination with the city council, seems to have persuaded CBDC of the merits of fair and negotiated settlements, of the benefits to CBDC in facilitating an orderly relocation of businesses from the key development sites, and, most importantly, of trying to protect the business vitality of the local economy. Indeed, the latter is of great significance in CBDC now acknowledging, in its strategy, one of the more important principles of postwar planning in the city, the maintenance of the docks as the manufacturing centre of Cardiff. While CBDC's original strategy envisaged sweeping away what was presented as 'the last vestiges' of manufacturing, the lack of mobile (alternative) investment, coupled with political pressure and persuasion by the city and CAVE, has led to a rethink.

Yet despite these arrangements, previous research has unearthed discontent and alienation among small firms affected by CBDC's plans (Imrie and Thomas, 1992), sentiments which help explain the emergence, in early 1992, of

the Cardiff Bay Small Business Forum (CBSBF) as a voice of *local* small firms.
The Forum has displayed a political astuteness not previously apparent among
the Bay's smaller firms, and has been at pains to protect itself as a responsible
body, able and willing to enter constructive discussions. It is generally
supportive of CBDC's strategy but concerned that local small firms are not yet
seeing any benefits from it, while the inevitable disruption hits them harder
than most. Because it is a newly formed body it is difficult for researchers to
get a firm idea of its sources of membership and support, but the impression
obtained is that it attracts a wide range of businesses, and particularly the very
small ones. Some of these, such as small shops and snack bars, have previously
had no obvious vehicle for representing their interests, while the small
engineering establishments or professional offices are evidently unhappy at the
lack of vigour with which their interests were pursued (if at all) by the formal
liaison committee with businesses set up by CBDC (membership by invitation)
and the Chamber of Commerce and Industry, which was one of its members.
There are indications that the Small Business Forum is gaining acceptance as
a legitimate voice of a stratum of the Bay's businesses; whether it can exercise
any influence over the development corporation remains to be seen; its very
existence suggests that, to date, smaller firms in the area remain unconvinced
of the benefits to them of CBDC's strategy for renewal.

While agencies like CAVE and the CBSBF are obviously influencing, at the
margins, aspects of CBDC's strategy, the most significant influence is central
government (i.e. the Welsh Office). Though all UDCs have had their
expenditures closely monitored and controlled, planning consultant David
Walton (1990a, p. 1) – who has worked with a number of UDCs – has
commented that 'central government . . . was more closely involved than would
be normal elsewhere in Britain'. Indeed, a central and controversial feature of
the regeneration strategy – namely, the massive barrage across Cardiff Bay –
'was in place from the outset' (p. 1). It is clear that, in Cardiff, central
government involvement has extended beyond financial regulation to directly
influencing a major element of the regeneration strategy and (we would
speculate) more subtle influence over the overall nature of the regeneration
package. However, perhaps this influence should not be conceived as an
imposition from above, but more as a particularly important voice in a discussion and debate, in local and central government, about the future of the
docklands which, as we have set out earlier, has been under way since the late
1970s. The Welsh Office, in this reading, is a regional actor, responsive to
regional circumstances, rather than simply a transmission mechanism for
national (UK) policies.

Yet, there are a number of significant instances in which the fiscal and
political controls of the Welsh Office are undermining the development
of a genuine local corporatism in the city's spatial development. This is best
illustrated in relation to CBDC's expenditure programmes concerning land
acquisition, compensation to companies, and their utilization of section 146 of
the 1980 Local Government, Planning and Land Act. In the latter instance,
CBDC have utilized a provision in the Act which seems to state that if you
have an organization (e.g. business) in the UDA that wishes to remain, then
the UDC can sell property to it at a subsidized rate. However, in using this,
CBDC has come into conflict with their original remit (making market returns

on sales, etc.) and were told by the Welsh Office (via a Treasury directive) not to use the provision on expense grounds. Indeed, CBDC were reminded by the Welsh Office of their obligation to 'get the best price possible' while exhorting CBDC to use the minimum assistance to achieve development. Nevertheless, CBDC have used the provision on one occasion but have concluded that it is 'too much hassle as we have to go to the Treasury in London each time for approval'.

Conclusions

The ambitious objectives which CBDC has been set by the Welsh Office fit into a view of Cardiff's role and trajectory which has been dominant politically in South Wales for over thirty years and has enjoyed consistent media support. Consequently, we should not be surprised that there has been no significant opposition to the idea of large scale urban renewal in south Cardiff; it has been portrayed, and widely accepted, as a natural continuation of the modernization project under way since the 1950s. Such opposition and discontent as has occurred has focused on aspects of the renewal strategy and its implementation – and, in particular, on the barrage and separately the disruption caused to small firms forced to relocate. The relationship of the disadvantaged Butetown community to the Cardiff Bay project is a source of embarrassing silence or platitudes from proponents and opponents of the Cardiff Bay strategy. In the face of criticisms, CBDC has shown some willingness to vary details, but no departure from the essence of its positions; and we speculate that Welsh Office interest and pressure is ready to stiffen its resolve should it show signs of weakening.

But if the project is one which has a local flavour, the implementation of it marks a departure with the practices of the 1960s and 1970s, and has caused some disquiet to local interests. It is clear that the Cardiff Bay regeneration is not, and will not be, managed by local authorities. The balance of influence over the details of land-use management and implementation have shifted from the local councils, with consequent frustrations on their part. This shift has accentuated the distance which would inevitably exist between the local resident and working populations and an agency set on creating an environment responsive to the needs and perceptions of national and international audiences, be they investors, tourists, journalists or politicians. There is a widespread feeling that advantages to the immediate community are either by-products of projects undertaken for other reasons, or sops to secure consent to the radical changes envisaged for the area.

Cardiff Bay's story also provides an interesting example of the interplay between local and extra-local forces. The huge barrage, and the grandiose scheme of which it is a part, reflect a particular, regionally significant, view of the city. But their effect has been to hamper and hinder development in the area as recession follows boom with the linchpin of CBDC's strategy yet to be approved by Parliament. Indeed, many local observers feel that the Corporation 'missed the boat' in the boom years because of its fixation on the barrage (a fixation, of course, which had strong Welsh Office backing). Moreover, many of CBDC's original aims, of superlative design, prestigious waterfront developments, and a new environment of international standing, seem unattainable due to a mix of property recession and ideals which were always going to struggle to attract the requisite levels of mobile (international) capital even in buoyant times. The irony of all this is that CBDC is looking more strongly towards the indigenous potential of the locality, recently restating some of the earlier modernization themes. In this sense, the break with the past, that CBDC seemed to stand for, is less assured.

Acknowledgements

We gratefully acknowledge the assistance of the Economic and Social Research Council grant R000 233525 in supporting some of the research underlying this chapter.

6

PROPERTY DEVELOPMENT AND PETTY MARKETS VERSUS MARITIME INDUSTRIALISM: PAST, PRESENT AND FUTURE

David Byrne

Introduction

. . . it is the distinction of this river that it is man-made. Literally, its tidal flow, no less than its busy banks, its capacious docks, its magnificent piers . . . are the handiwork of a generation of Tynesiders who have snatched a port from the North Sea and converted what was little better than a ditch into a great river. It is but fact to say that the Tyne of today is so vastly different from the Tyne of our grandfathers that its transformation offers one of the finest examples of applied local effort.

(Johnson, 1925, p. 5)

This chapter is about the recent operations of the Tyne and Wear (Urban) Development Corporation (TWDC). It will devote by far the greater part of its attention to the operations of that UDC on Tyneside, essentially because Wearside developments have been small-scale in comparison, and whilst the UDC assisted in the programme of destruction of marine industry on that river, it was not the prime mover. It is the prime de-industrializer on the River Tyne and that is the most important thing about it. The operations of the TWDC are quite distinct from those of the other estuarine UDCs. London Docklands and Merseyside Development Corporations have been dealing with areas of deepwater-fronting land which were formerly used for marine transport and which were clearly not any longer required for the same purpose. Teesside Development Corporation has an enormous amount of land forming a flat estuarine plain, most of which was not previously used for marine-related purposes. The Tyne and the Wear are different. These were and are rivers on which things were and are made, things (ships, topside engineering on rigs, etc.) which have to be made next to deep water because they are structures which go to sea. The Tyne is a port, and marine transport is important in relation to the operation of TWDC, but it is marine manufacturing which matters the most because that is the industrial activity around which the modern cities of Tyneside and Sunderland were made. See Figure 6.1.

To understand the operations and effects of the UDC we have to understand both what went before it and the context in which it is operating. The first is a

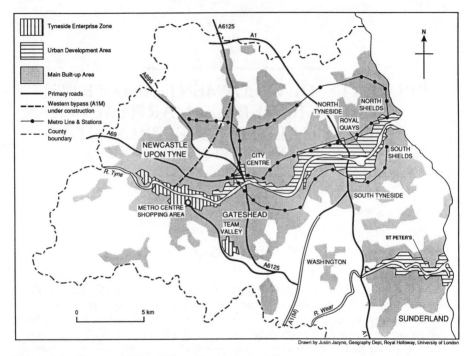

Drawn by Justin Jacyno, Geography Dept, Royal Holloway, University of London

Figure 6.1   Tyne and Wear Urban Development Plan.

matter of reviewing the history of the making of the modern Tyne and the
way in which national ports policy after 1965, part of a national programme
of modernization, delocalized control over the river around which the city
was constructed. The second requires a brief identification of the short-term,
supposedly market-oriented strategies, derived from a combination of new
right ideology and the specific interests of property developing capital, which
have underpinned urban development policy since 1979.

The chapter will proceed through a history of the modern Tyne to an account
of the operations of TWDC since its designation (set in relation to national
urban policy) which will pay most attention to its anti-industrial development
culture and the conflict between this and Tyneside's 'Civic Culture'. In the
course of this, unflattering comparisons will be drawn between the corrupt
mercantile culture of the ancient Newcastle Corporation, swept aside by progressive modernizing industrialism in the second half of the nineteenth century,
and the policy culture of TWDC and its allies (particularly the dominant group
in the present Newcastle City Council). The emphasis here is on the cultural
and political dimensions of a dispute between industrial production and financial
circulation through land development. The operations of TWDC also have
very great significance for differentiated reproduction/consumption, and issues
here will not be ignored, but the basal dispute is fundamental.

Industrialism versus Mercantilism – the Making of an Industrial River and City

From the twelfth century until 1850 the River Tyne was controlled by the Corporation of the City and County of Newcastle upon Tyne. Newcastle was the third medieval port of England after London and Bristol, as the Tyne was to be the third port of the modern UK after London and Liverpool. The basic activity was coal-shipping together with the shipbuilding and boatbuilding associated with this. By the end of the eighteenth century other industries had developed, especially chemicals and glass, but coal dominated. Newcastle's running of the river was corrupt and incompetent (the present author is a Shieldsman). The navigation was badly neglected. In the 1840s Shields Bar drew 6 foot at low tide and at an especially low tide it could be waded. The approach to Shields harbour was notoriously dangerous. Both the lifeboat and the rocket rescue line as used by volunteer life brigades were invented on the Tyne in response to particular inshore disasters.

Disputes over the running of the river date back to the thirteenth century, sometimes reaching a state of open warfare. Shipping interests in the two Shields (the twin ports on either side of the river mouth) wanted control taken from Newcastle City. This demand became the programme of radical Liberal Tyneside capitalism in the mid-nineteenth century. Of particular significance was Joseph Cowan, a former blacksmith who became a self-made industrial millionaire through brickmaking and radical journalism. He was identified by Marx as the example of a progressive and radical capitalist. The dispute was fought out through private parliamentary bills but in 1850 it was concluded with the establishment of the Tyne Improvement Commission (TIC) which took over responsibility for the river and was to coordinate its subsequent development. This involved publicly organized civil engineering works on an enormous scale. The river was deepened through dredging. New bridges and docks were constructed. Millions of tons of rock were blasted. Part of County Durham ended up north of the new river course. The ditch, by 1880, was able to float the largest modern battleship fifteen miles upstream from the river mouth.

These developments quite literally made modern Tyneside. The development of coal shipment docks, shipyards and shipping caused a massive influx of population and associated urban development. Between 1851 and 1901 the population of industrial Tyneside increased by a factor of more than three, reaching its modern level of a million in 1911. The word modern is not used here innocently. What was developed on Tyneside was precisely a modern, engineering/carboniferous capitalism, in the specific sense in which 'modern' is opposed to 'post-modern' and in the related sense in which organized is opposed to disorganized (see Lash and Urry, 1987). The basis of development was high technology and design. Indeed Tyneside was the UK birthplace of that most characteristically modern aspect of industrial production, the making of heavy electrical generating and transmitting equipment, in an industry which developed directly as a spin-off from marine engineering. The river and the railways were of course intimately interlinked. Tyneside was where rail met ship for the first time in the modern world with the construction of the Causey waggonway to Dunston in the 1770s and it was the birthplace of subsequent railway development.

All this development depended on the making of the river. The forces which made it were interesting. The actual form was a coalition of various industrial capitals and progressive local government, with representation also given to Newcastle. The TIC was composed of five shipowners elected from that group of capitalists, five coal-owners (and shippers) elected from that constituency, five traders (i.e. capitalists engaged in general import and export but taken by 1880 to include shipbuilding and related activities), five representatives of the council of the City of Newcastle, three each from the councils of the County Boroughs of Tynemouth and South Shields and one from the Municipal Borough of Jarrow. Membership was regarded as a serious business and principals of the largest firms in the respective sectors participated directly. This was very much an example of organized capitalism and it is worth noting that the British Shipping Federation, British Chamber of Shipping, and shipbuilding and engineering employers federations all developed on the Tyne. Likewise the Confederation of Engineering and Shipbuilding Trades Unions and National Union of Seamen and Firemen (forerunner of the late NUS and marine element of RMT) began on the north east coast. Johnson's 1925 book was very much a hagiography of those responsible for the innovative results of this organization.

The life of the modern Tyne corresponds to that of the TIC, i.e. from 1850 to 1968, although the modern river has had an afterlife and the potential for revival. In this period the river was for most of the time the second largest shipbuilding port in the world (second to the Clyde and, together with Sunderland, the largest), the third port in Britain (and on a world scale having a total trade in coal and general cargo equal to that of Shanghai, Lisbon, Algiers, Baltimore and Seattle), and a major centre for British shipping. This modern industrialism was severely affected by the depression of the 1930s, but, with the exception of Palmer's Jarrow Yard closed permanently by National Shipbuilding Securities, revived in the run-up to World War II and grew in absolute, if not relative, terms during the 1950s and 1960s. What did decrease massively after 1950 was the significance of coal exports, with the shift to oil and the decline in the great northern coalfield, leading to the abandonment of coal staithes.

In 1968 there was a very important administrative change. In the aftermath of George Brown's National Plan of 1965 there was a major reorganization of British ports. The operations of the TIC were drawn together with the separate corporation quays of Newcastle, Gateshead, Tynemouth (North Shields) and South Shields (the TIC having already taken over Tyne Dock from the LNER on railway nationalization) to form the Port of Tyne Authority (PTA). The significance lay not so much in the change in form as in the change in relationship. Before 1968 the Tyne was locally controlled by local bodies with local responsibilities. After 1968 it was part of a centrally directed (some would say, stalinist) planning system, and this subordination was reinforced in 1974 when the composition of the PTA was changed so as to eliminate local government and interest representatives and make the body a wholly subordinate group of ministerial nominees. In passing it should be noted that this is yet another example of the facility provided to the Tories after 1979 by Labour's efforts at national planning through the directive control of local government and related bodies. Labour never could control capital, but it facilitated centralization of the public sphere at the expense of local democracy, and even of local corporatism. The intention was to modernize the modern. In a previous piece (Byrne, 1992) I have suggested that Cooke's (1985) notion of an era of 'modernization' in UK planning policy, should be applied specifically to post-1960 efforts at reconstructing the base for industrial employment through nationally directed indicative planning and infrastructure investment. The creation of the modern was, in Johnson's words, an example of 'applied local effort'. Modernization was nationally dominated, with the subnational present only in the form of consultative Regional Economic Planning Councils, which had no directive power over key policies.

The Tyne declined as a port, not only because of the decline in coal shipping, but after 1968 because National Ports policy selected the Tees as the growth port for the North of England at the expense of the Tyne. In the 1970s and 1980s the Tyne had the worst of both worlds. It was part of the nationally planned sector, coterminous with the sector covered by the National Dock Labour Scheme, and was deliberately subordinated to the Tees. At the same time non-scheme ports, which were outside both the dock labour scheme and the planning process, were taking an increasing proportion of trade. In fact the Tyne's general trade held up, but the changes in cargo handling led to a massive decline in employment of dockers, etc., which was associated with the concentration of port activity at Albert, Edward and Tyne Docks in North and South Shields and the effective abandonment of the upriver quays.

From 1974, the Tyne saw a massive decline in shipbuilding, especially after nationalization. Much of the background to this is given in Hudson's *Wrecking a Region* (1989) but the essentials are that British shipbuilding suffered from both international competition (especially from South Korea) and the inveterate hostility of central government after 1979 to nationalized industries in general and those which provided a base for organized trade unionism in particular. It was this latter which led to the destruction of the potentially profitable Sunderland Shipbuilders in the teeth of opposition from private capitalists who wanted to purchase it as a going concern, in which business TWDC played a minor, but not unimportant, supporting role to national government. However at the same time as merchant shipbuilding declined, a new but related industry developed on the Tyne. This was the offshore industry, in which the Tyne specializes in topside engineering through the fitting of modules (both production and accommodation) to existing rig jackets. This industry is dependent on shipyard-based skills and the former shipyard labour force.

By the time of the establishment of TWDC in 1986, the Tyne was still a shipbuilding and repairing river, had a large and important offshore industry, and was still a port with an important roll-on, roll-off (ro-ro) and container trade with Scandinavia. However these activities were now all downriver of the Newcastle Bridges. It was clear that the Tyne above this point was not, and would not again be, an industrial river. This had been explicitly recognized in the preparation and development of the Tyne and Wear Structure Plan after 1974. Indeed, the Structure Plan is important in formal planning terms because it still constitutes the planning regime within which TWDC is supposed to act, although, in practice, it has been able to ignore it completely. For the purposes of this chapter it is even more important because it represents the last local significant statement of political priorities as expressed by land-use planning.

The County Council had considerable difficulties with the Port of Tyne Authority in the preparation of the Structure Plan as it had very little capacity to influence what the Port Authority would do, given the elimination of local authority representation from that body. There were a number of disputes, but their character was not indicative of the role that the Port Authority is now playing as a subordinate of TWDC. The basic position of the County was that it wanted the Port Authority to release some port land for general industrial uses, whereas the PTA insisted that any development of its land must be for uses which would generate significant port traffic, and, hence, port revenue. In the words of the PTA's first chairman:

> One of the main essentials is to retain and reserve sufficient land adjacent to the river berth to meet the variations in cargo handling techniques . . . The authority's policy of retaining and reclaiming land adjacent to deep water for developments which will generate traffic through the port is firm and necessary for the future viability of the port.
>
> (Shields Weekly News, November 1975)

The Structure Plan did recognize that deepwater fronting land was a unique resource, declaring that:

> Land with a deep water frontage represents a special and scarce resource. Structure plan studies have established that there is sufficient land potentially available for general use without using this port owned land. In view of the limited amount of such land . . . land owned by the Port Authority in the following general locations should normally be reserved for port related uses . . . Whitehill Point (and others).
>
> (Policy ED4, Tyne and Wear County Council, 1979)

Essentially, the County accepted the PTA's position as compatible with its general objective of maintaining industrial employment through industrial land development, although it would have liked more land released by the PTA for industrial estates. These sites were part of the overall county policy of designating 'strategic sites' on which piecemeal development was to be discouraged. They were intended for large, job-creating, industrial employers.

There was more to the dispute between county and PTA than simply a clash of bodies or personalities, although, of course, the actual developments took that apparent form. The conflict is best interpreted as a dispute between corporatist labourism and marine capitalism. Corporatist labourism wanted to maximize employment. Marine capitalism wanted to maximize returns. These two objectives were not necessarily incompatible. Some port-related developments, particularly in off-shore construction, would be job-rich. Others, especially the development of ro-ro and associated transport clearing, would have limited job development potential. The issue and the dispute were real, but compared with what was to come this was a family squabble.

Before leaving the local prehistory of TWDC we must deal with the issue of industrial culture. Reference has already been made to the contrast between the pre-modern mercantilist culture of the City of Newcastle in the first half of the nineteenth century, and the modernizing industrial culture which was to replace it. Newcastle Corporation stood for mere trading and was narrowly local. Its rival stood for industrial production and was world orientated. There is a striking reference to what this meant in Holden's recent book on *The Pacific* (1990) in which he refers to the fact that the first cables laid across that ocean were made 'in the most unPacific city of Newcastle upon Tyne' and laid by a ship built on Tyneside for the purpose. In this context it is really rather important to remember that until 1920 Walker and Benwell were separate Urban Districts. These are Newcastle's industrial East and West ends. Newcastle proper was primarily a shopping town, not a manufacturing one.

The culture of industrial Tyneside was complex. It contained within itself profound antagonisms. The nine-hour day dispute of 1871 in Armstrong's works was a crucial event in the development of the labour process, and the one example of practical assistance rendered by Marx to an industrial dispute. However it was also inclusive, particularly in terms of the role played by that interesting complex of male skilled-worker/technicians who were the basis of marine manufacturing and of shipping. Indeed, there has traditionally been very little distinction on Tyneside between skilled workers and the industrial service class. Until quite recently (within the adult life of the 44-year-old author) recruitment to the industrial service class usually began with a skilled craft apprenticeship, particularly as a fitter. Almost all marine engineering officers began as time-served apprentices in the yards and engine works.

On the deck side until the Second World War it was quite possible, in the tramp trades in which Tyneside specialized, for a deck hand to come aft as a navigating officer. The one truly proletarian group were the black gangs (firemen/trimmers). These were often Arab/Somali, and in North and South Shields it was common for men to go to sea in this capacity when young and after marriage to go into the pits. Indeed marine engineers would also go into the pits as colliery mechanics or into marine engine works or electrical generating works as supervisors, etc. This maritime culture was very different from one constructed around casual dock labour as described for Liverpool by Lane (1988). Tyneside did have dockers (and much less casualized coal trimmers and teamers) but they were a small minority compared with shipyard workers. Interestingly, seamen in the Tyne tramp and weekly trades were much less casualized than in the west coast liner trades.

This made for an integrated industrial culture with a strong maritime component. Tynesiders think of themselves as a seafaring people, and this is perhaps strongest within the relatively prosperous skilled worker/service class rather than among the poor (although some of Tyneside's poorest locales do, as we shall see, have strong marine connections). This complex is equally strong in Sunderland. The modern character of all this has to be emphasized. Even Tyneside's fishing industry is modern in this sense of being the derivative of engineering technology, in that it dates from Purdie's invention of steam trawling at North Shields in the 1880s. Tynesiders (and Wearsiders) built ships and sailed them. In the author's youth it used to be said that there were men in South Shields who had never been west of Tyne Dock Arches by land, but who had been round the world by sea.

Women were not entirely separated from all this. Apart from the advantages of having a seaman as a husband as opposed to a miner (an advantage even greater with regard to sons), one of Tyneside's modern industries, the great steam-drifting herring fishery of the interwar years, was absolutely dependent on female processing labour. The Scotch lasses followed the boats south, but many local women (usually of Shetland/Orcadian origin) worked in this quite respectable employment. People feel strongly about this aspect of their history, particularly in relation to the contribution their culture and its industrial base made to the most important part of the World War II British war effort, the battles of the North Atlantic and Russian convoys.

This complex was still more or less intact until the late 1960s. Aspects declined during that decade. The British pelagic whaling industry, based in South Shields, was abandoned in 1964. Restrictions on deep water fishing in Norwegian waters changed the nature of the fishing fleet towards smaller North Sea going vessels. However the big changes date from the 1980s with the collapse of shipbuilding and of the UK merchant navy. The important question is, is that collapse irreversible?

Enter the UDC

The premise on which TWDC has worked, is that it is. In his evidence to the House of Commons Select Committee on Employment, Balls, TWDC's Chief Executive, asserted that:

> ... industry within the river corridors is characterized by heavy marine-based manufacturing. Due to world market conditions causing decline in these sectors, there are also a growing number of derelict factories, warehouses, shipyards, slipways and dry docks along both rivers, with river or rail access primarily, many of which are unlikely ever to be used again for their original purpose.
>
> (1989 p. 309)

Indeed in *A Vision for the Future* (1990) TWDC went even further. Not only were the marine manufacturing sites derelict and 'unlikely ever again to be used for their original purpose', but the industrial culture created by the complex was holding back development:

> The economy of the North East has, until recently, depended on three industries: heavy engineering, coal mining and shipbuilding ... For too long the need for a more diversified regional economy was not seen as important or necessary ... Indeed the senior management of these three industries was so small relative to the numbers employed that the opportunities for aspiring talent were severely limited, so for the most part they left the region. The opportunities for local entrepreneurial activity, given the dominance of engineering, shipbuilding and coal in the market, were limited. With the decline of these three sectors, the banks of the Tyne and Wear, essential to the functioning of those industries, lapsed into dereliction.
>
> (1990 p. 4)

This is quite an extraordinary statement. Not only does it ignore the partnership corporatist strategy of industrial diversification which dates from the Special Areas initiatives of the 1930s, and which has generated enormous numbers of manufacturing jobs, albeit primarily in branch plants, but it caricatures the management structure and opportunities existing in the core regional structure. Even more importantly, it displays no sense of the way in which the county's core industrial structure has evolved through developments of the existing base in human capital and organizational knowledge. In particular it ignores the way in which shipbuilding, marine engineering and mining engineering have contributed to the development of offshore engineering, which activity is very important on the supposedly derelict banks of the Tyne.

The emphasis on derelict land is wholly in tune with national policy as contained in the legislation establishing UDCs and as expressed by various DOE ministers since. Ridley summed it all up in his evidence to the same House of Commons Select Committee on Employment, when he appeared before them to tell them off for the critical tone of their original report:

> *In the United States . . . on their list of objectives, employment comes first and the need to regenerate communities. The remit in our legislation does not mention employment at all, hinges on physical regeneration and talks of bringing land and buildings into effective use.*

(1989 p. 1)

The identification of a conflict between land regeneration using the development industry, and the needs and wishes of local residents, is general in critical comment on the operations of UDCs (see Stoker, 1989, p. 161). What is distinctive about the Tyne and Wear situation is that subsidized 'catalytic' non-industrial development has been encouraged in opposition to the large scale existing industrial uses present on the rivers.

Overall, four principles seem to inform contemporary national urban development policy (see Byrne, D., 1992). These are:

1. Elected local government is to have no control and at the most serve as an agent for other bodies or the DOE itself.
2. Planning is bad and markets are good.
3. The revival of the cities is the business of the private sector. Government may stimulate and subsidize but it should not direct.
4. The objective of policy is to maximize short-term market returns on land development. Inner city populations and existing inner city manufacturing are irrelevant to this and may be an obstacle to it. If so, they are to be sacrificed.

All these principles can be seen in operation in the doings of TWDC, informed, it seems, by an additional working adherence to the strong version of Murphy's first law: if it is possible to make a cock-up then that cock-up will be made!

TWDC has had four significant zones of operation. The first is in West Newcastle on and around the site of the former Vickers factories, where it has supported the development of a non-contentious industrial park. This is widely regarded by non-UDC commentators as a major achievement. TWDC actually managed to achieve development on an already serviced site with Enterprise Zone incentives and additional resources of its own. The real question is what took them so long.

The second is on and around Newcastle Quayside, and in particular the site downriver of the Tyne Bridge described as 'East Quayside'. This is an interesting site. It consists of the upriver Newcastle Quays backed up by the original commercial centre of the city and a mix of warehouses and light industrial premises. Most of the original population has been displaced by the slum clearances of both the 1930s and the 1960s. There are a good many existing jobs of varied kinds, particularly in quite mucky light industries. The TWDC regards this as a flagship site and has a major proposal for redevelopment. Unfortunately the builder component of the developing consortium has gone bust and TWDC has managed to get itself embroiled in a long-running dispute with an alternative Swiss developer, backed up by Proctor and Gamble who own a large key site and seem to have been infuriated by being misled by Balls early in the formulation of proposals. There has been an expensive public inquiry, followed by extensive litigation. Meanwhile little is happening, which may be just as well since knowledgeable local engineers suggest that ground conditions are questionable, given that much of the ground consists of the medieval rubbish of the city thrown into the river and 'consolidated' behind medieval and nineteenth century quay pilings.

East Quayside is an important case from an urban design point of view. There is a real conflict with the remaining inner city population and with working class leisure uses which are connected with marine culture. The form of development proposed by TWDC with a very high office/car-park content is quite contrary to long-established county (but not Newcastle City) policies asserting the significance of public transport and the desirability of locating large office development adjacent to peripheral Metro stations. The proposals are for offices with a yuppie gloss in retail, hotel provision etc. The yuppification, especially in the Bridges area, is riding on the back of an established trend. Otherwise not much is happening.

The other two zones are the industrial Tyne and industrial Wear. Not much is happening on the Wear, other than in the words of one Sunderland Conservative Councillor, the building of some backward-facing tat in Monkwearmouth, and the development at North Sands of which more anon. On the Tyne likewise, not much is happening but intentions are clearer. The local Chamber of Commerce magazine has identified '. . . the TWDC's strategy of turning the traditional uses of the river inside out'. (1990, p. 25).

TWDC is the planning authority for the whole of the North Bank of the Tyne to the rivermouth. It has had a series of proposals for development, beginning with those contained in its pre-designation brief. Although details, emphasis and, particularly, amount of action change repeatedly, clear principles can be established. Basically TWDC is seeking to insert non-industrial uses into previously industrial areas, largely on the grounds that these will maximize land value change returns. This is associated with the release of land for industrial uses, although the emphasis has been on B1 style business parks. However with the exception of the Walker Offshore Park on the site of the former Walker Navy Yard, which had already been designated by Newcastle City, there is no specification of maritime industrial uses. Walker Offshore Park has in any event now been abandoned by Newcastle who will permit any industrial development on this site.

TWDC's main achieved development is the isolated marina-centred St Peter's Village in Walker, which is a London Docklands-style yuppie development on a former shipyard site (Wigham Richardson's). Its 'flagship' site on the industrial north bank is the Whitehill Point land in North Shields, renamed for marketing reasons as Royal Quays. The saga of this development will form the next section of this chapter. South of the river the UDC has done little. It has supported the existing Hebburn Village development, initiated by South Tyneside Council, which again takes former shipyard land, but not now, as was originally intended, the Hebburn dry dock which is the largest such facility in the UK. A small hotel is being built on the former Velva liquids site at the South Shields rivermouth. Otherwise TWDC has left the PTA with Tyne Dock as the centre of port operations.

Jarrow Slack, which had been reclaimed by the county, has been touted as a site for a large offshore development, which would have involved excavating reclaimed land for a dock, but the proposed developers have disappeared into a haze of winding-up petitions and bankruptcy, as was expected by those with any knowledge of the offshore sector. In May 1988 TWDC threatened Tyne Ship Repair with compulsory purchase of the 'Middle Docks' at South Shields. This company, which has a core workforce of 280 and expands with orders in a cyclical trade, used this site as its flexible element for repairs, fitting out, and ship parking. It seems that this was not tidy enough for TWDC but no further action has been taken, although the event did stimulate the foundation of the Tyne Port Users Association.

In Sunderland TWDC's main contribution was to demand residential land values for a crucial site adjacent to the one of Sunderland Shipbuilders yards. This land, originally belonging to the local authority and intended for industrial development, had been taken over by TWDC. A Greek consortium, with local management and workforce backing, was seeking to acquire the site for a holding ship repair operation with a view to returning to shipbuilding in a world market context of a shortage of capacity for merchant shipbuilding. They have eventually succeeded despite TWDC's demanding originally £888,000 and then £450,000 for five acres, but the proposal was much delayed. Otherwise there is a small yuppie housing scheme at North Sands, industrial estate development (with Enterprise Zone incentives) along the Wear shore but back from the river.

Whitehill Point – Deindustrialization in the Face of Change

The crucial site, both symbolically and in practical terms, is the port authority land at Whitehill Point and around Albert Edward Dock in North Shields. Here TWDC has the capacity to do the most damage and has encountered the most developed and sustained opposition. This site consists of some 200 acres between Howden Road, which separates it from the 1930s slum clearance Meadowell Housing Estate, and the Tyne. It is centred around the twenty-seven acre Albert Edward Dock which is still operating and contains the ro-ro terminals for the Scandinavian passenger ferries together with other port facilities. Originally this area was the main location of coal drops for that part of the South Eastern Northumberland Coalfield which exported through the Tyne. The site was the terminus for the railway complex by which the coal was brought to it. It was also used for the importation of pit wood, which activity occupied fifty-eight acres. Finally it contained the shipyard operations of the TIC itself. This was not a manufacturing facility, but rather the service depot for the port. In the 1970s the Albert Edward Dock was the base for the distant water Ranger fishing company, and it is still used as an overspill facility for the North Shields fishing fleet.

The PTA has always regarded this site as one of its prime assets. It resisted any non-port development proposals from Tyne and Wear County, and seems to have agreed a sale to TWDC only subsequent to Tynemouth's Tory MP (Neville Trotter, the only Tory sitting for a Tyne-Wear constituency) blocking a PTA private bill which sought to extend its development powers. The TWDC could have vested the land but seems to have preferred a forced sale, under the terms of which TWDC obtained an option to purchase both the site and the Albert Edward Dock and associated quay frontage.

In late 1989 TWDC mounted a development competition based on an Invitation to Submit Proposals which stated:

> The Corporation's objective in inviting proposals is to achieve the rapid and successful regeneration of the site with high quality mixed use development, levering private investment and producing a satisfactory return to the public sector in terms of land price. Employment creation is also regarded as a major objective, and a target of 3,600 full time jobs is considered feasible.

Three developers submitted schemes which were put on exhibition for public comment, although TWDC made it plain that it was picking a development consortium rather than a scheme. In other words, the schemes were illustrations rather than intentions. The project was awarded to the Royal Quays Development ment Consortium which included Avatar as lead developer together with four builders, the management buyout group from Washington New Town, and an architects firm. Their original proposal was for 1,440 dwellings, 500,000 sq ft of business/industrial park, 390,000 sq ft of retails development and 390,000 sq ft for leisure related developments.

A vigorous opposition to these proposals was mounted by the North Shields Riverside Action Group. This was based around the Trades Council's TUC-sponsored North Shields Peoples Centre and included supporters from community groups in central North Shields and on the Meadowell Estate. This large 1930s slum clearance estate was built as a replacement for the bankside slums which were North Shields' traditional sailor-town. Many of the estate's residents were merchant seamen, fishermen or ship-repair workers, and these industrial connections persisted throughout the postwar period. However the estate was always the poorest part of North Shields and it has been the worst affected by deindustrialization (see Byrne, 1989). Formal male unemployment rates are now of the order of 50% and only about a third of all households are connected with regular wage labour. The other elements in the coalition represented traditional trade unionism and, in the form of the North Shields Chamber of Trade, traditional shopping interests in central North Shields.

The Riverside Action Group produced an alternative planning brief emphasizing marine industrial development, job creation and open riverside leisure access. It argued that the collapse of the Soviet empire (foreseeing this in 1989) would open up the Tyne's traditional trading connections with the Baltic and Arctic Russia, offering the possibility of large scale new port trade. The moving southwards of North Sea oil exploration meant the possibility of service jobs. Finally new offshore technologies, particularly wave-power, were identified as logical developments of the existing industrial structure and the basis for major industrial development after the year 2000. The group suggested that in the short-to-medium term the site could be used for port-development around Baltic trades and oil servicing together with light industry. The long-term potential would be developed around a wave-power research centre directed towards the development of production processes for this very promising technology. These proposals, including the leisure component, were compatible both with the Structure Plan and with the detailed River Tyne–Local Plan for Recreation and Amenity of 1983.

The group, together with North Tyneside Council, drew up a scheme layout based on these proposals, which would produce some 4,200 permanent jobs with minimal displacement component. These would be new jobs in the region. It was estimated that the total capital cost of developments, including a large offshore manufacturing facility, would be approximately £150 million. If this was all delivered as public subsidy it would give a cost per job of £29,000 compared with Nissan subsidies and Enterprise Zone permanent job creation equivalent costs of £35,000. These figures are actually in line with Department of Trade and Industry subsidy patterns of recent years, although any manu-facturing development would include private capital investment which would reduce the total public subvention. TWDC has proposed a total expenditure of some £170 million on the site, although not all of this will be public subsidy. The only clear identification of a gearing ratio (*Vision of The Future*, 1990, pp. 69–70) specifies 'pro-rata' for housing and industrial development. It would seem that at that stage retail and leisure developments were to be unsubsidized. On the conservative estimate public subsidy would be circa £75 million, exclusive of site development.

TWDC proceeded to an outline planning application, made of course to itself, in July 1990. This repeated the earlier proposals with some modifications. Housing development was to be 1,440 with 25% social housing. There was an increased leisure component. Carparking was a major land user with 2,350 spaces for leisure and retail. North Tyneside MBC considered that the proposal constituted a major departure from the Structure Plan, not only in relation to the change of use of a strategic industrial site, but also in terms of the retail element. The intention was to develop more than 250,000 sq ft gross and there was a clear likelihood of detrimental impact on existing shopping centres, particularly North Shields. The proposal also contradicted existing housing land policies, given that it represented 30% of development over an 8–10 year period. The scale of the proposed retail development is indicated by the fact that it was of almost exactly the same size as total retail space in North Shields Town Centre. In its formal response to TWDC North Tyneside observed that:

We are aware that the balance of the scheme has been determined to enable leverage ratios between public and private sector funding to be met. This, in our view, is an inappropriate way to plan the development of such a significant strategic site.

The other principal objectors were the Riverside Action Group who supported the Council's general line, and also objected to the social exclusion inherent in the housing and commercial leisure proposals, and the Tyne Port Users Association. This body has a membership which includes all the significant traditional industrial and trading users of the Port and had been established in 1988, in large part to keep a watching eye on TWDC and coordinate responses to its proposals. Its officers have indicated clearly that they see TWDC as hostile to the interests of existing industry, cavalier in its approach to it, and uninterested in the expertise which exists in it. The Association objected vigorously to the development proposals on the grounds of detriment to the future of the Tyne as a working river and port. Thus the coalition of opposition was existing local authority, existing (large-scale) industry, and the local community.

Despite this opposition, and despite the scale of the retail proposals, the Secretary of State did not see fit to submit the application to a public inquiry. TWDC was therefore able to award planning permission to itself. Development has proceeded but rather slowly. Most of the work undertaken so far has been site development and road access, which would be non-contentious for any use. The only industrial development has involved the movement of Twining's teabag factory from one side of the Tyne Tunnel Road to the other. This is a perfectly acceptable light industrial use, and Twining's would have been foolish not to take advantage of TWDC incentives in funding new premises, but it is not job creation. By the summer of 1991 the status of Avatar and its financial capacity were coming under question, a common occurrence in the history of development in North Tyneside!

As of today (Tuesday, 10 September 1992) the whole housing/leisure/retail use of the site is in question. The Meadowell riots do not make the site attractive, even for the most exclusive development. To a considerable extent the Meadowell riots have been the response of the excluded young poor to their relative deprivation. The proposals for 'Royal Quays' combined the injury of eliminating the land basis for real employment prospects with the insult of the development of a housing/leisure/retail complex which could only function if the likes of Meadowell residents were excluded from it. The original proposal even included a separate 'village school' despite the close proximity of two existing primary schools to the site. Progress is awaited.

Conclusion

TWDC has explicitly rejected a strategy for the regeneration of industrial Tyneside (and in practice, though not explicitly, industrial Wearside) which is based on the revival and further development of a marine manufacturing and port-trade base. Instead it has adopted a property-orientated approach, which seems to be based on imitating development 'successes' elsewhere. It is interesting to look at the proposal currently emerging for Unitary Development Plans in Tyne and Wear. All the MDCs apart from Newcastle seem to have adopted strategies which recognizably derive from the original Structure Plan, which in turn reflected the industrial orientation of the Northern Regional Strategy. Newcastle's strategy is summed up in its commitment to being a 'Regional Capital', and which is clearly non-, and indeed to some considerable extent, anti-industrial. This seems to reflect the considerable influence exerted in the ruling Labour group of that authority of property and property-related interests. Newcastle's activities no longer have the direct relevance to the industrial river that they once had, except to the extent that it has given up a commitment to offshore development just as the southern North Sea oil comes on stream! However the symbolic importance is significant.

It is not just that TWDC has got it wrong, although it has misjudged and mismanaged the property market to such an extent that the kind of developments to which it is committed are unlikely to materialize. It is not just that proposals, by emphasizing property-derived criteria of exclusivity, are actively against the interests of a number of poor riverside communities, and in particular the people of the Meadowell. TWDC has gone against the whole cultural bias of the county in which it is located. To quote one retired Chief Engineer of my acquaintance, 'these bozos are trying to piss to windward' and we know what happens to people who do that! TWDC is a classic illustration of the failures, not of free market capitalism with which it has little connection, but of anti-democratic central direction. If there is any lesson to learn from the experience, it is probably that Derek Senior got it absolutely right in his minority report of the Redcliffe Maude Commission on the reform of local government, and Peacock and Crowther-Hunt got in right in their minority report of the Royal Commission on the constitution. The government and planning of development in this country requires effective democratic processes which can handle whole cities and whole regions. The last things required are colonial administrations in the form of UDCs.

7

DEVELOPER-LED LAND USE STRATEGIES: THE BLACK COUNTRY DEVELOPMENT CORPORATION

Brendan Nevin

Introduction

The election of a Conservative government following the 1979 general election marked a radical reorientation of area-based urban policy initiatives. Urban policy after this date has sought to retain an area-based approach, but the Conservative government has redefined the cause of urban problems from one of market failure to that of public sector activities (local authorities in particular) inhibiting the working of the free market (Ambrose, 1986). In this context the government has seen the private sector as the means to its solution, with the role of local authorities marginalized to facilitating private sector investment through 'pump-priming' initiatives and much reduced local authority planning controls.

This reorientation of urban policy in the 1980s reflects the dominant ideological principle which underpins Conservative government thinking – privatism. According to this ideology the source of urban problems lies in the constraints that have been placed on private sector investment and activity, particularly by the state. Consequently, government initiatives, and Urban Development Corporations (UDCs) in particular, have sought to facilitate private investment through land acquisition and disposal, grant aid, infrastructure provision, land reclamation, environmental improvements and the ability to cut through red tape by much reduced local authority planning controls.

The overall reorientation of urban policy has occurred within a framework of ideological hostility between local and central government. The Conservative government's objectives have included a reduction in planning controls and public expenditure, and a retrenchment of the state at both national and local level. It is within this context that this chapter examines the impact of the Black Country Development Corporation (BCDC) during its first five years of existence. The second section examines the historical context of the Black Country and looks at recent economic trends in the area, examining the rationale for the declaration of a UDC, and briefly looks at the response of the local authorities to the designation. The third section evaluates the BCDC's regenerative activity over the first five years, and the fourth section details the effect that the Development Corporation has had on strategic planning within

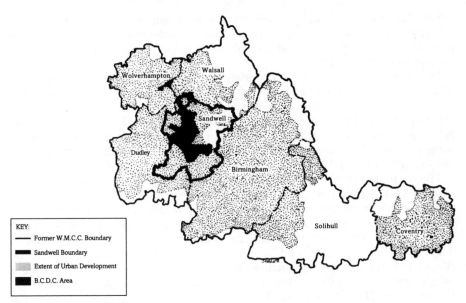

Figure 7.1 BCDC and surrounding districts.

the Black Country. The fifth section considers the extent of public sector expenditure necessary to regenerate the BCDC area. Finally the sixth section concludes with an assessment of BCDC's activities over the first five years.

The Background to the Designation of the Black Country UDC

The Black Country Development Corporation (BCDC) area is situated in the boroughs of Sandwell, Walsall and Wolverhampton, which in addition to the borough of Dudley, form an area known as the Black Country (see Figure 7.1). This heavily industrialized area to the north of Birmingham has a population of around one million people, who live in an inter-related network of long-standing urban villages which expanded because of local manufacturing specialisms.

The Black Country developed an industrial base in the eighteenth and nineteenth centuries, as industrialists located the manufacture of metal-related products near to the deposits of coal, limestone and clay which lay close to the surface and were therefore relatively cheap to extract. The Black Country benefited from the growth of Birmingham's manufacturing industry from the mid-nineteenth century, as it supplied both labour and materials to the rapidly expanding city. However, the trading relationship between Birmingham and the Black Country was an unequal one, with the former producing the finished goods from the latter's raw materials. The result of this unequal economic relationship was that higher wages prevailed in the Birmingham area, a fact which caused resentment amongst workers in the Black Country (Sutcliffe,

1986). The economic linkages with Birmingham continued to develop during the twentieth century as the Black Country's industrial base developed to provide engineering and metal-related produce which serviced Birmingham's expanding motor industry.

Given the Black Country's dependence on heavy manufacturing industry it suffered a considerable contraction of employment during the recession at the beginning of the 1980s, when industry nationally competed against an overvalued exchange rate and high interest rates. Between 1979 and 1981, for example, the Borough of Sandwell lost 34% of its employment base (Sandwell MBC, 1987), while in Wolverhampton more than 23% of employment in manufacturing was lost between 1981 and 1987 (Champion and Townsend, 1990).

The combination of recession and 200 years of activity by manufacturing and extractive industries have left a legacy of an exceptionally poor environment and a pattern of mixed residential and industrial land use which makes communications poor, even though the M5 and M6 motorways run through the area. In 1988, the worst-affected area, Sandwell, contained 403 hectares of derelict land, 4.7% of its total land surface. To tackle this huge problem the Black Country boroughs constructed a three year rolling derelict land reclamation programme, the first of its kind, which was ratified by the Department of the Environment (DOE) in 1986. This programme has consistently achieved a comparatively high level of expenditure, Sandwell being the second highest spender in England in respect of derelict land reclamation in 1986–87. Planned spending between 1986–89 was set to range between £11.7 million and £16.4 million. This ambitious programme, however, fell well short of the resources needed to achieve a real reduction in the total area of derelict land, which in Sandwell increased by 25% in the six years to 1988 (Sandwell MBC, 1988). In 1992 the chairman of the BCDC has estimated that a quarter of England's derelict land lies in the four Black Country boroughs (Francis, 1992).

Despite the evidence of structural decline in the local economy the Black Country still has a large manufacturing base, for example, in 1987, 45% of all jobs in Sandwell were still located in the manufacturing sector, with a sub-total of 23% who were employed in the metal goods, engineering and vehicle industries. There has been significant underinvestment in these industries in recent years, with total investment in 1987 being 21% below the UK average for the manufacturing sector. The metal manufacturing sector in Sandwell has been particularly badly affected by high interest rates, a high and unstable currency, and competition from substitute commodities. This structural decline is reflected in local income levels. In 1986, 40% of the workforce in Sandwell were low paid and average household income was only 67% of the British average (Sandwell MBC, 1990a).

Unemployment also remains high; in May 1987 the unemployment rate in the wards contained within the UDA was 19.2%. Locally, however, unemployment and its duration has not been equally distributed spatially, by social class or by ethnic origin. For example, in Smethwick (a district in the south-east of the UDA) the area's manufacturing base lost 43% of its employment between 1978 and 1981. Further research has shown that the labour market areas of Smethwick and West Bromwich had the worst levels of long-term unemployment in the country (Champion and Green, 1988).

Following the return of economic growth from 1981, it became apparent that

Table 7.1 Urban deprivation in selected urban areas 1981; the ten worst areas

	Z score
Manchester	4.19
Leicester	4.02
Wolverhampton	3.77
Birmingham	3.51
Liverpool	3.51
Coventry	3.17
Sandwell	3.15
Nottingham	3.14
Blackburn	3.08
Knowsley	2.67

This table does not include figures for individual London boroughs as the table compares free standing towns and cities. A Z score for London of 2.37 was derived from the composite figures of the London boroughs.

Source: Loftman and Nevin (1992).

many of the remaining factories in the Black Country were still vulnerable to structural economic change. In Sandwell in 1984, 8.3% of total employment was accounted for by the drop-forging sector, and output from this sector was three times more dependent on the automotive industry than the sector nationally. The output from the foundry and drop-forging sector destined for the automotive industry fell by 38% between the years 1983 and 1987 (Polytechnic of Wolverhampton, 1988). These negative economic factors outlined above had a significant impact upon private sector investment during the 1980s. For example, during 1988–89 there was not a single speculative industrial unit developed within the Sandwell area.

In addition to the problems of unemployment and low pay, the Black Country emerges as an area containing severe concentrations of deprivation compared to the national averages. Table 7.1 shows that both Wolverhampton and Sandwell are amongst the ten most deprived urban areas in England. Subsequent research has also revealed the widespread distribution of poverty within the sub-region. Figures released in 1990 show that 36% of the residents of Wolverhampton lived on or below a poverty line (defined as those people living in households entitled to Income Support or Housing Benefit). The respective figures for Sandwell and Walsall were 35% and 30% (Sandwell MBC, 1990b).

It was to this background that in 1987 the Secretary of State for the Environment announced an Urban Development Corporation (UDC) for the Black Country which encompassed 2,343 ha of land in Sandwell and Walsall. The Urban Development Area was later extended in 1988 to cover 253 ha in Wolverhampton. The Black Country UDA is unique outside London in possessing a large resident population, with over 35,000 residents living in 14,000 properties.

During 1986 the Secretary of State visited two areas within the West Midlands (East Birmingham and the Black Country) and it became known that one of these areas would be chosen to site a UDC. In December 1986, the DOE commissioned the consultants ECOTEC to construct an 'outline Development

Strategy' for the Black Country UDC. They reported in March 1987 that, with an injection of £130 million of public sector funds, £440 million of private sector investment could be realized, creating over 18,000 jobs (ECOTEC, 1987). Following the publication of this report the government moved swiftly, and on 8 April 1987, the statutory instrument was laid before Parliament which created the BCDC and defined the UDA. The government was clear that the UDC was to be a short-life agency and the Housing and Urban Affairs Minister promised that: 'I take the view that given five years it will be a great success . . . In ten years it will have gone. If it doesn't work in ten years it's not going to work' (Jones and Craig, 1987).

The plans to introduce a UDC in the Black Country were most strongly resisted by some elements within the Labour group in Sandwell and Walsall, but Wolverhampton (then Conservative controlled) lobbied for, and was granted an extension of the UDA into three small areas of the borough. In Sandwell the local authority went to the lengths of obtaining the opinion of a Queen's Counsel to investigate whether the Secretary of State's decision to declare a UDA could have been legally challenged. The government responded to local criticism of its decision by highlighting an Audit Commission report which criticized Sandwell for low spending, lacking an overall regeneration strategy and parochialism in capital programming (Jones and Craig, 1987). The disjointed political response of the local authorities to the threat of the imposition of a UDC reinforced a view, which is shared by officers of the BCDC, that a UDC was necessary to provide a unifying focus for a sub-region which is geographically and politically fragmented, thus creating a political and economic force that could challenge Birmingham's hegemony within the West Midlands (Nevin, 1991).

The initial opposition by Sandwell and Walsall to the UDC has, however, been tempered by a pragmatic approach to ensure that some of the councils' objectives are achieved within the UDA following designation. This more cooperative approach has involved the councils designing and implementing schemes for BCDC. 112 BCDC schemes had been started by 1989, of which 79 (70%) had been managed by Sandwell or Walsall MBC. In addition to this, BCDC funding has complemented local authority works initiated by resources from the Transport Policies and Programme, Housing Investment Programme and Urban Programme. Co-operation has been extended further to cover the day-to-day development control function, which is exercised by the local authorities' Planning Departments on an agency agreement negotiated with the Development Corporation.

The designation of the Black Country UDC has had a differential strategic impact upon the three local authorities. Table 7.2 shows that 73% of the UDA lies within Sandwell. This area contains 90% of the resident population of the UDA, 65% of the borough's derelict land and 74% of the forward supply of industrial land identified at 1990. The Walsall section of the UDA contains only 4.2% of the borough's total land area, however the strategic significance of the sites in this area are such that it contains 23% of derelict land and 39% of industrial land available to the borough at 1992. The Wolverhampton part of the UDA contains a small area adjacent to the town centre, and Bowmans Harbour, possibly the most polluted site within the Black Country UDA.

The characteristics of the UDA presented the Development Corporation

Table 7.2 The distribution of land within the BCDC area

	BCDC area HA	BCDC area as a % of the total land
Sandwell	1,903	24
Walsall	440	4.2
Wolverhampton	253	3.7

Source: Information supplied by Sandwell MBC, Walsall MBC and Wolverhampton MBC.

with an extremely complex task. The identified problems include a working population of 73,000, a diverse resident population of 36,500, problems relating to the fragmented ownership of derelict and underused land, a poor local transport infrastructure, and a proliferation of contaminated land (Morgan, 1992).

BCDC Strategy and Performance

During its first three years of operation the BCDC has developed the initial development framework created by the DOE's consultants, and set clear aims and objectives which will be achieved prior to the winding up of the Development Corporation. The emerging strategy was ambitious, setting out policies which would improve the environment, diversify the local economy, secure inward investment and improve the infrastructure of the UDA. BCDC's 1989 Corporate Plan stated that £167 million of public sector expenditure would be required by the UDC. It was expected that this would 'lever' a further £845 million of private investment, creating 28,000 jobs (BCDC, 1989). The 1990 Corporate Plan continued in optimistic tone, arguing that an increase in grant aid to £245 million would increase the jobs gains to 30,000 and the private sector investment total to £1.2 billion.

Given the extent of the dereliction and the widespread ownership of land within the UDA, the development process has been front loaded with public expenditure, as the BCDC assembles land packages for reclamation and disposal. In the financial years 1987–88 and 1988–89, £26 million was spent by BCDC, 60% of which was expended on land acquisition. The scale of the operation required to assemble a marketable land portfolio has been huge. The BCDC has identified 839 interested parties on 534 separate plots, which by 1992 had been subject to compulsory purchase orders or had been purchased by negotiation. The Development Corporation had acquired 800 acres of land by September 1991 and by 1994–95 it will have owned more than 1,000 acres. At March 1990 BCDC had the second highest land holdings of any UDC, being second only to the Merseyside UDC (CLES, 1990b).

The acquisition and reclamation of land has been the most time-consuming activity for the BCDC during its first five years. This activity has also proved to be expensive with much of the land being purchased during the property market 'boom' of the late 1980s, only to be released during a property market recession in the 1990s. A parliamentary answer to the Labour MP Steven Byers has revealed that the BCDC has spent £68 million on land acquisition, and the resulting land bank has now been revalued at £38.8 million because of the fall in property prices over the last two years (Swingler, 1992). By March 1991, BCDC had either completed or started the reclamation of 138 acres of the 800 acres in its ownership (17%) and sold or secured an agreement in principle to sell 75 acres or 9.3% of its land holdings (BCDC, 1991a).

Private sector housing development is a major end use for land which has been released by BCDC. This latent demand has been evident since the discussions surrounding the designation of the UDA. In 1987 ECOTEC noted that 'considerable interest has already been generated in the area by proposals for the Urban Development Corporation; especially amongst housebuilders' and 'if it is possible to accelerate the development, particularly of housing, this will have an impact on the investors perceptions of the area' (ECOTEC, 1987, p. 63). BCDC has sought to capitalize on this developer interest. By 1989 the housing development estimates for the first five years had been upgraded from 800 to 1,800 units, with the identification of sites for an additional 800 units in the Tividale area alone (BCDC, 1989).

By April 1990 the Development Corporation had reclaimed 76 acres of formerly derelict land of which 30 acres (39.5%) was being marketed for housing development. Additionally, BCDC has definite plans to facilitate the provision of 2,467 housing units within the UDA, of which 1,850 (75%) are located in the Sandwell area (BCDC, 1990). The 1990 Corporate Plan increased the total housing output to some 4,000 units over the life-time of the Development Corporation compared with a target of 1,660 units identified by ECOTEC in 1987. By April 1992 more than 1,400 units had been completed or were under construction and the Development Corporation had been encouraged by the DOE to increase its housing target by a further 1,000 to 5,000. The success of private sector housing development within the UDA can be explained by two factors; one is the strength of the housing market in the late 1980s, and the other is the concentration of building in the western part of the UDA which contains the only wards within Sandwell which were estimated to have experienced an increase in population between 1981 and 1987 (Sandwell MBC, 1988).

While the provision of housing, mainly within the south and western parts of the UDA, has improved the environment, this has not generated long-term employment prospects. These were to be delivered by the provision of development opportunities for retail, office and business parks. The largest development was to be at the 120 acre site of the former Patent Shaft Steelworks in Wednesbury. The proposal here was for a three million square foot retail and leisure facility known as Sandwell Mall which would dominate the West Midlands region. It was estimated that this scheme would attract £450 million of private sector investment and create 8,000 jobs. The proposal for the Patent Shaft site was bedevilled by the problems historically associated with the Black Country. Construction was unable to start in the 1980s because of the extensive contamination of the land, and there has been a considerable delay in providing transport infrastructure to the site. By 1991 the recession was firmly in place reducing consumer confidence and expenditure, and as a consequence of this, the proposal for Patent Shaft has been abandoned.

The 1989 Corporate Plan outlined the objective of securing a large government

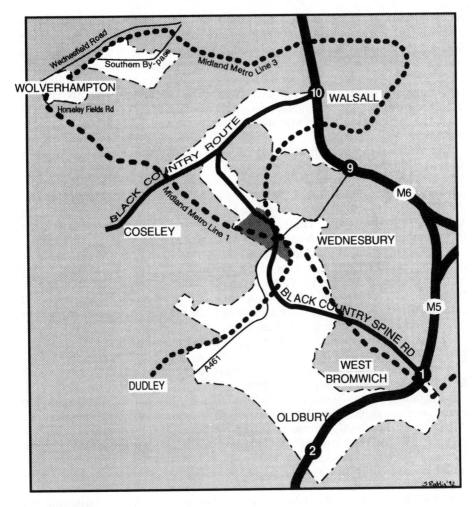

AREA KEY

Sandwell Mall Development

B.C.D.C.

NECESSARY TRANSPORT IMPROVEMENTS

●●●● Midland Metro / Rapid Transit Rail Link

New Roads which have Regional significance

New Roads which have significant Local impact

M5 / M6 Links

Figure 7.2 Transport infrastructure improvements required by BCDC.

office relocation from London. This would have impacted upon the UDA by creating favourable publicity, generating service employment and producing a demand for housing. However, a relocation of this kind has not occurred in the Black Country, and given the large surplus of office space in the London Docklands Development Corporation's area, the chances of this happening are now minimal. Nevertheless despite the loss of its prestige project, BCDC has been successful in securing interest in retail developments on the periphery of the UDA where transport links are good at the junctions of the M5 and M6 motorways.

The poor transport and communication systems within the UDA are a long-standing historical legacy, and therefore most of the major transport infrastructure projects planned for the area pre-date the UDC. The major projects are set out in Figure 7.2 which shows how the planned Spine Road and the Black Country Route provide a north/south and east/west link between the M5 and M6 motorways. These two important dual carriageways will open many land-locked sites for development which would otherwise remain derelict.

The BCDC recognizes that a vastly improved transport infrastructure is necessary, noting that 'the success of the promotion of major development sites in the vicinity of Wednesbury, for example Sandwell Mall and the Triplex Lloyd site, are very heavily dependent upon improved access arrangements at Junction 9' (BCDC, 1989, p. 14). Furthermore, the prospect of the construction of a rapid transit rail system through the area, in the opinion of the Development Corporation, 'fundamentally influences the development prospects at Sandwell Mall' (BCDC, 1989, p. 16).

Additionally, there are proposals to improve the main arterial routes which feed into the development sites within the UDA. In Sandwell this will entail the upgrading of the A461 from Dudley to the M6, and in Wolverhampton extensive improvement work is necessary to widen the access to the Heritage Area and to secure improvements in the Nechelles and Wednesfield area (see Figure 7.3). The total cost of the essential road building projects are itemized in Table 7.3, showing that over £362 million investment is required for road building in conjunction with a further £218 million necessary to fund the Rapid Transit System.

The construction of the Black Country Spine Road is a priority for the BCDC. However, during 1991 the Government announced that it was only to

Table 7.3 Total cost of essential transport improvements to the infrastructure of the UDA

Roads	£000s	Rail/rapid transit	£000s
A461	32,100	Line 1 Wolv-B'ham	137,000
Junction 7,10,M6	12,000	Line 3 Wolv-Dudley	81,000
Junction 1,2,M5	12,000		
Black Country Route	77,400		
Black Country Spine Road	200,000		
Wolverhampton UDA	28,800		
Total	362,300	Total	218,000
Total investment in road and rail	£580,300		

Source: Information supplied by: Sandwell Council; Wolverhampton Council; and Centro.

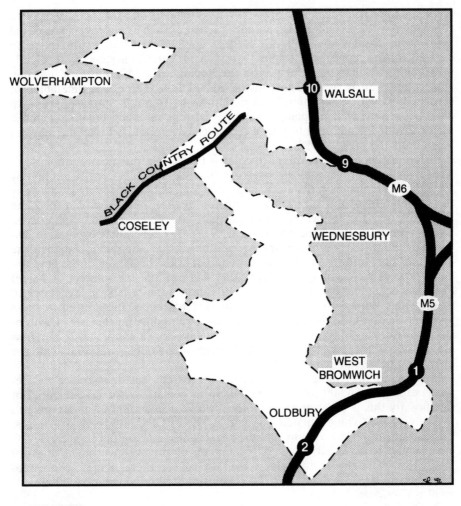

AREA KEY

⌐_⌐ B.C.D.C.

NECESSARY TRANSPORT IMPROVEMENTS

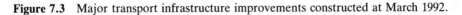 Black Country Route as at 1992

Figure 7.3 Major transport infrastructure improvements constructed at March 1992.

provide funds for 2.5 miles of the 4.7 mile dual carriageway, necessitating that the Spine Road be redesigned, with the road starting at Junction One of the M5 and finishing at the largest derelict site in the UDA, at Patent Shaft in Wednesbury. The total cost of the redesigned road will be £93 million, of which £25 million has been allocated from the BCDC's grant-in-aid. Construction work on the Black Country Spine Road is due to start in late 1992, with completion in 1995. Other local authority schemes such as improvements of the A461 from Dudley are unlikely to start until 1995. Centro, who hope to oversee construction of the Rapid Transit Light Railway System, were slightly more optimistic than the local authorities, hoping for a 1991 start for Line One, with completion in 1993. The construction of Line Three was timetabled to start in 1993 with completion in 1995. However, Centro's optimism seems to have been somewhat misplaced; with the current recession creating a public sector spending-squeeze it has been reported that a start on Line One may not begin until 1996 (Bell, 1992).

Failure by central government to commit funds to infrastructure projects has already delayed progress in regenerating the area. ECOTEC envisaged that by 1991 the Black Country Route would be completed, followed in 1992–93 by the completion of the substantive elements of the Spine Road. In 1992 the Black Country Route has only been partially completed, and the Spine Road has not been started (see Figure 7.3). The Development Corporation has entered 1992 with its original strategy and objectives being unobtainable. The large transport infrastructure projects required at the beginning of the development process have not materialized, the 'flagship' prestige project at Patent Shaft has been abandoned, and the UDC is now a major land holder trying to market sites during a severe property-market recession. In addition to these problems legislation relating to polluted land, contained in the 1990 Environmental Protection Act, is creating uncertainty for investors who are now unsure about the issues of legal and financial liability associated with the ownership of contaminated land.

In recognition of these adverse factors the BCDC has downgraded its lifetime outputs to 26,000 jobs and £1 billion of private sector investment. But significantly this is to be achieved with a two year extension of its life-time to twelve years, with an estimated exit date in 1999 (BCDC, 1991b, p. 6). Despite the slow-down in the economy and the reduced life-time output targets, BCDC has claimed to have attracted £219.4 million of private investment at April 1991. However, the methodology used to collect these figures is open to question and suggests that the BCDC's contribution to job creation and investment is considerably lower.

BCDC's figures for job creation and employment have been calculated by estimating the number of jobs which accrue to each scheme which is granted planning permission within the UDA. A similar exercise is conducted to estimate the value of private sector investment. However, the total investment figure of £219.4 million does not distinguish between public and private sector investment and jobs which have been created or merely transferred into or from within the Black Country (Prisim Research, 1991, p. 16). An example of this is the new £19 million administrative centre for Sandwell MBC which houses 650 local authority workers and is located within the UDA. This one public sector project, which involved the transfer and centralization of local authority office staff, accounts for nearly 10% of the 'private sector' investment and 'job creation' claimed by BCDC at April 1991 (BCDC, 1991a).

It is clear, therefore, that BCDC originally overestimated its ability to regenerate the UDA; however, there is a growing realization that the lifetime output targets will be difficult to achieve. This is highlighted by the fact that in terms of the quantity of development, the collapse of the retail proposal at Patent Shaft has meant that a greater proportion (38%) of projects granted planning permission since 1987 have been abandoned than have been completed (37.8%) (Prisim Research, 1991). Following the release of figures which showed a failure to achieve BCDC's targets for derelict land reclamation, road building and private investment during 1991–92, the Chairman of BCDC has stated that 'the recession has lasted longer than we thought and industrial and commercial development has been slow to materialise' (Gregan, 1992).

Urban Policy and the Locality

Much of the debate which surrounds the BCDC revolves around estimates of the number of jobs created and the quantity of private sector investment which has been attracted. However, of equal importance are issues relating to strategic planning, the distributional issues which surround its activities, and whether the economic development strategy pursued provides linkages between job opportunities and the local community. These issues are explained in more detail below.

The most successful development activity for the BCDC has been marketing land for housing development. However, the decision by the Development Corporation to pursue a vigorous programme of promoting private sector house building has important implications for strategic planning in the three boroughs in which the UDC operates. The Chief Executive of Wolverhampton MBC has commented that relationships between BCDC and the local authority:

are still marked by the differences in planning horizons with the Corporation favouring the early gain of housing and retail development as opposed to the commercial/leisure uses, which may take longer to achieve but for which Wolverhampton offers few better locations.

(Lyons, 1989)

BCDC is now committed to facilitating the construction of between 4,000 and 5,000 housing units over its twelve year life. However, the Unitary Development Plan (UDP) in Wolverhampton has allocated space for approximately 200 units, while in Walsall where 229 units have already been constructed with financial support from the BCDC, there are no additional sites allocated for housing development. Despite this the BCDC 1990 Corporate Plan identified 610 units of accommodation that will be constructed in the northern part of the UDA. It is likely, therefore, that there will be some conflict on this issue with the respective local authorities.

However, it is in Sandwell where there is the greatest potential for conflict between the policies contained in the UDP and the housing development intentions of BCDC. The borough has already increased its housing target within the UDP from 7,500 to 8,500 units of accommodation to the year 2000. This increase was meant to reflect the construction of 2,500 dwellings within the Sandwell UDA facilitated by BCDC. The new target of 4,000 to 5,000 dwellings adopted by the Development Corporation however, implies that between 1,000 and 2,000 more housing units will be constructed in the Sandwell

UDA than is provided for within the UDP. The spatial location of the additional dwellings will be a political issue as land, which is presently zoned for industrial or commercial use, will be reclassified by the Development Corporation.

The concept of social balance in the development of housing is not prominent in BCDC's publications, unlike, for example, the Cardiff Bay Development Corporation that hopes to facilitate the construction of 1,500 housing association units (Brookes, 1989). BCDC's attitude to the provision of social housing is ambivalent, stating that it 'expects to be able to market the land readily and does not intend to reserve land for housing that is not readily available' (BCDC, 1990, p. 17).

There is a body of evidence which suggests that not only has the Development Corporation failed to adopt proactive policies to improve the provision of low income housing, but also that it has failed to grasp the severity of the poor housing conditions experienced by low income groups within the UDA. During 1989–90, a survey of private sector housing built prior to 1919 was conducted by Sandwell MBC. The results, based on a 61% sample, showed the extent of housing disrepair amongst the owner-occupiers of older housing in the wards in which the UDA is located. Because the ward boundaries do not coincide exactly with the boundaries of the Development Corporation, a precise assessment of housing need was not possible. Nevertheless, an analysis of the data shows that of wards located in the UDA, all but one have an unfitness level of over 50% in the pre-1919 private housing stock. The figures relating to the Oldbury Ward which is the only ward wholly within the UDA, are also revealing. This ward contains 1,026 pre-1919 dwellings of which 57.5% are unfit and 72% require repairs costing in excess of £10,000, compared to the respective national figures of 4.8% and 5.9%. These figures show that there is a severe problem of marginal owner-occupation within the UDA, and this factor in conjunction with the prevalence of low income groups suggests that the BCDC's policies of encouraging build for sale will increase social polarity within the UDA (Nevin, 1991).

The BCDC's pragmatism and market-led approach to planning has also undermined Walsall Council's economic development strategy. This document states that:

> The Council will assist the revitalisation of the local economy by ensuring that land supply considerations do not unnecessarily constrain economic development and employment generating opportunities, and by creating a physical infrastructure which supports and encourages investment.
>
> (Walsall MBC, 1990, para.2.3)

The main point of contention has been over BCDC's allocation of industrial land for retail use in the north of the UDA around the M6 motorway. This area of land is mainly zoned for industry within the Walsall UDP, however it has been estimated that between one-fifth and one-quarter of Walsall's prime industrial sites have been allocated to alternative uses, primarily retail or leisure (information supplied by Walsall MBC). Furthermore the presence of BCDC has undermined Walsall's strategic planning process. BCDC has developed an Area Development Framework, which has overridden Walsall's Darlaston District Plan. This is highlighted in the case of the Bentley Mill site in Darlaston, which in the District Plan was designated as an employment site. Subsequently BCDC has granted planning permission for a leisure complex (Nevin and Loftman, 1992).

There is also a feeling amongst the local authorities that there is a dislocation in the process of local economic development. This is because the affected local authorities have consistently had resource support withdrawn from central government, while this source of support has increased for the Development Corporation. This differential level of resources has engendered a pessimistic view within Sandwell MBC of its ability to carry out industrial regeneration outside the UDA stating that 'against a climate of capital restraint and an overall reduction in DLG [Derelict Land Grant] resources outside the BCDC area, the impact the council can make on qualitative and quantitative issues of land availability is severely constrained' and furthermore 'it is unlikely that major improvement in the quality of the land portfolio can be achieved in the short term' (Sandwell MBC, 1990a, p. 30). This view from Sandwell complements the earlier statement from neighbouring Walsall that there is:

likely to be considerable diversion of start-ups, inward investment and local companies into the area [the UDA]. This is similar to the effect that has been observed in the vicinity of a number of Enterprise Zones which have sucked investment away from surrounding areas. This problem is not, of course, simply a function of the economic development initiatives proposed, but is to some extent an inevitable outcome of the existence of a UDC.

(Walsall MBC, 1987)

This view that the BCDC will divert investment away from the areas surrounding the UDA was confirmed recently by a survey by Chestertons which described the Tipton area as 'suffering "an Investment By Pass" reinforced by the BCDC's presence and an armoury of incentives' (Sandwell MBC, 1992, p.11).

A major criticism of the UDC model has been that it has failed to build links between employment opportunities resulting from the regenerative process and local people (CLES, 1990b). This criticism would appear valid in the case of the BCDC. Between May 1987 when the UDA was designated and December 1991, the relationship between the unemployment rate in the wards containing the UDA and the West Midlands County, remained constant at 30% above the county average (West Midlands Enterprise Board, 1987, 1991). This suggests that the BCDC has yet to make an impact on the employment prospects for residents in some of the poorest areas in the Black Country.

The BCDC has tried to build links with community groups through a financial support package. During 1989–90, this support amounted to 1.8% of the total spending, a proportion which placed the BCDC fourth out of the eleven UDCs nationally (CLES, 1989). This support was planned to total £2.9 million over the first five years of the Development Corporation's life-span. Its life-time social expenditure has now been increased to £9.8 million. There are however, structural difficulties for community groups wishing to be funded by the BCDC. As with the Urban Programme, most BCDC grants take the form of capital rather than revenue expenditure, and the Development Corporation will normally only fund 50% of the cost of any project proposed by a statutory agency. However, this is subject to some discretion.

There were, prior to the designation of Birmingham Heartlands as a UDC in

Table 7.4   UDC expenditure on community support: London Docklands, Black Country and Tyne
& Wear 1990/91

	UDC community per capita spending (£)	Population eligible for support
London Docklands	433.17	40,400
Black Country	24.99	35,405
Tyne & Wear	45.16	12,000

The population figures for the London Docklands and BCDC are based on figures at designation
while the figure for Tyne & Wear includes a population of 4,000 who, while not residents within the
UDA, are able to apply for community support grants.

Source: BCDC (1991a) Annual Report. Additional information supplied by Tyne & Wear and
London Docklands Development Corporations.

1992, only three UDCs which have a significant resident population; these are
the London Docklands Development Corporation (LDDC), the Tyne and
Wear Development Corporation (TWDC) and the BCDC. Table 7.4 shows the
per capita expenditure on community support by these three development
corporations in 1990–91, revealing that the BCDC social expenditure per head
of population was 5.7% of the LDDC and 55% of the TWDC.

Despite the low level of funding of community groups, the BCDC has
enjoyed good public relations with the local community until relatively recently.
Having spent the first four years purchasing and assembling land, BCDC has
now reached a phase where sites are being aggressively marketed. The result
has been a series of development proposals which have angered both community
groups and business organizations. Proposals to excavate 250,000 tons of coal
from the Bowmans Harbour site in Wolverhampton have generated a petition
containing 1,500 names (*Birmingham Evening Mail*, 1992), and additionally
proposals to develop the sites in the north of the UDA adjacent to the M6
for retail use, have drawn criticism from traders' associations, Labour and
Conservative councillors from both Sandwell and Walsall, and the Walsall
Chamber of Commerce. This difficult period for the Development Corporation
culminated in Sandwell's Chair of Planning calling for more local authority
representation on the board of BCDC and a greater emphasis on social regeneration (Collins, 1992).

Gearing Ratios and the Free Market Myth

Much of the discussion which has surrounded urban policy in the last decade
has involved the subject of gearing ratios. Success has often been measured by
the size of the ratio of private sector to public sector investment. Thus it has
been estimated that Urban Development Grants have secured a gearing ratio
of 4.4:1 (Campbell *et al*, 1990), and the UDCs at Cardiff, Central Manchester
and Tyne and Wear estimate ratios during their life span of 4:1, 5:1 and 4:1
respectively (*Estates Times*, 1988).

The BCDC has set similar investment targets to the Development Corporations
listed above. The 1990 Corporate Plan details expenditure by BCDC of £240.4

million, but it is hoped to secure an increase in grant-in-aid to boost this total to £288.4 million (information derived from the 1990 Corporate Plan with additional information supplied by BCDC). This level of funding would attract a private sector investment total of £1 billion, providing a gearing ratio of 3.5:1. This approach to calculating the success of urban regeneration is too narrow in concept and in its accounting practice. To realize the private sector investment total above, two things must occur: the national economy must grow at a speed which can sustain speculative housing, retail and industrial development; and central and local government would have to massively increase the level of infrastructure investment in and around the UDA to enable the area to benefit from this growth.

It has already been highlighted in this chapter that the total cost of the necessary transport infrastructure will be £580 million. In addition to this figure the local authorities will target expenditure to achieve objectives within the UDA. This is particularly true of Sandwell Council which has 90% of the UDA's population within its boundaries and has the statutory responsibility for providing education, housing and highway maintenance services. Between 1986–87 and 1989–90 the distribution of Sandwell's capital spending was analysed to identify the extent of expenditure on regenerative activities within the UDA by the local authority. This analysis found that the seven wards which lie wholly or mostly within the UDA have benefited from £53,577 million of local authority capital expenditure, this representing 41% of the total spend identified in an area which has 29.3% of the borough's resident population (Nevin, 1991, p. 26).

This represents a significant concentration of Sandwell Council's capital expenditure. The amount being invested in the wards within the UDC has increased in absolute terms from £11.875 million in 1986–87 to £18.206 million in 1989–90. However, this figure has been shrinking as a proportion of *total* capital expenditure from 37.6% in 1986–87 to 23.6% in 1989–90. These absolute figures mask shifts in departmental spending. For example, Sandwell's Derelict Land Reclamation Scheme has been reduced from £2.544 million in 1986–87 to £1.321 million (Sandwell MBC, 1990c) in 1989–90 as the BCDC land reclamation programme has progressed, while capital investment in housing has increased substantially. Figure 7.4 confirms that the UDC is located in a high expenditure band which stretches from Smethwick in the south-east to Princes End and Wednesbury in the north-west of the borough.

Table 7.5 shows a clearer picture of the potential cost to the public sector if central and local government incur the necessary complementary investment to enable BCDC to achieve its £1 billion private investment target. The bill for the essential roads and communications infrastructure is approximately £580 million. Additionally if Sandwell MBC continued to invest in the UDA to the year 2000 at the average sustained between 1986–87 and 1989–90, a further £187 million will have been targeted at the regeneration of the UDA. The total public expenditure bill for securing the £1 billion of private sector investment is likely therefore to be in the region of £1,055 billion, giving a true gearing ratio of 0.94:1 if the BCDC performs to its high expectations.

While the economic recession will undoubtedly delay the regenerative process, questions have been raised as to the realism of the concept of the Development Corporation as a short-life agency. A senior officer of the BCDC, following a

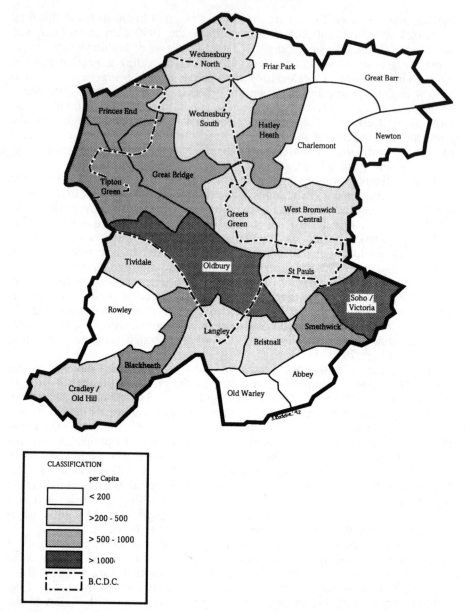

Legend:

CLASSIFICATION

per Capita

□ < 200

▨ >200 - 500

▨ > 500 - 1000

■ > 1000

⌐·─·⌐ B.C.D.C.

Figure 7.4 The distribution of local authority capital expenditure on housing land and infrastructure, 1986/87–1989/90 (source: Nevin, 1991).

Table 7.5 Total project public sector expenditure within the UDA 1986–87 to 1990–2000

	£000s
Transport infrastructure	580,000
BCDC expenditure	288,000
Local authority expenditure	187,000
Total	1,055,000

BCDC expenditure net of Black Country Spine Road costs.

visit to regeneration projects in Baltimore and Boston (USA), commented that it could take 35 years of concerted intervention to regenerate the Black Country (*Birmingham Post*, 1991).

Conclusion

The BCDC is now nearly halfway through its twelve year life-time having completed its first phase objective of land assembly and reclamation. It now faces a daunting task of securing large-scale land disposal and development in a severely depressed property market. BCDC's objectives in creating 30,000 jobs and levering £1.2 billion of private sector investment were always ambitious; however, the onset of recession has heralded a scaling down of employment and investment outputs and a two year extension to the limited lifetime.

The BCDC has begun however to reassess its output targets as the effects of the recession, the full extent of land contamination, and the Government's unwillingness to make funds available for major transport infrastructure improvements has become apparent. Furthermore, BCDC appear to have overestimated their impact on the local economy, by including public sector investment and job transfers in their 'private sector investment' and 'jobs created' totals.

The need to secure development quickly has influenced the BCDC into pursuing a developer-led land use strategy which is being shaped primarily by demand in the housing and retail sectors, with much prime industrial land being lost to speculative development particularly in the north of the UDA. The overwhelming concentration by the UDC on the physical redevelopment of land is a product of the narrow interpretation of regeneration adopted by UDCs and the short, fixed life span imposed on the Corporations by the central government. These factors combined with a myopic concentration of resources on the UDA, as if this area were an independent, autonomous spatial entity, has created the mechanism for a transfer of dereliction within the conurbation, rather than a springboard for urban regeneration. The focus on the development of land has diverted attention away from a linkage between job creation and the unemployed, and from ensuring that an economic development strategy is created which links the UDA into the regional, national and European economies.

There is, however, the possibility that the spatial transfer of dereliction following from the activities of BCDC will not occur. This is unlikely to be a result of improvements in the performance of regional policy or strategic planning but from a failure by BCDC to achieve its development and investment targets. This failure will have three main causes. An over-optimistic assessment of private sector interest in a heavily contaminated area; a decline in the trend line of national economic growth; and the failure of government departments and ministers to evaluate and plan for the requisite amount of public expenditure needed to build the infrastructure to support the activities of the BCDC.

The re-election of a Conservative government in April 1992 has brought to an end any speculation that the BCDC may be prematurely wound up. However, there are signs that the public sector funding totals of the Development Corporation are being closely scrutinized by the DOE. During 1991, the DOE informed the Black Country Development Corporation that £25 million of grant aid would be vired towards the costs of the truncated Black Country Spine Road. In 1992 the BCDC has been instructed to make provisions of £12 million to pay corporation tax to the Treasury. The total funding available to the BCDC has therefore been effectively reduced by £37 million. In July 1992 the government announced that the Tipton area in Sandwell containing a small part of the UDA would receive £37.5 million from the City Challenge competition over five years. This change in funding priorities by central government may signal a phase in the development of UDCs where public sector funding is much harder to obtain as the DOE and the Treasury modify urban policy in the light of changing economic and political circumstances.

8

AN URBAN POLICY FOR PEOPLE: LESSONS FROM SHEFFIELD

Gordon Dabinett and Peter Ramsden

Introduction

During the relaunch of urban policy in 1988, urban development corporations (UDCs) were described as the most important attack ever made on urban decay (Cabinet Office, 1988). Such a bold political claim throws open the debate about the role of UDCs to include fundamental questions about the nature of urban policy. In particular urban policy since its early conception in the 1960s has addressed issues of inequality between urban and non-urban areas, but, more significantly, within cities. Only a year before the exaggerated claim was being made for UDCs, Prime Minister Margaret Thatcher claimed that one nation of free prosperous and responsible families and people was being built, and that a Conservative dream was becoming a reality (Conservative Party Conference, 1987). Such a claim was in stark contrast to the views of Sheffield MP and former Council Leader David Blunkett. In 1987 he wrote that the country was more divided than ever before, that large sections of the population were dispirited and struggling for an opportunity to use their energies and talents responsibly, both at work and in the community (Blunkett and Jackson, 1987).

This chapter describes the delivery of urban policy in one specific locality. Sheffield was declared a programme authority in 1979–80, had a UDC imposed in 1988 and failed in a City Challenge bid in 1991. The City Council developed clear local policy responses to urban decline during the early 1980s. It took an antagonistic stance towards central government policy on urban local authorities and developed alternative strategies and approaches. The most notable of these were the staging of the World Student Games (WSG) in 1991, and the evolution of an economic regeneration strategy which was articulated in initiatives known as the Twin Valleys Strategy and more recently Sheffield 2000. Overall the experience shows that urban policy must return to some of its more basic objectives to assist people and communities in improving their quality of life by providing appropriate locality based assistance.

Urban Policy – The Sheffield Context

To understand the significance of the UDC declaration in Sheffield requires an appreciation of the historical context of urban policy in the city and in the Lower Don Valley, the area covered by the UDC (Lawless and Ramsden, 1990). This is best provided by examining the nature of the urban problem in Sheffield and the way that national policy was applied in response. Sheffield is the major urban centre of the South Yorkshire subregion. This region does not form a cohesive conurbation in geographical terms, but was united by the traditional industries of coal, steel and engineering. During the late 1970s Sheffield was regarded as an area of relative prosperity in this subregion. Sheffield, like all major urban areas, has always had a number of residents who suffer social, economic and political inequality. In relative terms, these groups were small and concentrated in a number of well-defined spatial areas, and urban programme funds were used after 1979 to tackle this urban-based inequality.

It can be argued that Sheffield only became strongly associated with depression and urban decline after 1981 (Lawless, 1986). At this time confidence within the city was very low. There was no new investment, housing and land markets were stagnant, employment falling and unemployment rising, and the main area of traditional employment, the Lower Don Valley, was becoming an enormous wasteland of vacant buildings and derelict sites. The level of unemployment in the city rose above the national average after a long period of stability. This was a direct result of job losses in steel, steel processing, engineering and cutlery. Therefore, the city's position changed rapidly and relatively recently, and this was explicitly linked to the state of the local economy.

This situation was fuelled by the conflict between central government and the city council about local government funding and local taxation. With David Blunkett as leader of the council, Sheffield was at the forefront of the national campaigns to save local authority jobs and services. The local authority refused to become involved in the deregulation experiments of Enterprise Zones and did not receive special status through Task Forces or City Action Teams. Conflict and division grew between the controlling Labour nexus (the council, the party and the wider movement) and private capital interests in the city (Duncan and Goodwin, 1988; Seyd, 1990). The Lower Don Valley itself became a powerful political symbol of this debate, as the issues incorporated the nature of economic policy as well as public expenditure controls.

This local economic and political situation was to change again late in the 1980s coinciding with the election of a further Conservative government, which saw the period 1986 to 1991 become distinguished by economic regeneration and partnership rather than industrial bargaining and old style corporatism (Lawless, 1990). It was only with the declaration of a UDC in 1988 that the main instruments of national urban policy were implemented in the city. Sheffield, therefore, remained an urban area where local policy responses dominated and central Conservative government urban initiatives were marginal, unlike their policies towards public expenditure and industry.

The main policy measures taken in the city are described next, concentrating on the period 1986 to 1991 since this coincides with the declaration of the UDC

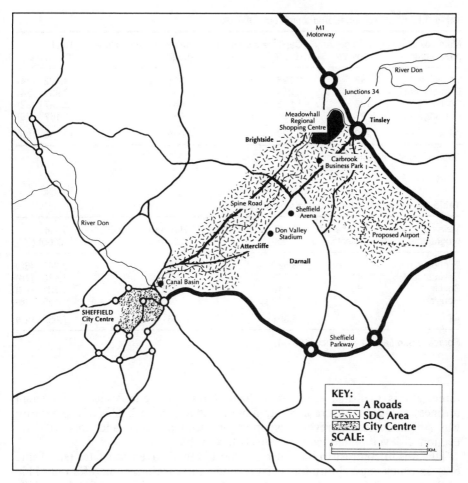

Figure 8.1 Sheffield's Lower Don Valley.

and a paradigm shift in local policy. The nature of these policy responses, the relation between local and central initiatives and the role of the UDC are well illustrated by the evolution of Sheffield's urban programme bid, the WSG, and the City Council's regeneration strategy.

Sheffield was first designated an urban programme authority in 1979 and it has consistently funded a breadth of projects generally of a small-scale nature yet orientated to specific local needs. Such approaches have been shown to be relatively effective in delivering local benefits and job opportunities (Turok and Wannop, 1990). Tables 8.1 and 8.2 show the basic breakdown for the bids made by Sheffield City Council for 1986–89 and 1991–94. The 1986–89 programme was the first to recognize explicitly the economic restructuring that had occurred in the city (Sheffield City Council, 1986). This programme included a supplementary bid for activities in the Lower Don Valley, and other major projects included proposals for a science park, a technology park, as well as

Table 8.1 Sheffield urban programme bid 1986–89

Main objective/ programme	Number of projects	Capital expenditure (£000)	Revenue expenditure (£000)	Total (£000) (%)
Economic	49	3,796	326	4,122 (34)
Environment	48	2,249	682	2,931 (24)
Social	108	1,266	2,661	3,927 (32)
Housing	27	828	339	1,167 (9)
All	232	8,139	4,058	12,198 (100)

Source: Sheffield City Council (1986).

Table 8.2 Sheffield urban programme bid 1991–94

Main objective/ programme	Number of projects	Capital expenditure (£000)	Revenue expenditure (£000)	Total (£000) (%)
Economic	36	3,523	424	3,947 (52)
Environment	44	1,239	239	1,478 (19)
Social	65	847	873	1,721 (22)
Housing	9	382	73	455 (6)
All	154	5,991	1,661	7,652 (100)

Source: Sheffield City Council (1991a).

direct grants to firms, either in Industrial Improvement Areas or for small businesses. Despite this reorientation of the bid in 1986–87, 22% of expenditure was still allocated to revenue support of social projects, and only 31% on economic development capital projects (see Table 8.1).

This was in contrast to the much smaller bid made five years later (see Table 8.2), in which expenditure for social revenue initiatives accounted for only 11% of the total bid, and capital projects seeking economic objectives made up 46% of the bid (Sheffield City Council, 1991a). With the exclusion of the Lower Don Valley, the 1991–94 bid focused on the wider economic strategy of the City Council, and in particular the attempts of this strategy to 'spread the benefits' of regeneration to the community as a whole. Some of the major projects in this bid included an Afro-Caribbean enterprise centre and an employment project on the Manor, a local authority housing estate. However, other major events were to have an impact on urban regeneration policy in the city between 1986 and 1991 including the staging of the WSG.

The WSG has been the most controversial of the initiatives in Sheffield. Very little research was done into the probable costs and benefits that the WSG would bring to the city at the time the decision was made (Smith, 1991). The construction of new facilities included an arena and a stadium in the Lower Don Valley and two new swimming pools. A cultural festival was also held and the Lyceum Theatre was renovated at a cost of £12 million. Overall, the cost of the construction work has been estimated at £147 million with relatively few financial benefits or contracts for Sheffield and region (Sheffield

City Council, 1991c). The management of the WSG ran into seve
when the public/private company set up to run the event ceased tra
1990. The Council subsequently took over the direct management c
at an unknown cost although estimates have varied between £5 and
(Foley, 1991). The WSG went ahead with some commentators cla......g great
benefits to Sheffield in terms of morale, image and new facilities. Opponents
have pointed out the cost to the city poll-tax payer, the concurrent closure of
schools, local sports facilities and libraries, and the elitist nature of the new
facilities.

Since the development of an economic strategy by the City Council set the
context for many policy matters during 1986–1991, it is worthwhile briefly
considering the nature of this strategy. The concept of an economic strategy
began to emerge in 1981, with the formation of an Employment Department
and Employment Committee. This was a clear political response to deepening
industrial decline and was essentially employment based rather than a coherent
industrial or regeneration strategy (Bennington, 1986). However in 1986 the
Council was forced to concede that private sector investment would be necessary
to meet the shortfall between available public resources and the investment
needed to complete agreed projects.

In order to secure such investment, a new development strategy and agency
were required. The agency was seen to be a public/private partnership which
could change the anti-business image of the Council, representing a significant
move away from municipal socialism (Dabinett, 1990). This turned out to
be the Sheffield Economic Regeneration Committee (SERC) with substantial
private and voluntary sector representation. SERC was charged with overseeing
the development of a collaborative approach to regeneration in the city, at that
point of time outlined in the Twin Valleys Strategy. This strategy was intimately
linked to Urban Programme and European Commission funding.

Later, in the light of the policy changes with respect to the Lower Don
Valley, the City Council began to recast this strategy to incorporate other
geographical areas of the city and to broaden the issues tackled. The outcome
was Sheffield 2000, a City Council-led initiative to develop positive proposals
for the city through to the year 2000 (Sheffield City Council, 1990b). The
organization of this strategy was also partnership based and represented an
extension of SERC's operations. The initiative may be regarded as an attempt
to reclaim the policy areas ignored by the UDC and conservative urban policy,
but the approach was managerial in its style and operation, and Sheffield 2000
represented more of a corporate working plan than an alternative employment,
economic or social policy.

The need to search for new, and additional, funding to implement Sheffield
2000 was well illustrated by the unsuccessful City Challenge bid prepared in
1991 containing proposals extracted from this strategy (Sheffield City Council,
1991b). Spatial targeting was again a feature of this bid which was largely based
on site-specific projects with combined capital and revenue costs of £180 million,
of which the private sector was to provide 74%. The bid in many ways
illustrated the strengths and weaknesses of the strategic approach adopted in
the city. It was criticized for being over-ambitious, in particular with respect to
the level of private sector funding for which there were few precedents in the
city. It was also argued that the bid had been prepared without full or proper

consultation, relying on the new corporatism of the city's organizations such as SERC for formulation and implementation of proposals, rather than using or setting up grass-roots participation.

Sheffield Development Corporation

In June 1987 SERC commissioned an independent report on economic regeneration in the Lower Don Valley. The City Council hoped that the report would convince the Government that a considerable amount of public money should be invested in the area and that the local authority could control the process. The report was published in November 1987 and recommended that an Urban Regeneration Authority should be established to oversee the regeneration of the valley (Coopers and Lybrand, 1987). On 7 March 1988 the Department of the Environment (DOE) announced the proposed establishment of a UDC to be located in the Lower Don Valley as part of the third round of designations. The order establishing the Sheffield Development Corporation (SDC) was approved by Parliament on 29 June 1988. The corporation was to have a life of seven years with £7 million to spend each year. The City Council opposed the setting up of a UDC but decided to negotiate terms rather than take their opposition to the House of Lords as Bristol were to do. The result was an agreement over consultation, a commitment to Section 71 of the Race Relations Act and a commitment to discuss possible agency agreements with the City Council. In addition three councillors took positions on the SDC board. A Community Director was also appointed being the first such post (Kirkham, 1990).

The SDC was directed to adopt the comprehensive and integrated approach to regenerating the Lower Don Valley recommended by the consultants the previous November, and its overall objective was 'to service the economic and physical regeneration of the Lower Don Valley at minimum cost to the public sector, levering maximum private investment into the area' (Deloitte, Haskins and Sells, 1989). The area covered by the SDC was 2,000 acres of land, of which 35% was derelict or vacant at declaration. It included some 800 firms employing 18,500 people, predominantly in metal manufacturing and engineering. There were only about 300 residents in the area although the valley was surrounded by areas of acute poverty and high unemployment (Kirkham, 1990).

The declaration of the SDC represented a significant development in the city in terms of the scale of the problems in the Lower Don Valley, the perceived requirement for new organizational structures and the new funding which would not have been available to the city without the declaration of a UDC. The SDC formulated its plans for the valley through its own corporate planning structure and through the publication of Planning Frameworks (SDC, 1989). These documents continued the flagship approach. Many of the major schemes including the Meadowhall shopping centre, and proposals for an airport and the Canal Basin office and leisure scheme, were initiated before the SDC was established. To date, the majority of actual expenditure has been on the purchase of old steel works sites in the valley (see Table 8.3). Initially the SDC took the view that developers should be responsible for all site preparation,

Table 8.3 Grant-in-aid received by SDC 1989–91

	1989–90		1990–91	
	£000	%	£000	%
Administration	2,020	21.2	2,120	11.1
Estate management	1	0.0	65	0.3
Environmental improvement	175	1.8	373	2.0
Land purchase	6,340	66.7	11,761	62.0
Reclamation/site preparation	0	0.0	580	3.1
Services	0	0.0	292	1.5
Transportation	436	4.6	1,937	10.2
Assistance to private sector	52	0.5	1,252	6.5
Support to voluntary sector	57	0.6	146	0.8
Promotion and publicity	419	4.4	441	2.3
Total	9,500	100	18,967	100

Source: Sheffield Development Corporation (1991).

reclamation and servicing works. This reflected the buoyant state of the market in 1988–89; in 1990–91 the Corporation, faced with the severity of the property recession, embarked on a programme of derelict land reclamation, clearance and infrastructure works to open up sites.

One major scheme that illustrates the market-led approach was the Canal Basin. Shearwater were the original winners of a City Council backed competition for the site, but after 1988, under the SDC, negotiated £10 million of City Grant for the scheme which included retail, housing, office, hotel and leisure development. Shearwater pulled out of this scheme in 1990 and a new competition was announced which was won by Norwest Holst. The new scheme had a higher office content with less retail and leisure, and was awarded an £8 million City Grant but no work had started by 1992. The shift from manufacturing to other uses for the valley is further illustrated by an application for a ten-screen cinema, a 200,000 sq ft retail park and a Tivoli Gardens scheme projected to cost £100 million on 70 acres to include mixed leisure uses, a hotel and conference centre.

In other directions the SDC has been less active and grants to the voluntary sector were less than 1% of the total allocation (see Table 8.3). The prevailing attitude towards existing businesses in the valley is shown by the low level of assistance and a proposal to build a new feeder road along the valley. The latter was to lead to great uncertainty in the area. Compulsory purchase orders (CPO) were placed on approximately 200 companies in early 1989 to make way for the dual carriageway and to improve premises in its vicinity. In 1990 the road was downgraded to single carriageway and at Easter 1991 many companies were reprieved leaving only 50 companies in the main CPO.

The operation of the SDC has therefore continued the drift towards a style of urban regeneration that included: site specific property flagship developments; a dependence on a much criticized concept of 'trickle down' to secure wider benefits; and a pragmatic strategy based on no clear industrial or economic analysis.

Appraisal of Urban Policy in Sheffield

Different commentators have identified a range of criteria for evaluating urban policy (Cameron, 1990; Turok, 1991). Our appraisal is not intended to be definitive but instead aims to bring into focus particular areas of debate. The first looks at business involvement and partnership. In this section the question of control, accountability and private sector involvement in the partnership is examined. The second focuses on funding regeneration and attempts to analyse the relationship between private and public investment and the changing balance of capital and revenue funding. Finally the third section looks at employment growth and distribution, examining arguments about equity and additionality in employment creation.

Business Involvement and Partnership

One view held by central government that underpinned the UDC approach was that urban local authorities had misused their power by excluding business from policy considerations, and allowing agendas to be shaped by particular political or factional interests. The use of a 'quango model' for the UDC structure was to overcome this (CLES, 1992). What role did the establishment of the SDC play in changing the role of business in formulating urban policy in Sheffield?

The Board of the SDC was appointed by central government and although three Sheffield councillors served on it, the majority of members were local businessmen. Many of these people were already involved in other public/private bodies set up to manage urban regeneration in the city including urban programme funded projects. There was considerable overlap between membership of the Sheffield Training and Enterprise Council Board, Sheffield Partnerships Ltd, Universiade GB Ltd, Sheffield Science and Technology Park Boards, Sheffield 2000 and, more significantly, SERC.

Representation on SERC was by appointment and after 1988 the SDC became a member. From 1986 onwards SERC attempted to become the lead organization in pursuing urban regeneration. Unlike the SDC it had no funds or executive powers and was subordinate to the central decision making bodies of the constituent organisations. Perhaps as a consequence of this, but also as a result of the leadership role taken by some members of SERC, the agendas were dominated by issues and discussions which avoided conflict. Any disputes were seen as potential deterrents to inward investment, a key objective of the group in the late 1980s. Consensus was seen as a necessary prerequisite to a favourable image for the city, an image which was fundamentally based on the criteria of private capital and business. Therefore, the establishment of the SDC can be regarded as simply taking the influence of the business sector a stage further, rather than creating a radical departure in the city's politics.

More work is needed to fully evaluate the nature of the emerging partnerships in the city, but a number of points do emerge with regard to the SDC's policies and approach to urban regeneration. Firstly, certain local business interests could be seen as having a clear claim on the benefits accruing from increased property values, a central objective of the SDC, since these benefited local capital accumulation and commercial profits rather than industrial performance or social objectives. Secondly, some groups undoubtedly lost influence, notably backbench councillors, members of the wider labour movement in the city and possibly some community groups. Thirdly, the local authority's role in the partnerships remained largely as strategic leadership since its ability to implement projects became increasingly restricted by the lack of resources. The private sector secured a loose integration into a major area of policy formulation but could not replace the local authority.

A final comment on the nature of partnership concerns the wider interpretation that can be placed on these events in terms of central government objectives. It is of interest that the early establishment of a public/private body in Sheffield was not directly supported by central government. Despite the contrary views of SERC a government-appointed UDC was seen as necessary. This might represent some expression of central control over local autonomy, and the SDC has very few delegated powers and has to seek approval from the DOE on many decisions. This bears strong parallels with the operation of the Urban Programme. Alternatively the events might be interpreted as an attempt to split the partnership in order to marginalize the role of the council even further. This later view was reinforced by the failure of the first City Challenge bid and previous inability to secure central government funds for the WSG. Therefore, the Sheffield experience mirrors the national transition in the changing role of the business sector in urban policy, but perhaps more significantly is a commentary on the changing relation between central and local government.

Funding Regeneration

The physical decay of the inner city is inherently linked to patterns of new private capital investment and the maintenance of existing capital stock. The main aim of the UDCs has been to bring about urban regeneration. In practice the vehicle for this has been property development. Although not returning to the physical determinism of planning in the 1950s and 1960s, this approach has placed private investment at the centre of urban policy in the last decade. In Sheffield private investment has been encouraged through partnership, and in particular the promotion of the city as an economically competitive location for investment, through the property market led policies of the UDC and through subsidies in the form of Derelict Land and City Grants. This approach requires further evaluation, which should examine comparative levels of actual investment, leverage and distributional impacts.

Private sector investment and its relationship to public sector spending through the notion of leverage has been used by central government throughout the 1980s as a way of judging the success of urban policy. However, despite the commitment from the City Council in Sheffield to partnership, it is in the delivery of private capital investment that this approach has most obviously failed. This might reflect the nature of the partnership in the city. It was based on local political consensus and joint promotion activities rather than a property or regeneration company as in other areas such as Wakefield and Birmingham (Askew, 1991; Carley, 1991). It might more fundamentally reflect the lack of competitive advantage of the city to mobile capital.

One exception to this pattern was the Meadowhall development, a £250 million investment supported by public transport infrastructure and £2.5 million of Derelict Land Grant. Most other major initiatives during the 1980s ended up being paid for by the public sector. This was dramatically illustrated by the staging of the WSG in 1991 where the private sector contribution was minimal. In 1988 the Chief Planning Officer claimed that £1.3 billion of development was proposed for the city (Sheffield City Council, 1988). This included Meadowhall and public funded projects for the WSG. By 1992 only a small proportion of that development had materialized. By 1992 only one major inward investment from outside the city had been attracted to the SDC area. This was the Abbey National share dealing service with the potential to create 203 jobs. Otherwise investment was severely affected by the recession and the majority of developments were abandoned or delayed. These included the prestigious Canal Basin project which was to have been the largest recipient of City Grant in the city.

The contribution of private sector capital in urban policy and urban regeneration initiatives raises questions about the basis of private sector involvement. For investors there has to be a direct or tangible gain in return for the commitment. For some events, like the WSG, this may come in publicity and an improvement in the city's image, but spending in this area has to be commensurate with the returns. For private sector investment in development proposals, the main aim is to lever out public sector money in the form of grants and infrastructure work in order to increase returns on capital and reduce the risk. The question of who is levering whom is clearly crucial. The other issue to raise here is what community or distributional benefits are obtained in return for the public sector support.

There seem to be two major outcomes from the policy towards urban regeneration pursued in the period examined. Firstly, there was a tendency to go for bigger and bigger solutions, perhaps exemplified by the WSG, SDC and City Challenge proposals. The inverse of this was less activity in promoting the fine grained and small scale projects, that, taken together, could have made a difference in deprived areas of the city. Secondly, the type of projects supported increasingly incurred capital costs rather than revenue expenditure. This became a feature of the Urban Programme. Projects supported by the SDC were capital intensive from the outset and only 4% of the total 1991 City Challenge budget covered revenue expenditure. This reflected the concentration on property-led regeneration, which, in turn, was a major reason why the benefits failed to reach the poor neighbourhoods of Sheffield.

Employment Growth and Distribution

The contribution of urban regeneration projects in Sheffield to employment growth in the city had been marginal up to 1992. Of the Urban Programme projects, the Technology Park, the Cultural Industries Quarter and the Science Park had problems filling their space and tended to be occupied by relocations or expansions of local enterprises. Other employment related initiatives include a technology training complex and a black business centre. These initiatives were small scale and were working against the grain of the local economy. As a consequence, wider employment impacts were only likely to be felt after a long gestation period.

The major gains in terms of employment creation were not a result of urban policy initiatives. The notable manufacturing inward investments tended to occur on the urban fringe on greenfield sites. For example Northern Foods built their new 'cook-chill' food factory at a greenfield site in the new township of Mosborough, south east of the city. The plant utilized a highly localized work force well away from the inner city. In the service sector the major gain to the city was the attraction of Norwich Union, who moved over 1,000 head office staff to an inner city site. Perhaps significantly, in 1992 they were already expanding at a new site on the prosperous west side of the city. Norwich Union were the first company to utilize the SDC's 'Quickstart' recruitment initiative which incorporated an explicit equal opportunities emphasis in preliminary selection, but did not target spatially.

In retailing employment, the gains from Meadowhall were offset by losses elsewhere. Marks & Spencer's announced the closure of two nearby branches to coincide with their opening at Meadowhall and city centre retailers reported a drop in sales of 17% resulting from the opening of Meadowhall and the impact of the recession. Prior to the complex opening a register of people who wished to work there was established. Reportedly over 15,000 people registered, however of these less than 1,000 secured jobs. Many of the 5–7,000 jobs that were created were filled by people who were already working in other branches of chain stores that set up at the centre. This provoked an angry reaction from community groups in the area. Despite this, recent research indicated that many employees at Meadowhall lived on the poorer east side of the city (Meadowhall Retail Academy, 1991).

The third area of gain was in the construction sector. Here the city showed above average growth of 17% in employment between 1987 and 1989 (Sheffield City Council, 1991c). This figure compared to a national average of 7%. Much of this employment was for the construction of the WSG facilities and Meadowhall. The WSG alone is thought to have created 5,500 job years (Sheffield City Council, 1990a). The City Council pledged a local job content of 20% and monitored employment at the major sites, but the building industry increasingly moves key people from project to project rather than recruit locally. In addition, many of the facilities required specialist construction companies which were not based locally.

The holding of the Games created few direct job gains. Some expansion did take place in the hotel sector but employment in recreation showed a more varied performance. Three swimming pools were closed in the city in the run up to the Games and many staff were redeployed in the process. Management of the arena and stadium was contracted out to a specialist Canadian firm who employed 50 people. Most of the required services, such as car-parking, were subcontracted, often to firms based outside the city. Overall, few spin-off jobs were created either through business growth or inward investment, although it is probable that the external perception of the city has been altered which might translate into inward investment in the future.

The SDC originally set itself a target of 12,000 new full time equivalent jobs by 1995. This was increased to 20,000 in 1989 because of expectations about the Meadowhall shopping centre. In 1990 and 1991 the SDC commissioned research to estimate employment in the development area. For 1990 this research produced an estimate of employment in the area of 18,800 which had increased to 23,700 by 1991 largely as a result of the opening of Meadowhall

(Lawless *et al*, 1990). This growth disguises net losses in surviving firms in the area who have faced difficult trading conditions during the recession. Over 10% of businesses moved away or closed down in the 15 months between the two surveys.

The sectoral employment composition of the development area has been changing in response to the opening of Meadowhall, the new retail park, whatever leisure component ends up adjacent to Meadowhall and the limited growth in office development. More part-time work and more female employment were developing in an area of traditional high-waged male employment. There were potential threats to remaining manufacturing industry from the growth in the tertiary economy in the area. The glossy world of Meadowhall sits uneasily next to the black sheds of Sheffield Forgemasters. It remains to be seen whether such diverse land uses can happily coexist or whether the continued growth of the tertiary sector in the valley will be at the expense of remaining manufacturing industry and manufacturing jobs.

Urban Policy for Cities as if People Matter

The Sheffield case study illustrates many of the problems of national urban policy in the 1980s and 1990s. The local response expressed through 'Partnership' was also undoubtedly a visionary initiative, and one shared to a large extent by the SDC. But the question remains, was it the right vision? Fundamentally the main purpose of urban policy should be to improve the quality of life of people who live in cities, and, in particular, those who experience disadvantage. All projects funded out of public sector resources made available through urban policy should be able to illustrate clear and substantial benefits to the disadvantaged groups in the city region. The failure to adequately fulfil such criteria is illustrated by the facilities provided in Sheffield for the WSG and proposals being considered by the SDC to establish major 'theme leisure parks' in the Lower Don Valley.

This failure has been based on the false analysis of the 'trickle-down effect', which assumes that major developments will create benefits that, in time, will provide opportunities for the urban populace to take advantage of. This, in turn, has led to urban policy becoming fixated on site-specific projects, an approach that dominates the planning framework of the SDC. Too much money from the urban policy purse has gone into property-based flagship projects. These have relatively high capital costs. Such projects are often a reaction to malfunctions in local property markets, which could be dealt with by appropriate planning policies and property investment measures such as tax benefits or derelict land grant mechanisms.

This particular analysis and approach has also led to the targeting of resources in small spatial areas to become less a mode of policy delivery and more an element in image creation and the bidding for resources. Often the scale of the urban problem and its physical manifestations has led to such an approach. In Sheffield there has been the City Council led Twin Valley Strategy, the SDC area of the Lower Don Valley and, more recently, the Three Valleys in the first City Challenge bid. This concentration in areas has increasingly excluded disadvantaged people who live outside the boundaries. An urban policy for people should seek a balance between area-based initiatives and those which look instead to target initiatives on groups and sectors.

A way ahead in developing such an urban policy needs to address the debates concerning the future of local government and delivery of local services (Leach, 1992). In this context urban policy would look to secure its objective of reducing inequality by supporting projects that empower and enable individuals and groups to have services delivered in a more equitable way, in particular housing, education and employment/income support. This would see more initiatives such as law centres, adult education projects, debt advice agencies, community and development trusts.

One key to ensuring urban policy addresses this concept of enabling is to promote innovation. The scope for innovative projects to develop and survive is very much determined by control. The establishment of UDCs, perhaps more than any other policy, gave the wrong message with respect to local people's perceptions of their ability to control, and hence improve the quality of their lives and situations (CLES, 1992). Within urban policy during the 1980s, local agencies have not been allowed to make decisions about spending without first seeking approval from central government. This has applied to both Urban Programme and Development Corporation expenditure. The result is to stifle initiative, encourage officers to play safe, and increase the average size of projects. A future urban policy for people would delegate powers to city-based agencies, and encourage them to delegate further through trusts and other arrangements. Urban policy should be locally determined and locally led; central government's role in the process should be to agree overall priorities and overall budgets and avoid the detailed issues of project management and control altogether.

An enabling and innovative urban policy would change the scope of projects. The recent experience of delays with major physical development projects, dependent on property market cycles, vindicates such a scaling down of objectives. Urban policy has become the preserve of powerful people who can operate at this flagship scale. In essence that is what public/private sector partnership was about in Sheffield. An urban policy for people would be smaller in ambition, broader in scope, and more neighbourhood based than city centre or flagship based. Above all it would deliver policies through the involvement of people and communities rather than simply seeking tokenist community representation to support transforming visions.

Finally there is the issue of resources. Urban policy will always be marginal in spending terms to both local and central government activities. However, the 1980s saw a flood of legislation designed to change the role of local government and to reduce public expenditure. In this context the reduction in Urban Programme spending and diversion of funds to UDCs represented a significant and ill-judged movement away from the allocation of resources to cities in proportion to the scale of their problems. Similarly, UDCs were unable to fill the gaps left by the absence of well-resourced industrial, infrastructure and regional policies. The failure of the 1980s illustrates the significance of bending main-line expenditure to urban areas' needs, a response called for in 1977. After fifteen years of urban policy, the UDC paradigm has represented the most significant shift in moving urban policy away from the objective of creating 'a humane city, cities as if people matter' (Short, 1989).

9

REALIZING THE POTENTIAL OF URBAN POLICY: THE CASE OF THE BRISTOL DEVELOPMENT CORPORATION

Nick Oatley

Introduction

Following considerable speculation during 1987 that Bristol was one of a number of cities under consideration for an Urban Development Corporation (UDC), on 7 December 1987 Nicholas Ridley, the then Secretary of State for the Department of the Environment (DOE), announced his intention to set up a third generation of UDCs, including one in the city of Bristol. This decision, the process leading to the establishment of Bristol Development Corporation (BDC), and its subsequent mode of operation, illustrate a number of key themes which have run through urban policy in the 1980s and into the 1990s. These include:

1. The restructuring of central–local government relations and the central-ization of urban policy.
2. The use of urban policy in the 1980s to facilitate a process of economic restructuring, particularly the transformation of vacant/derelict industrial land and industrial premises to other commercial uses.
3. The emphasis on large scale, comprehensive redevelopments aimed at revitalizing inner city environments.
4. The centrality of the role of private sector led regeneration and the reliance on market criteria in the application of urban policy and the neglect of local needs and accountability.

The government has described the UDC programme as 'the most important attack ever made on urban decay' (DOE, 1988, p. 4). The programme has been presented by central government as the new solution to a problem which local authorities have signally failed to resolve. Whilst much of the early literature on UDCs tended to focus on their common characteristics – their powers, their structure of accountability, their relationship to the DOE and their purpose under the Local Government Planning and Land Act 1980 – there has been an acknowledgement recently that whilst UDCs may share the same powers and *raison d'être*, the way they operate in practice varies con-siderably (Batley, 1989; Brownill, 1990; Stoker, 1989; see Table 9.1).

For instance, Stoker (1989) argues that 'differences between UDCs reflect

Table 9.1   Frameworks for analysing local variation in UDCs' operations

Stoker (1989)	*Batley (1989)*
1. Nature of land and property market.	1. Differing histories of decline.
2. Relationship with local authority.	2. Different local agencies and elected local governments with varied political biases, practices and traditions of collaboration with business and government.
3. Approach of key board members and UDC officials.	
Brownill (1990)	3. Varying and sometimes conflicting expectations on the part of central government.
1. The restructuring of planning and urban policy.	
2. The state, local areas and urban change – 'locality' dimension.	4. The way organizational procedures and personnel mediate or interpret the problems, pressures and opportunities presented by the external environment.
3. Central – local government relations.	

among other things the particular nature of the land and property market in their area; the character of their relationship with local authorities; and the approach of key Board members and UDC officials' (p. 160). Batley (1989) has developed a more sophisticated framework for comparing the experience of the various UDCs which attempts to consider the interaction between 'external' pressures and the internal dynamics of an organization which mediates between social interests and policy outcomes. Brownill (1990) suggests a wider analytical context within which an understanding of the differing experiences of UDCs needs to be developed. Her approach acknowledges that to understand how UDCs operate they must be seen as part of the process by which the built environment is constantly changing due to economic, political and social processes operating at a level wider than the local. It is this approach which is used to analyse BDC. This analysis may be seen as premature with BDC only three years into its six year lifespan. However, significant events have occurred and BDC has developed a history worthy of analysis.

This chapter seeks to explore this history by looking at how the socio-economic configuration in Bristol, and the culture it sustains, has influenced the establishment and subsequent operation of BDC. The chapter is divided into the following sections: an analysis of the local economy together with an account of the local political context and the role of urban policy in Bristol; a summary of the debate surrounding the contested establishment of BDC; a discussion of the formulation of plans and policies of BDC and the conflicts this has generated; the extent to which BDC has attempted to link into existing networks and develop a local constituency; and lastly, an assessment of achievements to date and a reflection on the appropriateness of this form of urban policy for Bristol.

The Local Socio-Economic Context and the Role of Urban Policy: Gilding the Ghetto in 'Success City'

The city of Bristol lies about 120 miles west of London and is the gateway to the South-West region. It has a population of 374,300 and currently lies within the County of Avon which has a population of 952,000 (Avon County Council 1990 mid-year estimates). It is a major manufacturing and commercial centre

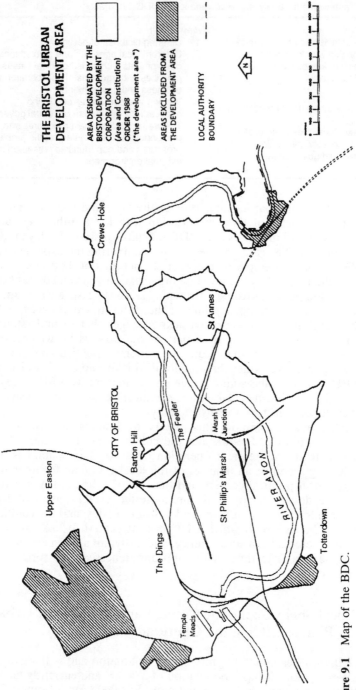

Figure 9.1 Map of the BDC.

and along with East Anglia has been one of the fastest growing regions in Britain. Changes in the local economy of Bristol have mirrored those in the national economy over the last twenty years and have been well documented (Boddy *et al*, 1986). As a consequence, Bristol has out-performed other cities in terms of employment growth and the containment of decline. However, Bristol – like other cities – has experienced the loss of manufacturing employ-ment: between 1981 and 1989 the number of people employed in manufacturing in the Bristol District fell by over a third (a loss of 17,000 jobs) following closures, relocations and redundancies in its key manufacturing industries of paper and packaging, food and drink, and tobacco.

More recently, there have been major losses from the defence-related indu-stries (Bristol City Council/University of Bristol/Confederation of Shipbuilding and Engineering Unions, 1989; Braddon *et al*, 1991). The rate of decline in these industries, during the late 1970s and early 1980s, was significantly below the national average and the loss of jobs was partly compensated by the growth in employment in the service sector, particularly in insurance, banking and finance, medical and dental services, and hotels and catering. The expansion and consolidation of the city, as a major administrative centre, was brought about by the decisions of a number of major banking, insurance and finance companies to relocate to Bristol. Between 1971 and 1986 office-based employ-ment in the city increased from 27,000 to 42,000. Whilst most of this growth has occurred in the city centre there has been a steady expansion of service sector employment on the north fringe of Bristol with decentralization of offices from the centre (e.g. Sun Life) and new developments such as the relocation of the Ministry of Defence Procurements Division.

Given the relative buoyancy of the Bristol local economy, and the reputation of 'success city' that it gained during the 1980s, it is perhaps not surprising that it did not appear on the map of national urban policy initiatives until 1986, when the DOE established an Inner Area Task Force and the DOE invited Bristol to apply for Inner Area Programme funding. Stewart (1990) has suggested four reasons why the city, having been excluded from policy initiatives for eight years from 1977 and having weathered the storm of recession in the early 1980s, warranted urban policy attention in 1986. First, there was an awareness of a growing segmentation in the labour market between a core of professional occupations and a more peripheral, lower paid and less skilled workforce, demonstrating that the benefits of growth had not been equally distributed. Second, there was an increasing awareness of an emerging pattern of polarization and segregation between different parts of the city, and between different social groups, as measured by indicators of deprivation. Third, Bristol was seen as posing a real and continuing threat to social order after the first 'urban riot' in St Paul's in 1980 and following the 'disturbances' in Handsworth and else-where in 1985. Fourth, Bristol was becoming the focus for growing tensions between central and local government.

The Labour-controlled City Council experienced a number of confrontations with national government over local financial discretion. In 1986 the City Council established a new Employment and Community Development Com-mittee that attempted to progress a range of 'radical' policy initiatives. The introduction of central government policy initiatives was a way of influencing this policy agenda and ameliorating the larger cuts in local authority main programmes. In addition to Inner Area Programme funding (worth between £1.25 million and £1.5 million per annum since 1986) and the establishment of a Task Force in 1986, Bristol also benefited from Derelict Land Grant, City Grant, and Estate Action. In 1990 central government also set up a Training and Enterprise Council (TEC) – a new private company which has taken over responsibility for all training and enterprise support in the County of Avon. The most controversial urban initiative was the designation of a UDC in 1987 covering part of inner Bristol (partly overlapping the Task Force and Inner Area Programme areas) running eastward from Temple Meads station along the River Avon valley to the city boundary (Figure 9.1).

Local Political Opposition to BDC

In December 1987 an announcement was made to establish a third round of Development Corporations in the cities of Manchester, Leeds, Sheffield, and Bristol. In a written answer to a Parliamentary question, Nicholas Ridley stated: 'I have chosen these areas because they all have significant amounts of derelict disused land and vacant buildings'. The Secretary of State decided that it was in the national interest that a UDC be established in Bristol in order to ensure that the area was regenerated and its development potential realized. The decision by the DOE was justified on four criteria:

1. A problem of accessibility, with much of the area having an old inadequate road pattern.
2. Physical difficulties with the land including contamination at Crews Hole.
3. Fragmented land ownership.
4. One of the poorest environments in Bristol.

The City Council's initial response was that the decision to set up a UDC represented 'an unwarranted intrusion into democratic local government planning and development powers'. The proposed use of public funding to promote the UDC was, in the Council's view, 'highly questionable given the obvious alternative of promoting local authority capital projects for infrastructure and implementation of development'. During the following six months city councillors met with the Minister (David Trippier), his civil servants, consultants, and the Chairperson Designate (Christopher Thomas) of the UDC, in order to establish the reasoning behind, and the purpose of, the proposed UDC in Bristol. The outcome of these discussions was, in the view of the City Council, unsatisfactory and a number of concerns of the City Council remained unresolved such as the undemocratic and unaccountable nature of the UDC, the lack of any obligation to follow existing local authority policies, and a concept of regeneration that was defined not by local/community needs but by the needs of the property market.

The City Council concluded that a UDC for Bristol, a city with a buoyant, thriving local economy, was unnecessary and could even be harmful to the long-term interests of the proposed Urban Development Area (UDA) and the city as a whole. Moreover, the City Council could not ensure a proper public debate other than by petitioning Parliament and, on 6 June 1988, a petition was presented to Parliament on the City's behalf. On 22 June 1988, the Hybrid

Instruments Committee of the House of Lords examined the Council's petition and decided that there were substantial grounds for complaint. A Select Committee of the House of Lords was established to investigate the Secretary of State's case for the establishment of a UDC and to hear detailed evidence in support of the Council's petition.

In the ensuing months, there were a number of polemical exchanges which highlighted the ideological position of both central and local government and clearly demonstrated one of the underlying themes in the designation of UDCs – that of the restructuring of central–local government relations. This theme was further exemplified in a speech which the Bristol West MP, William Waldegrave, delivered at a conference on the establishment of BDC convened by Hartnell Taylor Cook (a local property agent) at the Grand Hotel in Bristol on 9 September 1988 called 'The Debate'. In a speech billed as 'Why Bristol? What the Government Expects', Waldegrave referred to a number of points which revealed the intention of the Conservative government to discredit and bypass the Labour local authority. In the main text of his speech, and in response to questions, Waldegrave justified the proposed UDC by referring to the increased militancy of the local authority; perceptions of Bristol City Council as parochial, inward-looking and resistant to change; and the poor performance of the planning authority, which, he stated, had been on and off the list of slowest authorities in determining planning applications.

In petitioning the House of Lords, the City Council attempted to challenge each of the justifications given by the DOE and the specific terms of reference for a UDC. It was argued that ten out of eleven major unused/underused sites offering redevelopment potential in the area proposed were in single ownership and that *fragmented land ownership* was not a problem. There were no major problems of widespread *contamination* with only two out of the twelve key sites polluted (the former Distillers site and Crews Hole Road site) and the problems on the Crews Hole Road site were dealt with by the developer before the UDC was established. Furthermore, Bristol, unlike other UDAs, had very little *derelict land* amounting to no more than 150 acres out of a total proposed area of 1,050 acres (14%) including 70 acres on one site (the old St Anne's Board Mills factory site).

The DOE argued that the UDA contained some of the *poorest environments* in the city but the Council pointed out that the proposed UDA also contained some of its finest, such as the natural environments of the Avon Valley Conservation Area and the Old Market Conservation Area (a key historic area of the city where a careful and sensitive partnership has existed over the last ten years between the city council, English Heritage, housing associations and private owners). With respect to *housing* the City Council argued that several small areas of public housing included in the proposed area should all be excluded from the area. There were also other areas where development was either under way or about to start and where there was no need for the UDC.

While one of the main aims of a UDC is *to encourage the development of existing and new industry* for Bristol, the preservation of the existing industrial activities in the area was of crucial importance. The Council argued that St Philip's Marsh, a large area within the UDA, represented the industrial heart of the city with approximately 8,500 jobs. Whilst Bristol, as a whole, has lost 37,000 manufacturing jobs since 1970 the level of manufacturing employment in this area has remained relatively stable. It was said, by those proposing a UDC, that a Corporation was necessary to attract investment into the area, yet it was ignored that although the UDC area has less than 3% of the land of the city it has generated over 25% of the industrial investment in the city over the last 15 years. The area is also an important source of industrial land in the city and, over the last five years, it has had a considerable amount of industrial development. The 460,000 sq ft of industrial and warehouse floorspace completed in the area between 1982 and 1987 was 30% of the total industrial development completed in the city over the period. The area is thus continuing to attract investment. At designation three schemes were under construction, all on public sector owned land. At October 1987 (just prior to the designation of BDC) industrial and warehousing floorspace with planning permission totalled over 700,000 sq ft, including 463,000 sq ft on the former St Anne's Board Mills site and 155,000 sq ft (high technology units) on Temple Way.

The City Council was attacked for not having any plans to redevelop this area wholesale. However, the City Council maintained that there should be no major proposals to destroy or displace the firms in this area, many of whom are small firms who can only afford the kind of rents generated by the type of premises found in this area. The sum total of the argument put forward by Bristol City Council was that area by area, site by site, the case for a UDC could not legitimately be made. The Secretary of State defended his decision to designate a UDC in Bristol on grounds of national interest, and a belief that a Development Corporation would be better equipped to overcome the legacy of long-vacant and derelict sites and the infrastructure constraints of the area with a single-minded approach, powers of land assembly and additional resources, in order to realize the area's full potential. These views were expressed in representations to the Hybrid Instruments Committee of the House of Lords which considered the petitions made by the City Council (Representations of the Secretary of State to the House of Lords Hybrid Instruments Committee; The Bristol Development Corporation (Area and Constitution Order) 1989, p. 6).

The Committee accepted the argument that the proposed designation of the area as a UDA was expedient in the national interest, and that the government had justified the designation of the UDA but that four areas should be excluded from the proposed boundary (see Figure 9.1). The City Council was also given assurances by the DOE that BDC would not replicate the approach taken by the London Docklands Development Corporation and that a more sensitive approach would be taken:

I would like to draw the Committee's attention to the inclusion of . . . social objectives in the list of means . . . It is not the aim of a UDC to act solely as a commercially minded organisation . . . to maximising profits. It is not as it were, Government's private property company. In regenerating an area a UDC should take a broad view and supply the UDA with whatever is needed for a better quality of life there . . . the task of the UDC is not, as we see it, to pump in large sums of public investment supported by aggressive marketing in order to attract developers. Nor is it to undertake massive redevelopment. Nor is it to drive out existing employers and existing jobs in the area. We do not expect the emphasis of the UDC to be on the large scale acquisition of land or construction of major works. We are not looking for a Docklands Railway or a Canary Wharf.

(Minutes of the Hearing at the House of Lords,
Tuesday 11 October 1988, p. 47 and 61).

In spite of these assurances

- Public investment (grant-in-aid) has risen from an original figure of £15 million over five years to a commitment of £57 million over six years.
- In the period January 1989 – March 1990 the Corporation spent over £0.5 million on marketing and since this period a further £1 million is said to have been awarded to marketing consultants Chapman Thornton Belgrove Garratt to develop a campaign intended 'to inform local people about development in the area and to attract more people to the city'.
- Massive redevelopments have been proposed in the Temple Meads/Kingsley Village area with further disruption occurring in the wake of the Spine Road proposal. None of the 300 jobs in the existing modern industrial units in the Phase I area of the Temple Meads/Kingsley Village CPO area to be retained; and the one major manufacturing firm in the Phase II area, also employing 300 people, is also to be moved out.
- Over 90 existing companies and 2,200 jobs have been threatened by the BDC's plan for the Spine Road and Temple Meads development and associated CPOs. How many of these jobs survive the process of relocation and other disruption remains to be seen.

Furthermore, in spite of the inclusion of social objectives a prominent Board Member of BDC recently stated, in connection with the social housing issue, that 'BDC is not a Housing Authority. There is a low housing population in the area and social housing would have to be part of a wider need as there is no provision to fund social housing' (Report made by Councillor Fisk to full Council on 14 May 1991). In addition, on the matter of local unemployment, BDC has not demonstrated how the neighbouring populations are to benefit beyond assumptions about the trickle down of new jobs created.

On the 20 February 1989, BDC formally took up its powers and duties in relation to the 850 acres of land within the amended boundary. The House of Lords hearing had provided the opportunity for a thorough examination of the justification of establishing a UDC in Bristol. It also provided a high profile political arena where ideological differences between central and local government were contested. The detailed arguments put forward by the City Council for each site in the area had clearly persuaded the Committee to exclude certain areas – hence limiting the scope of UDC activity by reducing the area within the UDA and limiting the development opportunities it would inherit. The City Council had never really expected to prevent the UDA from being established but felt that it had won a major victory in obtaining exclusions from the original proposed UDA. Particularly significant was the exclusion of the Old Market Area which contained most of the land owned by the City Council and the strategic site of Bond Street – the site identified for the extension of Broadmead Shopping Centre.

Plans and Policies of BDC

When BDC took up its powers it employed consultants LDR, the well-known American based company responsible for many of the Baltimore regeneration concepts, to draw up a 'Vision for Bristol', a Corporate Plan for their area. At a later date it was decided to employ other consultants to draw up more detailed 'area frameworks'. To date, the BDC has produced a series of policy documents:

1. The Vision for Bristol (July 1989a)
2. Corporate Plan (July 1989b)
3. Revised Development Strategy (Summer 1990a)
4. Temple Meads/Kingsley Village Area Framework (August 1990b)
5. Central Development Area Framework (March 1991).

The Corporation's Corporate Plan of 1989 stressed responsiveness to the market, private initiative, the generation of new economic activities and a determined concentration on the promotion of physical development. The strategy sought to transform the image of Bristol to one of the great cities of Europe, able to compete for trade and international investment in the economic markets of the 1990s. It aimed to promote this by encouraging 'a dazzling, modern style of architecture' which would reflect the uses of financial services, hi-technology industry and medical technology supplies industries. BDC was not afraid to admit that their ambitious employment growth strategy would create problems for indigenous industrial and commercial activities. Commenting, in *The Vision for Bristol* document (1989a, p. 15), BDC stated: 'One area of difficulty will be the inevitable disruption created by major activities. The corporation is therefore developing a policy for relocation when it either proves necessary or desirable.'

The plans of the Development Corporation can be seen as an attempt to facilitate restructuring within the local economy of Bristol centred around the traditional industrial heartland of the city. BDC saw itself as spearheading the physical and economic regeneration of the area focusing particularly on the attraction of high value added economic activities, while the city council aligned itself much more with the traditional manufacturing industries already present in the area and the need to encourage and support this type of economic activity.

In a report to the Planning and Traffic Committee on 20 September 1989, setting out the City Council's response to BDC's strategy it was stated that:

> Regrettably the Corporate Plan is a confirmation that the City Council's objections were justified ... An unquantified number of businesses in the area will have to be relocated ... Far more worrying is the fact that the Corporation's Strategy will do precisely the damage to the City's economy that the City Council had previously feared.
>
> (Bristol City Council, 1989a, para. 3.2 and 4.1)

One of the prime concerns of local authorities, community organizations, industrialists, traders, and local people, was the nature of the economic regeneration that was proposed for the area. The threat to existing employment was evident in a number of the proposals. For example, although it is said that the industrial/business zonings in the St Philip's Marsh area are *not* aimed at substituting offices for industrial or similar uses, there is a fear that market pressure will force industrial uses out of the area. The UDC has stated that it is intent on preparing specific policies to support the retention of existing industry in the core of the St Philip's Marsh area and for the relocation of displaced industries. But large numbers of jobs are still threatened directly by the compulsory purchase orders (CPO) associated with the Spine Road and Temple Meads proposals, which pose a threat to over 2,200 jobs and over 90 firms. It also poses a threat indirectly through raising aspirations that feed into the land and property market, raising rents and land values beyond the level of affordability of existing users. There is evidence that some property owners in the area have terminated leases in the hope of selling off the land/property for more profitable uses.

When concerns were raised about the threat of the Spine Road to existing employment during the consultation process on the initial strategy, BDC stated that 'no residential properties and a maximum of *15* companies will be affected' (BDC, 1990c). Yet, in the opinion of the City and County Councils, the CPO threatens 78 companies and 1,900 industrial jobs while no specific sites or resources have been earmarked by BDC to relocate them. Indeed, relocation itself has been an issue and while a statement on it is now included in BDC's revised strategy the City Council's Director of Economic Development has concluded that the policy is likely to fail to retain displaced firms within Bristol because of a shortage of the type of premises required and an unwillingness on the part of the UDC to set aside land within the UDA for companies to relocate (BDC Development Strategy, 1990a, para. 5.31).

This issue of the future of employment in the area demonstrates the contested nature of plans and priorities for the area. BDC wishes to restructure the area by changing the profile of economic activities, but the local authorities, local traders, industrialists and certain community groups wish to see the existing employment maintained and enhanced. It also demonstrates the way in which UDCs have been used to restructure local government planning approaches in an era of rapid economic restructuring. By producing high-profile strategies, and identifying special opportunities and flagship projects as the basis for marketing and promotion, UDCs constitute a major break with the regulatory local government planning approaches. As Healey *et al* (1988) have stated, 'the impact of the forceful assertion of market criteria and development interests represented by UDCs has been to challenge the policy consensus on urban regeneration and to remove the constraints on economic restructuring' (p. 29).

A further example of the neglect of existing planning policy can also be seen in the proposals (using a CPO) to redevelop about 90 acres of land for mixed uses, on either side of the Floating Harbour near Temple Meads. BDC envisage 1.3 million sq ft of offices and more than 0.5 million sq ft of retail development. The City Council and County Council have jointly argued that these proposals would undermine the statutory planning framework in Bristol and central government policy. In particular, it threatens the future vitality and viability of Broadmead Shopping Centre and the city centre as a whole, the future of sixteen businesses with approximately 300 employees, while providing car parking well in excess of the standards contained in Bristol City's Draft City Centre Local Plan. Moreover, it appears that the CPO would also affect land which is held by the County Council for highway improvement.

The City and County councils, therefore, objected against the CPO, both as property owners and on fundamental planning grounds, but were unable to prevent it. Despite BDC's statutory duty to conform to the objectives of the approved Structure Plan, almost no reference is made in the strategy document, or Corporate Plan, to the planning policies of the County Council or, for that matter, those of the City Council. While this omission has been drawn to the Corporation's attention on a number of occasions there is little evidence that BDC has had regard to Structure Plan or Local Plan policies in the formulation of the latest Corporate Plan or published frameworks. Indeed BDC has claimed that the approved Structure Plan is not an up-to-date plan and has been overtaken by events despite the fact that two alterations have been approved and that a third is currently with the DOE. This view is refuted by Avon County Council and elements of the BDC's strategy in the Corporate Plan and Kingsley Village/Temple Meads Framework appear to conflict with Structure Plan policy as approved by the Secretary of State.

BDC has also focused primarily on its physical regeneration strategy. In addition to promoting the development of key sites, and securing the funding for physical infrastructure projects (e.g. the Spine Road and the Avon Weir), it has funded Bristol/Avon Groundwork Trust to produce a Landscape Strategy which identifies the main landscape corridors, linking pockets of open space, etc. BDC has already made substantial payments towards environmental improvement works, including £90,000 on two schemes with British Rail (including the cleaning of Temple Meads station building), £44,000 in tree planting at Netham Park in a joint venture project with Bristol City Council, and a £20,000 contribution to the resurfacing and landscaping of Avon Walkway at Crews Hole.

In contrast, little time and money has been spent on addressing the needs of disadvantaged groups. BDC rejected the City Council's suggestion that in new housing development it should adopt a target of 40% low cost housing. BDC has not established a 'social support programme', as suggested by the City Council, but has accepted the request of local community organizations for a regular and structured method of consultation. The UDC has not decided whether to fund the steering group which has been formed to represent the views of local communities and voluntary organizations. BDC's policy framework, and opposition posed by local authorities and other groups and agencies, illustrates the tensions inherent in the process of restructuring planning and urban policy. It also demonstrates how a national agenda has been followed, often against the views of local groups and organizations. This is explored further in the next section which deals with the way BDC has attempted to integrate itself into existing networks through consultation and other exercises.

Developing a Local Constituency?

The establishment of BDC signalled a change in the underlying ideological principles guiding activity in the UDA, from attempting to cater for the needs of existing local businesses and housing communities to providing the conditions where commercial land and property interests could flourish and generate profits. Marks (1988) expressed a widespread concern that the UDC's prime purpose was to serve property and commercial interests. Even the Chamber of Commerce feared 'that the UDC will respond to market demands which is not in the long term interests of Bristol – we have to keep in mind what has happened in LDDC and Merseyside'. The Phoenix Initiative (a consortium of local business interests) attempted to persuade Nicholas Ridley not to establish a UDC in Bristol fearing that it might broaden the gap between the local authority and the private sector. From the beginning the UDC presented its approach as being in the 'national interest', by embracing the government's major policy objective of promoting private investment as the solution to the inner city problem (DOE, 1988; BDC, 1989a, p. 1). Its organizational style, and mode of interest mediation, is geared towards responsiveness to the market, promoting regeneration freed from local accountability and statutory service provision and unburdened by the constraints which govern local authorities.

Consulting with Local Authorities

Under section 140 of the Local Government Planning and Land Act 1980 a UDC is obliged to 'prepare a Code of Practice as to Consultation with the relevant local authorities about the exercise of its powers.' In Bristol this has been the focus of much debate and political controversy, reflecting the tensions inherent in central–local government conflicts over participation and accountability.

On the 18 January 1989, before the UDC was formally established, the City Planning Officer put a report to the Planning and Traffic Committee urging the UDC to conduct its affairs in an open manner and to carry out proper consultation about its plans for the area under its control. This action arose out of the City Council's concern over the extent of consultation both with local authorities and the local community and recommended that BDC adopt a Code of Consultation based on the code agreed between Sheffield City Council and Sheffield UDC. The report stated that 'the example of Sheffield City Council serves to illustrate what can be achieved to "democratise" what many see as a potentially undemocratic and unaccountable body' (Bristol City Council, 1989b, para. 2.5).

BDC did not adopt the Sheffield Code. Six months later on 24 November 1989 Bristol City Council received BDC's first draft of a proposed Code of Consultation. The response of the City Council to this proposed code was critical. In a Committee report to the Planning and Traffic Committee (Bristol City Council, 1989c) it was stated:

There are still fundamental differences between the generally secretive approaches of the BDC and the 'open government' approaches of the City Council. It is unacceptable that the press, the general public and business community will be unable to obtain full and accurate information on the decisions made by the BDC or to know when they do receive information from the BDC that the Corporation is not being economical with the truth . . . As a consequence, the influence which the general public and local businesses can exert on BDC decisions will be very limited, perhaps even negligible.

(Bristol City Council, 1989c, paras. 5.1–5.2)

There have been regular City Council/Board member meetings and regular Development Control consultation meetings. But the commitment to consult on the basis set out in the code does not seem to have materialized and policies and strategies have been published without prior consultation. Both the City and Avon County Councils have maintained a hostile approach to the UDC although recently the City's politicians have been making conciliatory statements. The City has been forced to take this pragmatic approach after the fourth general election victory by the Conservative party and the need to create the impression of partnership to win the City Challenge bid for an area in the south of the city (Hatcliffe and Withywood).

Consulting with the Community

Consultation with community groups has been *ad hoc* and focused on specific development proposals. So far the major consultation exercise undertaken by BDC was carried out on the basis of the 'Vision for Bristol' document which drew together information from a variety of sources. BDC conducted a public consultation exercise in which 65,000 questionnaires were circulated to local businesses, residents and adjacent communities and a market research study which consisted of discussion groups and home interviews. A response rate of 7% was achieved from the questionnaires (4,800 responses).

In March 1990 BDC published a response to the points raised. Whilst it was generally supported on issues such as proposals for the new weir, opening of pedestrian walkways along the river, and the provision of cycle routes, a wide range of critical comments were received on the economic, housing, social, environmental and transport strategies. Five major areas of concern emerged: the compatibility with established planning policies; the physical impact of proposals within the UDA on the immediate and adjacent areas; the neglect of social needs; the impact of the Corporation's proposals upon the social infrastructure (schools, health facilities, leisure facilities, etc.) within and outside the UDA, much of which was already perceived to be inadequate; and the effects of the north/south link road, both on the UDA itself, and on areas outside the UDA (Bristol Development Corporation *Report on Public Consultation*, March 1990c, para. 2.1).

In spite of these concerns raised by local authorities and other local groups, BDC stated that 'None of the responses to the consultation indicates, in the view of the Development Corporation, that major changes should be made to the strategy' (BDC *Report on Public Consultation*, March 1990c, para. 1.3).

This established the style of consultation operated by BDC which has led to a number of unresolved issues and on-going conflicts concerning the various plans and policies proposed. It was felt that the 'Vision' document was too vague and general – raising more questions than it answered and gave the impression that the UDC had no real intention to do more than engage in a public relations exercise. The exhibitions were sketchy with little interpretation alongside the pictures, the maps were difficult to interpret, and the exhibition staff were not knowledgeable enough to discuss the details with local people. Furthermore, BDC has not given a real response, or produced a more detailed discussion of the issues raised. The same points could be made about subsequent consultations over plans for Temple Meads/Kingsley Village and proposals for the Spine Road.

BDC's apparently defensive attitude towards consultation with the community has created a negative impression of the UDC and Bristol's community groups are still waiting for a clear sign that BDC intends to be open and truly participative in its consultation approaches. The UDC has shown willing by agreeing to a concordat with Bristol Council for Racial Equality (BCRE). BCRE's remit is to promote equal opportunities and eliminate racism in the City and the concordat, signed in June 1990, commits BDC and BCRE

> to work jointly to ensure that policies and practices of the Corporation do not discriminate against black people and to ensure that as far as reasonably possible black people benefit from the Corporation's regeneration strategy.

However, as Skinner (1990, p. 15) points out, unless further work is done to operationalize these aspirations it will remain at the level of good intention. Although the concordat has not been tested with any major development, BCRE has stated that BDC has already contravened some of the principles laid down in this agreement in the recruitment of its *own* staff.

Consulting Local Businesses and Land and Property Interests

Some constituencies of interest have been given more attention than others. BDC's commercial director coordinated a survey of all 700 businesses in the area – the purpose of which was twofold: firstly, to collect basic information from the companies about their plans for expansion, their views on the Development Corporation, the nature of their workforce, and the nature of their business; secondly, it provided an opportunity to impart information about the UDC and to win over companies that were uncertain or anxious about some of the Corporation's proposals. The time and effort given to interviewing over 700 companies and courting private sector interests is in stark contrast to the effort expended on canvassing community organizations' opinions. BDC has also staged a number of expensive high profile events to promote their plans and proposals among the land and property interests. There was an exclusive launch of the Corporate Plan at the Hilton Hotel in Bristol (by invitation only) and a boat trip organized to promote the Avon Weir proposal. If one analyses the composition of the original Board there is a further bias in favour of private sector interests (with five of the eight members of the Board from the private sector).

What impact have these consultations had on BDC's activities? Very little has actually happened on the ground. The public consultation exercises, carried out on major proposals, appear to have been designed more to inform and persuade than to engage in a critical dialogue about alternatives. As a non-local body BDC has been aware of the need to win over public opinion. It was widely reported in the local press that a £1 million contract had been awarded to public relations consultants Chapman Thornton Belgrove Garratt to undertake a campaign 'to inform local people about development in the area and to attract more people to the City.' This is in addition to the £522,000 spent on marketing between January 1989 and March 1990 (BDC, 1990). Whereas their plans and proposals are expressed in language that is meant to appeal to private capital, entrepreneurs and national interests, they have recently responded to local criticism by placing full page advertisements in the local evening press to alter people's perceptions.

These show how the UDC has resorted to the language of persuasion to convey the impression that BDC is working for the people of Bristol. It is a clear demonstration of what Edelman (quoted in Edelman, M. 1987, p. xxi) calls symbolic policy:

> *The material impact of policy is likely to favour dominant groups, while the symbolic aspects of policy falsely reassure mass publics that their interests are protected against the rapaciousness of powerful groups.*

In this respect BDC has clearly demonstrated its priorities to engage with land and property interests and to create an image to attract private investment rather than to enter into a meaningful dialogue with the community over social needs.

Realizing the Potential?

Aspirations and Expectations

In May 1988, ECOTEC Research and Consulting Ltd reported to the DOE on the economic potential of the proposed UDA and set out a strategy to unlock the development potential of the area. BDC was established to realize this potential, to cut through the perceived bureaucratic regulation and 'burdensome' planning to bring about the redevelopment of the area. Newspaper reports, before the House of Lords hearing, testify to these expectations. The *Western Daily Post* (1987) reported a visit by Inner Cities Minister, David Trippier, who

> *took one look at dereliction beside the River Avon in Bristol and called it disgraceful. 'What has happened here in recent years is very little', he said at a former Tar Works Site in Crews Hole. 'We want speedy development in the area to rejuvenate it and make it prosperous once again'.*

Similarly, the *Bristol Evening Post* reported Nicholas Ridley as saying, as he stood on derelict land in the UDA:

> *I want to come back here in three years time and see a thriving area . . . I am more than ever convinced the UDC is necessary. What this area needs is money up front to develop it. I can see warehousing, offices, housing, recreation, shopping and a whole new community here . . . I want to get on and get this area moving. It will go like a bomb. I want to see bulldozers moving in here by the end of the year.*

Reality

Three years after the first announcements many of these sites remain derelict. In contrast to the speedy development that was hoped for completed development within the UDA has been negligible (as at April 1992). St Anne's Board Mills still stands derelict, although a start was made on the development in July 1992. Marsh Junction still stands vacant, while sites around Temple Meads are still undeveloped. Over the last three years BDC has become involved in costly and time-consuming public inquiries regarding its controversial plans and CPOs associated with Marsh Junction, the Spine Road proposal and the development of Temple Meads/Kingsley Village. Only one major development has been partially completed, the Unicorn Business Park on Whitby Road, although this was set up by the city council before the designation of BDC.

Not surprisingly, the DOE is concerned at the lack of progress. The Junior Minister, Mr Key, accepted the criticisms that projects had been slow in getting off the ground. A senior government source was quoted as saying that 'The state of affairs in Bristol is moribund' (*Bristol Evening Post*, 1991). The record on development is poor, comprising 58 units of housing, 200,260 square feet of industrial/warehousing and 93,000 square feet of offices which were completed during the period January 1989–April 1992. All of these are developments granted planning permission by the city council (with the exception of 68,465 square feet of industrial/warehousing developed at the Unicorn Business Park).

It would be wrong to attribute this performance simply to BDC. The poor economic climate, the slump in the property market and the high cost of money has seen developer-interest and commitment reduce over the last two years, coinciding with the lifetime of BDC. However, these problems clearly demonstrate the limitations of relying solely on market-led development strategies. As the Centre for Local Economic Strategies (1990) note, there is no easy solution as too much depends on key sites and on investment by large developers and institutions. UDCs cannot proceed simply on the basis of marketing brochures and strategy documents. Since developers' interest has been receding, UDCs generally have been finding it much more difficult to get development going, and as yet, have no alternative strategy for regeneration. One might question the wisdom of an approach to regeneration that relies so heavily on the private property market. If recent reports are to be believed, about UDCs being requested to draw up exit strategies and the creation of an Urban Regeneration Agency, it would seem that the DOE and government are also having serious doubts about their effectiveness.

Conclusions

This study has shown how the activities of BDC need to be understood in the context of changing economic, political and ideological relations. BDC has given market criteria a higher priority, challenging the policy of the City and County Councils. However, the market has failed BDC. During the last three years of recession BDC has failed to realize the potential of the area. It aimed for a leverage ratio of 12:1 but has only managed to achieve 4.7:1 (Potter, 1990). This has been the overriding factor in determining the outcome of BDC activities although local political opposition has also been a significant factor. The UDC style of operation clashed with the local authorities' principles of accountability and local participation and became a central theme of Bristol City Council's opposition to the establishment of BDC.

If BDC is to be understood as an attempt to challenge the urban planning approaches in Bristol, by introducing a new market-led ideology, it can also be seen as an attempt to facilitate the economic restructuring of the traditional manufacturing heart of Bristol. In other areas, UDCs have played an important part in attempting to facilitate economic change. They have often been established in areas of industrial dereliction or decline. This is perhaps more obvious in areas like the London Docklands or the Black Country where there has been dramatic decline in the traditional industries creating the opportunity for a new geography of production. The Bristol UDA is not a vast tract of derelict land but an area of mixed industrial use with some key sites prime for redevelopment.

By proposing flexible planning regimes attempting to attract high value added uses, BDC was breaking with the tradition of the area. But an approach based on levering in private investment at a time of recession in the land and property market was doomed to failure, particularly in a city that had boomed in the prosperous years of the 1980s leading to over-provision of commercial space in the inner area. In spite of the central importance of this area in terms of industrial activity, the BDC has sought to exploit its locational potential, adjacent to the city centre, by adopting a strategy which favours office/commercial investment. Although Bristol City Council has encouraged office growth in the central area in recent years, it has viewed the plans of the UDC with some concern due to the potential impact on the existing traditional manufacturing employment in the area and the potential damage it could cause for redevelopment plans elsewhere in the city (e.g. Broadmead Initiative and city centre office developments).

This clash between the city council and BDC over what the City has called the Development Corporation's 'anti-industry' attitude has been an important theme and arena of conflict. This set of circumstances revealed the failings of the approach and prompted the government to increase its funding commitment from £15 million to £57 million with an extension to 6 years – sending clear signals to landowners and property investors. This demonstrates the essentially political nature of urban policy and the commitment that has been given to BDC's programmes despite many of the criticisms and weaknesses associated with it. However, recent announcements have shown how UDCs may not continue to occupy such a privileged position in the government's urban policy.

Yet in Bristol, the increasing militancy of a significant proportion of Labour Councillors led to greater opposition to central government during the 1980s. The City Council complained about cut-backs in the Urban Programme funding and failed to support the Employment Training Initiatives. The local authority was criticized by local Conservative MPs, particularly J. Sayeed, who claimed he was largely responsible for persuading the Minister to designate a UDC for the central area of Bristol. Criticism focused on accusations of inefficiency, anti-developer attitudes and neglect. David Trippier branded the City Council a 'loony left wing' authority in the run-up to the House of Lords inquiry and set the tone for subsequent relations between BDC and the city council.

However, given the experience of the conflict-ridden 1980s the present government may have reviewed their earlier position 'that existing arrangements involving local authorities were inadequate to deal with the complex task of regeneration' (National Audit Office, 1988). Local authorities' enthusiasm for recovering its central role in regeneration efforts, as the Bristol case illustrates, does not seem to have been dampened by the attempts of central government to challenge the role of local government, to reduce many of its functions and to exclude it from the corporatist alliance formed between central government arm's-length agencies and the business community. For example, CLES (1990b) identifies five elements of an alternative to UDCs:

1. If local authorities had the prime responsibility for development, there would be a more democratic basis for defining regeneration, drawing up the strategy and making decisions, with local authorities playing a key role.
2. There would be a broader approach to intervening in the local economy which would include much more emphasis on industrial regeneration, community enterprise, and the labour market. Market-led development would play a role but as part of a much wider concept of inner city renewal.
3. There would be specific targeting of employment and housing to those in need through training programmes, affordable housing schemes, and community development programmes.
4. Planning would play a key role, not as marketing documents but setting out social, environmental and economic objectives for the city and the regeneration area.
5. Local authority led regeneration would benefit from the coordination of physical development within their locality with housing, social, educational, and economic programmes. Local authorities are in a better position to create these links than UDCs.

Bristol City Council has recently outlined similar principles. In responding to the recent National Audit Office questionnaire on UDCs, it stated that if the local authority retained local democratic control over the regeneration process, was given special government funds and power, and, adopted 'fast-track' decision-making procedures, including staff teams dedicated to the UDA work

that such an approach would combine the clear advantages enjoyed by a UDC, some of which are indeed of positive value in regeneration, with the positive attributes of local authority approaches; particularly the regard for the well-being of the urban area as a whole, the experience in working alongside existing communities to further their involvement in developments in which they will have a stake and the long term commitment to the area which will transcend cycles of boom and recession

(Bristol City Council response to the NAO questionnaire, 1991, para 10.4)

It is towards such an integrative approach that urban policy in Bristol, and beyond, must look in the 1990s.

10

THE NEW PARTNERSHIP: INTER-AGENCY COOPERATION AND URBAN POLICY IN LEEDS

Peter Roberts and David Whitney

Introduction

The Leeds Urban Development Corporation (LDC) was established in June 1988 as one of the 'third generation mini-UDCs' and, as such, it was afforded a relatively brief lifespan in which to achieve its objectives. As a relatively short-term agency for change in the inner areas of Leeds, its capacity for action must be judged against the broader prevailing economic circumstances in the city and the Yorkshire and Humberside Region. The LDC, in common with a number of other development agencies in the city and region, has experienced considerable difficulty in bringing forward development during a period of recession and therefore its achievements should be judged within an appropriate frame of measurement.

Having set the context for the initial designation of the LDC, this chapter then outlines and assesses the designation of the LDC, including the definition of its boundaries. The third section of the chapter examines the strategy which was adopted by the LDC and provides a commentary on its initial implementation, the further elaboration of the strategy and its achievements. Finally, some initial conclusions are drawn; this final section of the chapter also attempts to relate the evaluation of the LDC to the broader trends which can be observed in the UDCs and in UK urban policy more generally. By its very nature, especially given the unfavourable economic conditions prevailing during the past three years, this outline of the origins and operation of the LDC offers a provisional rather than final assessment. Further research is now under way which will offer a further appreciation of the LDC and other modes of partnership for development in West Yorkshire.

Economic and Political Context

Economic Background

Yorkshire and Humberside is often viewed as an 'average' region within the UK. A diverse range of urban and rural environments are contained within

Table 10.1 Employment in Yorkshire and Humberside 1981–87

Category	Employment net change		
	1987	1981–84	1984–87
All primary industry	98,182	−17,519	−30,882
All manufacturing	482,090	−94,200	−2,682
All construction	90,137	−1,352	−3,181
All service industry	1,112,870	44,100	46,142
All employment	1,783,279	−68,809	9,397

Source: Leigh *et al* (1990).

the region; common perceptions of environments within the region vary from abandoned coal mines and derelict land in the central belt, to the dales of Herriot country. During the early 1980s many of the region's traditional industries shed labour at a rapidly increasing rate (Table 10.1), with a loss of over 94,000 jobs in manufacturing between 1981 and 1984. This trend of job loss in manufacturing decelerated during the period from 1984 to 1987 and the sector experienced the loss of 2,600 jobs. Meanwhile, employment in the service sector grew with an additional 44,000 jobs added to the regional total employment in this sector between 1981 and 1984 and a further 46,000 jobs in the period from 1984 up to 1987 (Leigh *et al*, 1990).

The population of the region was 4,950,000 in 1981 having grown by less than 0.4% between 1971 and 1981 (compared with a rate of growth in the UK as a whole of 3.8%). Within the region the largest proportion of the population was, and still is, resident in West Yorkshire (over 2 million of the regional total of 4.9 million in 1981). Preliminary estimates from the 1991 census indicate that the region's population declined by 1.8% between 1981 and 1991 (compared to a fall of 0.1% in England and Wales as a whole) and that the population of West Yorkshire fell by 2.6% over this period. In 1991 the population of Leeds was estimated at 702,000. Leeds is the major city of the region and of West Yorkshire, and has at the time of the initial announcement of the LDC, had a higher proportion of its total employment in service occupations (67% in 1987) than in the region as a whole (62% in 1987). This development of the service base of the city reflects both its role as the 'regional capital' of Yorkshire and Humberside and the trend of service growth observable throughout the 1980s where it was seen to compete with Manchester for the status of the 'Business Capital of the North' (Townroe, 1992).

It was within this context that the UDC was proposed. In May 1988 the consultants (PIEDA) in their preparatory study concluded that: 'By comparison with other northern industrial cities, Leeds has a relatively well balanced economic structure. This provides a sound basis for future employment growth' (PIEDA, 1988, p. 3). In particular the consultants pointed to the potential for the further expansion of the financial services sector, the enhanced development of Leeds as a regional distribution location for Northern England, the development and retention of a strong and diversified manufacturing base, and the exploitation of hitherto underdeveloped potential for leisure and service activities. This broadly optimistic assessment was confirmed by other appraisals undertaken at the time. For example, a recent study concluded that in coming years: 'It is reasonable to assume that the most prosperous areas (Leeds and parts of North Yorkshire, for example) will have growth rates comparable with many areas of the South East' (Leigh *et al*, 1990, p. 57). In a similar vein, Cambridge Econometrics in the 1988 edition of *Regional Economic Prospects* considered that: 'As indicators point to a continuation of relatively buoyant conditions in North Yorkshire, so they do for Leeds' (Cambridge Econometrics, 1988, p. 77).

Development Potential

Within this context of relative buoyancy in the local economy it is understandable that the consultants concluded that considerable potential existed for the further development of the Leeds local economy. They argued, correctly at the time, that Leeds, by comparison with other cities in the region, had demonstrated a degree of resilience in the face of the economic recession of the early 1980s, and that unsatisfied demand existed for the provision of further office, industrial and warehousing floorspace. This view of the development prospects for Leeds was confirmed by other observers. The Cambridge Econometrics review (1988) of the Yorkshire and Humberside Region, observed that an increase in pressure upon land and property resources could be discerned and that in areas of high activity, such as Leeds, commercial and industrial properties were scarce and

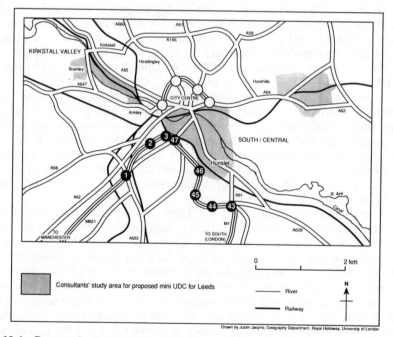

Figure 10.1 Proposed mini-UDC for Leeds: consultants' study area.

rents were rising. This rise in the level of rents was seen to enhance the viability of speculative developments (Cambridge Econometrics, 1988).

Rising pressure on land and premises, the enhanced viability of land and property developments and the desire to unlock the potential of hitherto under-utilized land, especially in the central areas of cities such as Leeds, led to the announcement in December 1987 of the three 'mini UDCs'. The objective of the Leeds UDC was to secure economic and physical regeneration by:

- bringing land and buildings into effective use;
- encouraging the development of existing and new industry and commerce;
- creating an attractive environment;
- ensuring that housing and social facilities are available to encourage people to live and work in the area (PIEDA, 1988).

The preliminary boundaries for the Leeds UDC (as announced in December 1987) included land in three areas: the Kirkstall Valley, South/Central Leeds, and Killingbeck/Seacroft (Figure 10.1). This definition of three areas of search for the UDC area was unusual, especially when compared with the single unified areas announced for Bristol and Manchester. It reflected the difficulties which had been experienced in Leeds in identifying land both with potential for development and which was capable of being brought into productive use in a relatively short time. In the final analysis only two of the areas – the Kirkstall Valley and South/Central Leeds – were included within the designated area of the LDC. Further details of the consultant's report and the process of designation are given in the following section of this chapter.

Political and Organizational Context

The announcement in December 1987 that a UDC was to be established in Leeds added an additional agency to the somewhat 'crowded platform' of organizations seeking to stimulate development in the Leeds area. It also created further difficulties and tensions between agencies, each seeking to define its own specific role and functions. Within the city, and the region more generally, a multiplicity of development agencies existed prior to the designation of the LDC. Interventions in the local economy of Leeds varied from those undertaken by the region's promotional and inward investment organization (the Yorkshire and Humberside Development Association), to the provision of equity capital (through the West Yorkshire Enterprise Board, which was established by West Yorkshire County Council in 1984) and the establishment by Leeds City Council during the early 1980s, and publicly launched in 1988, of the Leeds City Development Company (LCDC). These function-specific agencies existed alongside the more conventional institutions such as the City Council, the Chamber of Commerce and Industry and a range of nationally-funded agencies including the Leeds and Bradford City Action Team.

Inevitably the entry of a new organization into an already complex institutional infrastructure exacerbated the desire of each body to enhance and clarify its own particular function and role. In the case of the designation of the LDC, and the definition of its area, an immediate source of contention was, for example, the development strategy which was proposed for the Kirkstall Valley. This area of land – the developed area of which was in a multiplicity of ownerships, whilst the open land was mainly within the ownership of Leeds City Council and the Central Electricity Generating Board – had been in an underdeveloped and blighted state for some years. In 1980 the Kirkstall Valley Local Plan had proposed the concept of the recreational development of the Valley; this had later been further promoted by the City Council through the suggested development of the Kirkstall Valley Park. A later development brief, which had promoted the notion of new prestigious mixed development in the Valley (commercial, leisure, retail, residential and business uses), had been taken up by the LCDC and its partner Mountleigh in the face of opposition from local residents. It was into this area of conflict that the LDC entered in 1988.

This illustration is provided in order to demonstrate the tensions which were inherent in the addition of a new actor to an already 'crowded platform' of development agencies. The proposal for the creation of a UDC in Leeds initially led to a period of challenge and confrontation, with the Labour-controlled City Council claiming that it had already established a planning framework and organizational structure through the creation of the LCDC, which was capable of promoting urban development. However, despite some critical acrimonious posturing, the LDC soon established itself within the development community of the city and region. This rapid reconciliation of interests between the City Council and the LDC was to a certain extent enabled by the inclusion of City Councillors on the Board of the LDC, and also through effective collaboration at officer level.

The relative harmony in the working relationship between the City Council and the LDC has been assisted by the relatively brief lifespan which was given to the LDC (with the subsequent need to bring about development quickly) and the necessity, therefore, for it to operate within the already evolving partnership within the city. This process has resulted in the evolution of a style of operation which is characterized by negotiation and collaboration. Further incentives for cooperation were the already successful record of the LCDC in bringing about development within the UDC area, and the reality that certain big areas of land within the UDC were owned by the City Council.

A further evolution of the joint working relationship resulted from the creation in 1990 of the Leeds Initiative. The City Council, the LDC and the Chamber of Commerce and Industry are represented on the Leeds Initiative, together with leaders of development, educational, governmental and other key sectors in the city. The Initiative meets regularly, with the Leader of the City Council taking the Chair, the Deputy Chair coming from the Chamber of Commerce. A Project Director was appointed in 1990.

The inclusion of the LDC within the Leeds Initiative symbolized the partnership mode of operation which has typified the recent evolution of the institutional infrastructure for urban development in Leeds. This is not intended to suggest that individual agencies do not have an individual role, mission and particular style of operation, rather it indicates the realism which has evolved during recent years as development opportunities have become more difficult to exploit. It also indicates the complexity of bringing forward developments, especially in South/Central Leeds where infrastructure improvements, environmental enhancement and land and property development necessitates multi-agency cooperation and integrated investment.

Why was the LDC Designated?

By comparison with many other cities and districts in Yorkshire and Humberside, Leeds was relatively late in entering the field of integrated economic and physical development and promotion. Despite having fostered a complex and well-developed series of departmental initiatives the City Council had struggled for some years to discover the correct blend and mode of policy delivery, especially in difficult-to-develop areas such as the Kirkstall Valley and South/Central Leeds. In addition, the city had lacked any significant or consistent input of assistance from nationally funded initiatives or policy means; it had not been given assisted area status, nor had it attracted other incentives such as Enterprise Zones, even though it had attracted substantial funds from the Urban Programme and other policies.

However, the city was perceived by central government as a place where the private and public sectors were willing to invest and develop, but also as a place where constraints upon development had hindered the release of this inherent potential. The designation of the LDC was therefore seen as a means of cutting through the constraints to development and creating a framework for the enablement and integration of development opportunities. This is not to suggest that the LDC has compromised its specific mission, rather it suggests that the designation of a UDC in the city can be seen as complementary to the efforts of other actors within the city. There have been instances where, for example, the LDC has served Compulsory Purchase Orders on land owned and intended for development by the LCDC, but, in general terms, despite conflicts of opinion about the means adopted, the various actors present within the city share common goals.

An additional factor which must be considered is the extent to which central government sought to designate a UDC in a location which promised guaranteed success. As has been demonstrated earlier in this chapter, the economy and development potential of the central area of Leeds was considered in 1987 to offer fertile ground for the establishment of a UDC. A large part of the designated area was within or adjacent to the thriving central area and this was seen to offer a platform from which other more difficult-to-develop schemes could be launched. Although, as experience has shown in more recent years, the existence of potential is no guarantee of rapid success, the strategy in designating the UDC was to capitalize upon an established trend of development which was spreading outwards from the central area.

Furthermore, the designation of a UDC was viewed by government as representing an additional allocation of resources to the city. Although it is possible to argue that the direct allocation of these resources to the City Council or other existing agencies may have achieved the same effect as the designation of a UDC, the political reality of the time was such that any alternative mechanism for the distribution of resources was not countenanced and the only politically acceptable way to ensure an additional allocation of resources to the city was through the establishment of the LDC. This explanation may fail to convince political theorists and it does not take into account the switch of resources from the Urban Programme to the UDCs, but in the somewhat pragmatic political economy of Leeds it is an important consideration.

The final consideration and explanation for the relative ease of designation of the LDC, and its rapid assimilation into the partnership of the Leeds Initiative, is the relatively small size of the population resident within the UDC area at the time of designation (800 in an area of 375 ha). This removed one of the principal objections frequently levelled at UDCs, that is that the designation of a UDC removes electoral accountability.

Defining the UDC Area

Areas of Search

As noted above, the initial area of search for a suitable designated area was defined within three broad study areas – to the north west in the Kirkstall Valley, to the north east in the Killingbeck/Seacroft area and south of the city centre. The consultants appointed to carry out the preparatory study for the UDC excluded Killingbeck/Seacroft on the basis that the area's restricted development opportunities, and a low level of potential commercial interest, would not make optimum use of UDC resources. It is significant to note that in making adjustment to the draft boundaries, the consultants (PIEDA, 1988) only included land and buildings which were considered to have sufficient potential to benefit from UDC action or which were necessary to the proper planning and development of the UDC area. Existing housing areas were excluded deliberately, together with sites where UDC intervention was not deemed crucial to satisfactory development. Quite clearly the guiding assumptions of the consultants about the purposes of the UDC, and hence the definition of the UDC area, related chiefly to the development potential of commercial and industrial areas.

This aspect of the work of the UDC was given priority in order to maximize the developability of the area through the available powers and to heighten its coherent image within the wider urban area. The Killingbeck/Seacroft area was deemed to be 'backland' in environmental terms where it would be difficult to develop a positive image, whilst the remaining two areas had scope for the creation of strong images which could be enhanced by including 'gateway sites' for environmental improvement. The proposals for specific UDC boundaries did not themselves provoke extensive controversy. During the initial period Leeds City Council held the view strongly that in principle there was no economic rationale for the establishment of the UDC in the city and it made many public statements to that effect. Political pragmatism however led to early recognition that the designation of a UDC represented the reality of national urban policy. It was further recognized that the UDC represented a considerable additional resource to the city (even if not through a favoured policy delivery mechanism) and that attention was to be given to key problem areas with which the city had struggled for many years.

Other development related agencies in Leeds were more positive about the designation of the UDC area. The Chamber of Commerce took the view that the city as a whole had insufficiently taken advantage of the strong upturn in the regional economy during the late 1980s, and that planning policies had indeed restricted development. There was the perception for example that the city centre was not expanding fast enough to the south, and more specifically

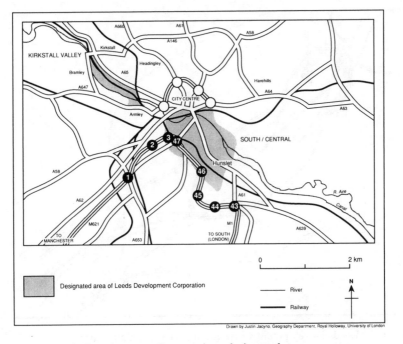

Figure 10.2   Leeds Development Corporation: designated area.

that the improvement of derelict land and buildings had not been accorded sufficient priority attention. In the event, the final designated area for the UDC comprised two areas of the city; the Kirkstall Valley and South/Central Leeds (see Figure 10.2).

The Defined Area

The first area as defined by the consultants comprised 164 ha to the north west of the city centre in the Kirkstall Valley (see Figure 10.3). Key features of this zone included a large area of derelict open land in the valley bottom once used by a former Central Electricity Generating Board (CEGB) power station, existing industrial uses at the eastern end and some leisure-related uses such as the Armley Industrial Museum, the River Aire and the Leeds and Liverpool Canal. Whilst there was little residential population within the Kirkstall Valley area, there were long-established housing areas surrounding it. The main area of open land was in the ownership of the CEGB and the City Council, as mentioned previously, with institutional investors also having a strong interest in a number of the principal development sites.

The valley area had been, and was, poorly served by the highway network, suffering from considerable peak period overloading on a number of roads serving it. To release development potential within the valley it was also anticipated that considerable investment was necessary in foul and surface water drainage in the valley bottom. Additionally, it was clear that ground

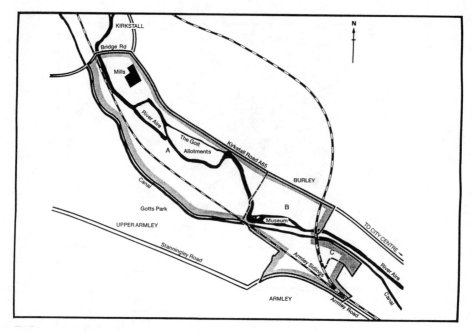

Figure 10.3   Leeds Development Corporation: Kirkstall Valley area.

conditions relating to the former CEGB power station site created major constraints upon development, including the need for the removal of retained electricity installations and concrete foundations while dealing with extensive former ash lagoons. Taken as a whole the Kirkstall Valley site represented, in one sense, a major opportunity for comprehensive regeneration, where land had been in a derelict or under-used state for a long period. It had also been clear to the City Council for many years that extensive and coordinated investment would be needed to overcome major highway, ground and infrastructure constraints. What is also significant to underline in terms of development perceptions – and noted previously – were the strong views held by neighbouring communities about developments appropriate to the valley. Proposals by the LCDC prior to the inception of the UDC had galvanized a latent community movement into a proactive campaigning group seeking to maximize a 'green future' for the valley. The UDC therefore inherited not only difficult physical constraints to development, but well organized and articulate interests holding strong views about the future of the valley.

The second area as defined by the consultants comprised 376 ha south of the city centre, known as South/Central Leeds (see Figure 10.4). Key features included its large extent of derelict, disused or low grade uses, resulting in a generally poor environment, its predominance of industrial and commercial uses accommodated in a wide variety of purpose-built or traditional mill properties, its severance from the city centre by the railway viaduct and the River Aire and finally its small amount of housing resulting from long-standing housing clearance and other demolition programmes.

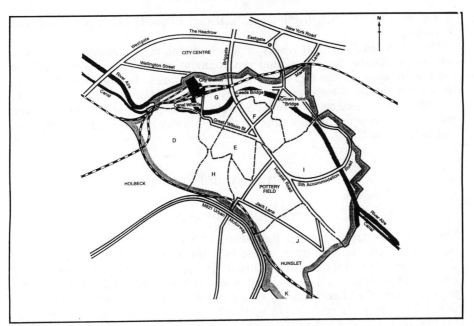

Figure 10.4   Leeds Development Corporation: south/central Leeds area.

Land ownerships were highly fragmented, although there were some significant public (or formerly public sector) holdings. The area lay at the northern end of the M1 which offered a clear strategic development advantage. On the other hand there were observable deficiencies in the strategic and principal highway network. An East Leeds radial and the southern section of the inner ring road were not programmed for development until the mid 1990s, and there was no timetable, at the time of the consultants' study, for a link between the M621 and the M1 in order to relieve congestion at the end of the M1. There were also the key problems of how to enhance the physical integration of the area with the city centre across the major barriers of railway station, railway viaducts and river. Pedestrian access from the city centre to the south side of the railway viaduct was both physically difficult and difficult to perceive.

In recent years development interest in the Riverside area had increased, to the extent of giving the lie to accusations that the City Council had devoted insufficient attention to these city centre fringe areas. The new ASDA head-quarters and a number of housing developments on the Aire waterfront, represented key projects which demonstrated and reinforced the potential of the area. With some exceptions of business or warehousing schemes taking place on sites adjacent to the M1, this area as a whole contained many sites both derelict or unused, and typified the sort of development difficulties which UDCs as development agencies were seen by the DOE as best qualified to tackle – that is areas blighted by uncertain road proposals, areas where development was inhibited by site fragmentation and areas of long-standing dereliction or with a negative image which were in need of both promotion and marketing.

The large South/Central Leeds area was therefore recognized by the consultants as having major existing development momentum which could be capitalized upon as having key strategic advantages. In addition, they also recognized the need for concentrated investment and attention to be given to various actions necessary in order to release the potential for business and retail uses of prominent sites close to the motorway network, and for housing and industry in Hunslet.

UDC Strategy and Practice

Overall Approach

The LDC's Strategic Plan was published in October 1988. The opening statement by the Board Chairman established the stance to be adopted by the Corporation: 'The Development Corporation is here to help, encourage and enable the private sector to improve businesses in Leeds and join those who already know that Leeds means better business' (LDC, 1988). At the same time there was early recognition that to be effective in its short lifetime, the Corporation would need to be positive and proactive in order to stimulate development, and would need to act in concert with the full range of relevant development organizations and agencies in the city. In other words, the Corporation sought to establish a consensual approach with existing agencies and organizations. In fact, in recognition of the general antipathy to the perceived imposition of the Corporation upon the city by both officers and members of the Council, the early public profile of the UDC was strongly one of cooperation and even partnership.

The Corporation rapidly shifted from its early more robust style of operation to one which was generally more open and consultative with development and community organizations. Planning meetings and Board meetings were made open to the public by the second year of the operation of the LDC. Extensive periods and mechanisms for consultation with business, development and public interests were built into working methods as area planning frameworks were progressively completed. This mode of operation was also adopted in the development of other major proposals, even though no formal consultation code existed. In those sub-areas which contained any existing population (very small within the UDC area as a whole) the Corporation has very deliberately established community forums in order to ensure that a consultative mechanism was available and, in addition, the UDC has ensured regular contact with ward members.

Whilst the apparent priorities of the LDC and those of the City Council may have proved to be in conflict – almost inevitable given their contrasting constituencies and perspectives – no significantly contentious differences have emerged with respect to the content of the land use and development strategy. In this sense the Corporation has largely followed the area strategies which had previously been established by Leeds City Council, the key point of contention between the City Council and the Corporation being the latter's propensity to bias some of its area planning frameworks towards office development. Otherwise there has been a strong measure of support for inherited City Council policy, with the exception of limited site specific proposals.

Area Strategies

In South/Central Leeds the Corporation has carried forward the broad thrust of the City Council for a southwards expansion of the city centre towards the River Aire, and has supported the potential of the developing business area in the vicinity of the M1/M621 for high quality office uses, while reinforcing long-standing industrial and housing regeneration policies in Hunslet. In the Kirkstall Valley, the Corporation inherited what it recognized to be a less coherent policy background, namely the non-statutory Kirkstall Valley Local Plan and the Kirkstall Valley Park Plan (also approved 1980), together with a subsequent development brief which had been issued by the City Council in order to invite 'imaginative schemes' for this 'major and outstanding development opportunity'.

The LDC encountered strongly articulated views from the local community in Kirkstall Valley about what they perceived to be an acceptable form and scale of development. The community groups produced an influential alternative local development plan (Kirkstall Valley Campaign, 1990) and the Corporation took account of this and other representations. In response the LDC produced a revised planning framework for the Valley in 1991 which, on balance, recommended that a 'greener' planning solution should be adopted. The nature reserve, which was initially recommended by the City Council in the 1980 Park Plan (and strongly advocated by the Kirkstall Valley Campaign Group), has been retained, and a Steering Committee (shortly to be superseded by a widely based Management Committee) has been set up to oversee its implementation. This Steering Committee meets at regular monthly intervals in order to check progress.

Discussions continue at the time of writing regarding the key issue of open space provision, which local community interests strongly advocate should be included as a counterweight to the proposed development of new high density housing. The crux of the issue revolves around the extent to which the Corporation is willing to inject appropriate resources in order to remedy the perceptions held by local community groups of open space deficiencies.

Implementation

The statement of priorities in the LDC's Strategic Plan provided overall guidance for the programme of the Corporation. During the first year of operation (up to 31 March 1989) the Corporation established the operational structure and base, and had undertaken preparatory work for a programme of land requisition and development. By April 1990, the Corporation confirmed that progress had occurred in relation to its policy of site assembly needed for comprehensive redevelopment (32.7 ha had been acquired). Developers had been selected or short-listed for sites which would be subject to competition, design work had been completed on various road proposals and five planning frameworks had been completed. On the economic development side, four City Grants had been offered. Grant assistance to owners of under-used land and buildings was being made available through its Sites and Property Grants Scheme. A property and business development package had been launched with Yorkshire Enterprise Ltd, providing access to venture capital for small businesses.

Agreements had been made with the Tourist Board, British Waterways and Leeds City Council to fund a three year Tourist Development Action Programme to realize the tourist potential of the Waterways corridor. A local community sponsorship grant scheme had been devised. More strategically, advertising and marketing campaigns were being directed locally, nationally and internationally. By April 1991, the Corporation had prepared planning frameworks for all but one of its sub-areas. By the end of March, 1991, 37.4 ha of land had been acquired. The first phase of the M1/M621 Interchange site was marketed as a hotel site in November, 1990, and the first phase of the Hunslet Business Park was similarly marketed in January, 1991. Some forty-three environmental improvements schemes covering 128,000 sq. m of landscaping had been undertaken, and twenty-nine Environmental Improvements Grants had been awarded. At the end of the 1991–92 financial year the Corporation reported that further progress had been made on a number of fronts, including the reclamation and improvement of derelict and underused land, the completion during the year of over 37,000 sq. m of floorspace, an increased rate of investment in new infrastructure and the completion of a 40-bedroomed hotel. In addition, the Corporation had started work on the creation of the Kirkstall Valley Nature Reserve and had made a major contribution to the Royal Armouries project.

On a cumulative basis the LDC had, by the end of March 1992, attracted over £39 million of grant-in-aid, £116 million of private sector investment and had acquired over 41 ha of land. Over 37 ha of land had been reclaimed, 215,000 sq. m of landscaping had been undertaken and 4.25 km of infrastructure had been completed. Some 6,514 gross new jobs had been created, resulting in the generation of 3,875 net new jobs (see Table 10.2). Although steady progress has been maintained during the past four years in terms of land reclamation, landscaping, infrastructure provision and the completion of floorspace, the rate of both gross and net job creation has slowed, and in the case of net job generation actually fallen, during the period of deep recession. The

Table 10.2   Leeds Development Corporation targets and performance 1988–92

	Output forecast*	Actual 1988–92[†]
Land developed (ha)	106.5	N/A
Land reclaimed (ha)	N/A	37.36
Housing units completed	990	180
New and improved roads (km)	3.43	N/A
Infrastructure put in place (km)	N/A	4.25
Jobs created gross	9,450	6,514
Jobs created net	6,600	3,875
Private sector investment (£ million)	233	116
Public expenditure (£ million)	30[‡]	39[§]

* From PIEDA (1988) for seven year period.
[†] From LDC Annual Report (1992) for four year period.
[‡] Net public expenditure from PIEDA (1988) for five year period.
[§] Grant-in-aid paid from independent (1992) for four year period.

gearing ratio of public to private investment (1:2.97 by the end of March 1992) has remained favourable throughout the period of operation of the LDC.

Modes of Operation

It is clear that there was a realization from the outset of the LDC that practical politics dictated that the Corporation, as a new imposition, would need to come together with established agencies and institutions. Increasingly and progressively, the definition and implementation of strategies for economic development, local planning and highway development matters proved stronger driving forces than formalized development control agency arrangements, in achieving coordinated activity on a daily basis. Increasingly too, working relationships developed on a multi-level basis between individuals and agencies in the city. In addition to daily technical collaboration between agencies and departments, the Corporation at Board and Director level has become a lead partner in the Leeds Initiative, a collaborator with the LCDC in a number of schemes and a working partner with The English Tourist Board, The British Waterways Board and Leeds City Council in the Waterfront development programme.

This transformation of a relationship, which could have been dominated by rivalry and antipathy, to one of relative cooperation, is exemplified by the establishment of the Leeds Initiative. Although there is still competition for the development of projects and although there have been accusations, especially in the early years, by the Corporation that the LCDC favoured the development 'plums' rather than 'lemons' (Whitney and Haughton, 1990), the general thrust of development agencies within the city has been towards the creation of a partnership mode of operation.

Such a mode of operation, which can be seen in Leeds, reflects the general evolution of urban development operations elsewhere in West Yorkshire (Roberts and Whitney, 1991). During the difficult years of the late 1980s and early 1990s it is not surprising that such a mode of operation has emerged. This is in part explained by the desire of agencies to share the burden of creating the conditions for development and the recognition that major schemes require mutual cooperation in order to assemble and implement the necessary elements for development to proceed. The real test of partnership may well occur in a more favourable economic climate where heightened competition for projects and funds could generate increased rivalry between agencies.

Four Years In: Some Initial Conclusions

As was stated in the introduction to this chapter, any assessment and review of the progress and operational features of an individual UDC must be informed by other more general characteristics and methods of approach which are common to all UDCs. It must also be informed by a knowledge of the general strengths and failings of urban policy.

Given the normal lead times in development, together with the recent slowdown in the property market and the somewhat unpropitious way in which the Corporation was designated in a staunchly Labour-controlled city, the relatively low level of tangible achievement in the LDC area (when compared to the outputs anticipated in the consultants' initial study) is probably not surprising. The LDC has stepped relatively swiftly, and in a relaxed fashion, onto the platform of Leeds urban development agencies. Clearly, there was a degree of acrimonious posturing at the outset, particularly by the leaders of the LDC and of the City Council, belying much effective officer collaboration at a more technical level. The activities of LCDC, whose resurrection was most likely prompted by the threat of the designation of the LDC, reinforced the antagonisms expressed at leader level by both Corporation and Council. There was a swift learning process by both bodies and a realistic acknowledgement that negative attitudes and disputes could only be harmful to both interests.

The arrival of the Corporation, to a degree, also coincided with the wishes of a new Council leader that the city should take a greater lead in project initiation in collaboration with other city interests. Clearly there was a change from the old 'Labour stronghold city-boss' style of the former incumbent. In one sense, the designation of a UDC initially worsened inter-agency working, and yet played its own part in stimulating the setting up of the Leeds Initiative as a widely-based partnership of economic, social and physical development interests within the city. It is perhaps also a little surprising and ironic that one of the most obvious achievements of the Corporation has been the extent of its systematic and consultative plan-making activities for all sub-areas within the designated area of the LDC. New and more coherent strategic attention has thereby been given to two areas of the city where plans were variously, and to differing extents, outdated and somewhat fragmented.

In addition to making plans, the Corporation has progressed a number of key 'cornerstone' sites through development agreements, it has also collaborated extensively with the City Council in marketing certain difficult sites and it has supported certain longstanding highway proposals through their being inserted into the Corporation's own programme. In a number of notable instances, such as the longstanding generation of development interest on the waterfront, the Corporation has continued the momentum previously set by the City Council. As in all cases where a multiplicity of agencies are at work, a number of parties, including the LDC, claim the credit for successful development of such areas.

Standing perhaps as the key 'achievement' of the Corporation has been the recent attraction of the Royal Armouries museum to the Leeds waterfront at Clarence Dock. Although it was important to the LDC to achieve a major success such as this, it also represents the results of close collaboration between a range of interests in the city through the Leeds Initiative. Recession may have slowed the progress of certain schemes, but this reduction in the pace of development in Leeds is not unique to those projects which have been promoted by the LDC. Accusations that the LDC (in common with a number of other UDCs) was engaged in the business of promoting 'instant success' (Fatchett, 1991) may have some foundation, but difficult economic conditions have made success much more difficult to guarantee in recent years.

In short, perhaps one of the key contributions to date of the LDC has been its catalytic and energizing effect upon the City Council in resurrecting its almost moribund development company and in assisting in the construction of a leadership forum for partnership working in the city. There were certainly

other factors contributing to these institutional innovations, but the arrival of
the Corporation would seem to have exerted a significant influence. The Leeds
Initiative has brought together the leaders of sectors not hitherto associated
with creative collaboration and in a city rather more marked by complacency
than strategic proactivity.

This takes this chapter back to its starting point and begs the questions as to
the overall level of achievement of the LDC, set against the features common
to all UDCs, and the broader geography of UK urban policy. In the introduction
to this chapter it was stated that it is somewhat premature to offer a full
critique of the operation of the LDC. However, crucial issues for urban policy
analysts when confronted by the need to assess the performance of a single
agency or initiative are related to:

- issues of democracy and accountability;
- policy effectiveness relative to objectives;
- the role of partnership in policy delivery;
- the spatial validity and integrity of the policy; and
- the distribution of benefits.

In considering each of these issues in turn, it is not possible at present to arrive
at a conclusive answer on every point. It is, for example, far too early to really
examine the question of 'who benefits' or the extent of any spread effects
generated by the LDC. Therefore, this section of the chapter offers some
initial observations which are likely to be of more help in defining the research
agenda than in providing definitive answers.

In relation to the first issue, the operation of the LDC presents fewer
difficulties than is the case in many other UDCs. There was and is only a very
small residential population within the designated area. Nevertheless, there is
resident concern at the scale and type of development proposed, particularly in
the Kirkstall Valley area, although it should be noted that this is a concern of
long standing and was also voiced in relation to earlier pre-LDC proposals for
development.

With regard to the second issue, it is difficult part way through the LDC's
relatively short operational lifespan to fully judge if it has achieved its objectives.
The onset of recession has dampened the heady development euphoria of the
late 1980s, and the noticeable, but not severe, downturn in demand has equally
affected areas of the city both within and outwith the LDC boundary. That the
LDC has brought additional resources to the city cannot be doubted and, as
this chapter has indicated above, it has helped to galvanize the various 'partners'
within the city into action.

This takes these conclusions to the third issue which is related to the role of
partnership in the operation of the LDC. Clearly, the development 'platform'
in Leeds, and West Yorkshire more generally, was already 'crowded' prior to
the designation of the LDC. However, the LDC has found and defined a niche
for its activities, and to this extent can be seen as complementary to existing
agencies. As has been discussed earlier in this chapter and elsewhere (Whitney
and Haughton, 1990; Roberts and Whitney, 1991) the question of who is
leading the collaboration is less clear. The bringing together of partners in the
Leeds Initiative is seen to offer a chance for the creation of an interactive mode

of partnership where belonging is more important (for the longer term benefit of the city) than leading.

On the question of the spatial validity of the LDC as an instrument of urban policy, certain doubts remain. The present authors have argued elsewhere (Haughton and Roberts, 1990, Roberts, 1990) that there is a case, on the one hand, for a less nationally dominated urban policy – it might prove more effective over the long haul to foster and fund strategic development partnerships of the kind found in some parts of the USA or, on the other hand, to cultivate and finance community-based development programmes of the kind proposed many years ago by the SNAP Report (McConaghy, 1972). This, however, is a superior research question which is not exclusive to the Leeds case and, as such, it would be unfair to criticize the LDC for following a centrally determined mode of policy delivery.

Finally, there is the question of the distribution of benefits. As noted above, it is premature to judge the LDC on this issue. However, the measurement and social mapping of any benefits which occur, especially the additional benefits which emanate from activities which can be clearly attributed to the LDC, is an important research task. As others have observed (for example, Parkinson and Evans, 1990) it may be unfair to judge the performance as a UDC, encumbered with relatively narrow terms of reference on criteria which can only be achieved by a total or comprehensive urban development agency. Nevertheless, the LDC in common with some other UDCs, has increasingly emphasized the social and community elements of its programme – the number of community sponsorship grants awarded more than doubled during 1991–92 compared with previous years – and it has enhanced its working relationships with community and voluntary groups (CLES, 1992). This may, in part, be a reflection of a reduction in the number of ready commercial development opportunities in the Leeds area, but it also reflects a trend observable in other UDCs. As CLES (1992) has stated, this indicates the emerging understanding 'that the achievement of private sector development opportunities is not incompatible with social goals'. This trend also reflects the growing realization that there are limits to property-led urban renewal – which have been so crucially demonstrated during the present recession – and that investment in human capital is an equally important element in urban development.

The LDC may have failed to achieve all of the property-related objectives which were set for it in the heady days of 1988, but it has acted as a catalyst for development action in certain difficult-to-develop areas of the city. Questions as to the cost effectiveness of the activities of the LDC vis-à-vis the alternative, such as providing additional resources to the City Council for it to spend on urban regeneration, will continue to be asked. However, the precise assessment of such hypothetical alternative policy options is both difficult to achieve and to a certain extent it is somewhat meaningless in terms of the actual progress which the LDC and the other agencies have made during the difficult years of recession. Issues of social justice and democratic accountability remain as matters for further research and debate.

In overall terms, the LDC, which was introduced as an agent for change and action in two somewhat moribund areas of Leeds, has done well to establish for itself a clear role and identity within the development community of Leeds. It has proved to be a key member of the Leeds Initiative and it has provided a degree of strategic clarity for the future development of the two areas of the city for which it is responsible. Maybe all of this could have been achieved through an expanded City Council brief and budget, but such a mechanism for development was not available as a policy-delivery option in 1988. Practical as ever, the business and development community of Leeds and West Yorkshire has accommodated and incorporated the LDC into its activities and has gained additional 'brass' to help to clean-up the confusion and 'muck' that had hindered the development of the Kirkstall Valley and South/Central Leeds for many years.

The introduction of a greater social and community element by the LDC, including an enhanced emphasis on training has further tempered the role of the Corporation. The LDC is now a fully accepted member of the city partnership in Leeds; perhaps the most explicit public recognition of this is contained in the recently published Unitary Development Plan which, when discussing the importance of policy coordination, acknowledges that:

> *This collaborative approach extends beyond the Council to the private sector, voluntary organisations and statutory bodies including Leeds Development Corporation [bold in original] the local planning authority for part of the area covered by the proposals.*

(Leeds City Council, 1992)

Although the LDC may, in the first instance, have been imposed upon Leeds, it has brought additional resources to a city which had previously lacked any special urban policy initiatives or assisted area status. During its short life span the LDC has contributed to the establishment of a new mode of partnership in the city which will continue beyond the existence of the Corporation. Perhaps that will prove to be its greatest achievement.

PART THREE

Prospects for Urban Policy

11

AFTER THE URBAN DEVELOPMENT CORPORATIONS? DEVELOPMENT ELITES OR PEOPLE-BASED REGENERATION?

Bob Colenutt

Introduction

The financial collapse of the Canary Wharf project in London Docklands symbolized the end of an era for urban regeneration in the 1980s. A new rhetoric of partnership between local government and business has emerged, contrasting sharply with the confrontation between central and local government in the Thatcher years. The questions this chapter asks are: what are the factors which have led to these changes in urban policy, and, more importantly, will they make any difference to hard pressed residents of the inner cities – are the new policies for the inner cities simply the same strategies as before wrapped in more beguiling clothes, or are real shifts in policy taking place? In particular, this chapter asks whether partnership signals a move towards the creation of undemocratic development 'elites' or to greater democratization of urban regeneration?

There is undoubtedly a different language of urban regeneration in the 1990s. There is less talk in government circles of deregulating planning and removing obstacles to the property market. The phase of out-and-out denigration of the local authority role in regeneration appears to be over – even if it is not over in other (related) spheres such as education and housing. There is also a new economic context. Instead of rising demand for land and property, there is a prolonged recession with a long period fall in land values and lack of property demand in many parts of the country. Thus, the 'demand-led' regeneration strategies of the mid-1980s, which formed the driving force behind Urban Development Corporations (UDCs) and Enterprise Zones do not work in the present economic circumstances.

Inner city local authorities for their part are no longer opposing government inner city initiatives such as UDCs, Housing Action Trusts or Priority Estates. On the contrary, they are desperate to bring government money into their areas. Faced with huge cuts in their budgets, most feel they have no alternative but to work with central government and get what they can for their communities. The confrontation between Labour-controlled local government and Whitehall has subsided for the time being. A cautious pragmatism prevails.

These changes are making a significant difference to urban policy and how it is evolving on the ground. On the one hand, urban policy as handed down by government is somewhat more 'local government friendly', but, on the other, the recession and public spending cuts are making the task of regeneration much more difficult for both developers and government alike. The purpose of this chapter is to consider how these changes in urban policy are likely to affect inner city communities.

The Decline of Urban Development Corporations

One feature of urban policy in the early 1990s is a move away from the highly centralized demand-led UDCs which were set up by Michael Heseltine and Nicholas Ridley while they were at the Department of the Environment (DOE) in the 1980s. The UDCs are to be wound down – albeit over a number of years. It is unlikely that more 'old style' UDCs will be created. The main reasons for this change are:

1. Change in the political climate of local government. This is perhaps the most important reason. Local authorities have suffered huge cuts in their capital and revenue programmes. Their legal powers to intervene in economic development, by setting up their own development companies or by spending money on economic regeneration are severely limited by the Local Government Act 1989.

    Local authorities in the inner cities also find it difficult (and prohibitively costly) to win planning appeals against development they do not believe will benefit their areas. This is because government has introduced planning circulars and planning guidance that prohibit local authorities putting forward policies that conflict with its policy. At the same time, most local authorities believe there is no longer a popular base to justify leading a revolt against government policies. A significant example of how the fear of costs affects planning policy is Camden Council's decision in 1992 to reach an agreement with the developers of the Kings Cross Railway lands instead of forcing a public inquiry which could potentially lead to costs being awarded against the Council if they lost the inquiry.

    Under these circumstances, central government can, and does, get its own way over planning, development and inner city policy without having to resort to the threat of a UDC. This is plainly evident from the positive reception given by local authorities to City Challenge and the creation of development partnerships between local authorities and the private sector in many parts of the country.

2. The costs of UDCs have proved to be much higher than the government originally anticipated. It was thought by the Treasury that with rising land values created by UDC investments, the costs of land reclamation and infrastructure would be recouped. But because of the recession and the rising costs of infrastructure like the £167 million Cardiff Bay Barrage, the £600 million Docklands Highway, or the £150 million Black Country Spine Road, UDCs have become something of a bottomless pit for public expenditure.

Indeed, grant-in-aid to UDCs as a proportion of all Urban Funds rose throughout the 1980s, and absolute levels to each UDC have increased steadily throughout this period (DCC, 1991a). Between 1981 and 1992, government grant-in-aid to the UDCs in England and Wales was over £1.8 billion. In 1991–92, it was £539.4 million with the LDDC receiving £248.7 million. Public spending restrictions in the early 1990s are now forcing a review of this level of urban expenditure. It is significant that new initiatives, such as the English Urban Regeneration Agency, and City Challenge, do not come with extra funds but simply take over existing programmes or use funds that are 'top sliced' from other urban programmes.

3. The prolonged recession has thrown the property-led approach into disarray. UDC flagship projects such as the Royal Docks Regional Shopping Centre in London, the Canal Basin scheme in Sheffield, the Middlesbrough Dock development, Twelve Quays housing scheme on Merseyside, Sandwell 2000 Shopping Centre in the Black Country, and Centre Gate office centre in Leeds, have not got off the ground. Other schemes which have started, for example, Teesside Park, or Canary Wharf, are stalled. The financial collapse of Canary Wharf, an office development of 4.6 million square feet on the Isle of Dogs, in May 1992, sent shock waves through the London property market. It was a symbol of the demand-led approach of the 1980s and stands now as a monument to it, only 14% of the space being occupied in September 1992.

4. Instead of UDCs creating a political climate favourable to the government, the political impact of UDCs has either been neutralized by local authority strategies of 'containing' UDCs and bending them to their own objectives, or by popular criticism of UDC schemes (such as the Spine Road in Bristol or the Docklands Highway in London). The Docklands scheme, which at one time was lauded as an international model of how to regenerate the inner cities, is now widely regarded as a model of how not to do it. Thus, the original aim of government, to spearhead a change in the electoral geography of inner city Labour-held areas, and in the politics of urban regeneration, has not been realized.

These factors do not, however, mean that government has given up its centralizing, and property market-led approach to urban regeneration altogether. This is evident from the remit and role of the newly created Urban Regeneration Agency (URA) that will operate in England. Though primarily concerned with reclaiming vacant land, its remit would allow it to become a sort of 'mobile UDC'. It has powers to acquire land by compulsory purchase or vesting, and has reserve powers to take over planning controls from local authorities. By 'designating' areas for reclamation, the URA can act as a UDC with respect to designated areas, with local boards appointed by the Secretary of State for the Environment.

The URA is a hangover from Heseltine's short stay at the DOE in 1991–92, and it may turn out that in a different political climate, it plays a lower profile ideological role than the UDCs. On the other hand, it may represent the iron fist of central intervention, with urban partnerships being the velvet glove.

Analysing Partnership

The urban partnership idea appears, at first sight, to be a more 'people friendly' concept than central government UDCs, Task Forces or similar agencies. Partnerships between central and local government and the private sector have a long history going back to the town centre redevelopments of the 1960s. In the 1970s, there were Inner City Partnerships for designated inner city areas involving central and local government. But partnership became a 'new issue' in the Thatcher years. Faced with the imposition of UDCs and direct control from Westminster, both local authorities and business organizations, such as local Chambers of Commerce, began demanding inclusion in decisions over urban regeneration. They wanted to be partners in urban regeneration rather than being ignored or at best looking in from the outside.

One of the champions of the partnership approach, later embodied in City Challenge, was paradoxically Michael Heseltine. Heseltine was the instigator of UDCs when he became Secretary of State for the Environment in 1979 and was responsible for setting up the 'First Generation' UDCs in Merseyside and Docklands. Later, out of office, he began proclaiming the virtues of partnership. What had happened? Had he changed, or were partnerships meeting the same aims as UDCs but by other means? An examination of Heseltine's speeches and actions reveals a complex reality behind the partnership idea which is far from reassuring for residents of the inner cities (see DCC 1991b). To take each of the 'buzz words' in the Heseltine lexicon of urban development in turn:

'*Partnership*'. The Heseltine idea of a partnership is one that is brought together under specific conditions – the most important being that the partnership operates under the effective supervision of the DOE. The DOE wants to be assured that business interests are given a high status. For example, the implementation agencies for City Challenge, though including representatives of the local community, do not in practice give the same status to local residents as to business. The reason for this is that DOE funding is given largely on the understanding that local business is happy with the arrangements. Partnership in this case does not necessarily mean the community's definition of regeneration will be given the same weight as that of business leaders, or indeed, the local authority.

'*Strategy*'. This term embodies the overall direction of the project. It is a management tool aimed at coordinating the main actors, and includes a statement of long-term aims. It can also embrace spatial strategic planning (for example, for the East Thames Corridor), for in contrast with some ministers, Heseltine advocates a degree of spatial planning, particularly for transport infrastructure and major reclamation works.

'*Leadership*' is regarded as critically important by Heseltine, for it is responsible for coordination, direction, and inspiration. It is a role that Heseltine believes business leaders should naturally play in urban regeneration. Local authorities are also regarded as having an important leadership role – with one critical condition, that they do not attempt to exercise 'control' over regeneration, and do not use their planning powers to block or delay regeneration.

'*Inducement to compete*' is the fourth feature. The carrot of public resources is the driving force behind the competition between local authorities for City Challenge and Urban Programme money. Local councils have to 'play the game' and play it well in order to get funding from the DOE. Thus, public money is a central part of partnership but it is carefully directed at the Department's definition of regeneration, and is not available for other purposes.

'*Management*' is another key factor. Michael Heseltine believes he achieved the introduction of modern business management methods to public policy while he was Secretary of State for Defence in the early 1980s, and is convinced that the management methods that have made his own private companies successful in the 1980s can be applied to urban regeneration and other areas of public policy. The City Challenge bids put into the DOE by local authorities in Urban Programme areas are steeped in 'management speak' to satisfy this new requirement.

'*Community*' is a word that is used more and more frequently in government publications on inner cities. City Challenge and Priority Estates money is conditional upon local authorities showing that they have involved the community. Thus, local authorities undertake public participation exercises as part of the preparation of their City Challenge bids. Implementation agencies are required to include community representation.

But why does the government bother with community involvement, if its main aim is to bring in the private sector? The answer is complex. Partly, it may be due to its perception that 'taming' Labour-controlled authorities is not, in fact, over and that further checks and balances are needed. Certainly, it is true that encouraging tenants' power reduces local authority control over inner city management. Another explanation is that community participation is a response to politically damaging criticism of UDCs, in particular, that they are not locally accountable and ignore local needs.

At the same time, 'community' is given a wider meaning by Heseltine and other ministers to embrace a coalition of local business, local authority and institutional leaders who have common objectives for regeneration across the city or region as a whole. Community in this sense does not mean 'neighbourhood' or place, but institutional common interests across the region.

Significantly, there is little to be found in Heseltine's writings about who benefits from urban regeneration, or about how the physical regeneration he espouses helps residents of the inner city get out of poverty, or into jobs, or better housing. He, or indeed the government generally, has shown little interest in evaluating the impact of regeneration. Success is typically judged by improvements to the image of inner city areas, by increased business confidence, and also by the taming of local authorities. During his 'adoption' of Liverpool in the early 1980s when he set up the Liverpool Task Force, he did show a concern about poverty. But he has resisted measuring how much his initiatives alleviate poverty and deprivation.

There is an assumption in government urban policy that the way in which inner city residents will benefit is from better management of public resources, and by 'trickle down' of benefits from private sector investment. But surprisingly perhaps, there is no analysis by the DOE of how trickle down works, or how it can be made to work better.

Because of Ministerial pressure, the DOE has not undertaken a systematic evaluation of urban programmes, in spite of recommendations from research it has commissioned that urban policy should be more tightly targeted (Barnekov *et al*, 1990). The National Audit Office (1988) and the Audit Commission (1989) have looked at aspects of urban policy (at the UDCs and at the coordination of urban policy initiatives), but these do not add up to a systematic or objective evaluation of the impact of urban policy on the inner cities.

The evaluation that has taken place is superficial. For example, for UDCs, the DOE has produced a list of performance indicators on which UDCs must provide information each year. The indicators are: land reclaimed, infrastructure built, dwellings completed, floorspace of non-housing develop-ment, private sector investment, and permanent jobs created. They give a measure of physical impact but they do not tell us anything about the costs and benefits for inner city communities through, for example, jobs for the unemployed, or affordable housing constructed, or resources put into community development.

In summary then, the aim of urban policy as put forward by ministers appears to be threefold; to target public expenditure, to restrict the discretion of local authorities over expenditure, and to redirect local economic develop-ment and town planning to business and Tory social policy objectives. The standard Heseltine or DOE questions when talking to local authorities about their regeneration schemes (such as City Challenge) are, 'Who are your private sector partners; and what is the tenure mix?'

If this analysis is correct, then urban policy in the 1990s may be as regressive for the inner cities as in the 1980s. Though Urban Partnerships hold out some hope of a shift in power and emphasis towards the inner cities, in practice, the DOE places a very tight rein on these agencies, and ensures that their aims are not, in fact, much different from urban policy in the 1980s. Moreover, though some shift in power may occur within some localities, it is taking place against a background of policy and legislation limiting local authority action, and, at the same time, with macro-economic measures which are arguably increasing poverty and disadvantage in the inner cities.

The struggle for inner city communities must continue unabated. One direction for this struggle will be to explore some of the contradictions of the new approach, and perhaps take advantage of them where possible. Particular elements could comprise the following:

1. Strategy can be simply a management tool, but it also can be interpreted as long-term planning for urban areas. This itself can imply a clearer statement of public objectives and hence some public direction of private sector investment. Unitary Development Plans and Strategic Guidance for the Metropolitan areas allow some aspects of this debate to take place, but because they are part of a legalistic planning structure, they do not provide an opportunity for an overall strategic debate about visions and priorities. Yet if it was possible to have a public debate about overall strategy for a region or a city this could be a very important new dimension to urban regeneration.
2. The rhetoric of community can be turned to the advantage of deprived

inner city communities, if residents make clear their own demands, and resist being marginalized in partnership arrangements. The danger of partnerships like City Challenge is that involving local people becomes a token. The corporate interests of the partnership, which are geared to spending City Challenge money, levering in the private sector, and creating a political profile for the local authority can easily take over.

3. The lack of proper evaluation of who benefits can be exposed by the community if they are able to undertake their own audits. These audits can show how public money is spent and whether community needs are being met. The results can be used in community campaigns and as a way of putting pressure on for more resources directed at meeting local needs. The dilemma is that communities rarely have the financial resources to undertake monitoring and analysis.

4. Prioritizing management objectives can focus on the quality and delivery of public services, as an integral part of urban regeneration. Public services are often divorced from urban regeneration because regeneration focuses on levering in property investment. But if improving public services for both new and existing communities becomes a principal aim of regeneration, this would amount to a radical reconceptualization.

5. The elevation of environmental aims and standards for the public and private sector can be turned by the community to focus on the environmental costs and benefits of development schemes. Very often the aim of achieving environmental quality is limited to the design of new buildings in regeneration areas like Cardiff Bay, Docklands or Liverpool. The quality of the environment for existing residents on surrounding council estates or the polluting effect of new roads, or disturbance from construction works, are all too often ignored.

The New Elites

One danger for urban partnerships in the UK is that they may evolve into US-style business oriented 'growth coalitions'. In Baltimore, Pittsburgh, and Cleveland for example, a network of major local institutions, government bodies, business, top politicians and community leaders form a committee for the renewal or regeneration of the city or city-region. Their purpose is to bring together powerful organizations in the city to promote urban regeneration opportunities, and target public and private sector funds to flagship development projects. Waterfront development of upmarket shops and penthouses and office developments in Baltimore, and Toronto and Pittsburgh owe much to this approach.

We have already noted that British government ministers often equate 'community' with a city-wide network of institutional common interests and speak approvingly of urban regeneration schemes in the USA. Networking between key figures and organizations has operated for many years in some regions of the UK. For example, in the North East, the Northern Development Agency, an agency made up of civic leaders and leading businessmen, performs this function. More recently, individual cities have formed city wide development committees to promote the city and coordinate action over regeneration. In Sheffield, for example, the Sheffield Economic Regeneration Committee consists of representatives from the public, private and voluntary sectors. In Leeds, the Leeds Initiative is a similar body with representatives from the Council, business, the UDC and the Training and Enterprise Council.

These agencies have not taken root so deeply, nor do they play the same high profile, overtly business led, role as those in the US and Canada. They are coordinating forums rather than implementation agencies, but there are some similarities. First, they are consensus creating bodies with a primary objective of making the city or region attractive to private investment, while at the same time presenting a politically acceptable face to central government. Controversial aspects of government policy on the inner cities, such as privatization of public services, cuts in public housing investment, or the undemocratic aspects of UDCs, are hidden by the aim of attracting private investment and support from government officials and Ministers. Problems of social regeneration with a severe impact on the lives of inner city residents, such as the condition of public housing or the quality of public services are not directly discussed because they may break the consensus.

Unless representatives on partnership committees are especially vigilant and bold, the partnership can create an illusion of common interests over the aims and means of urban regeneration. This is especially so when approaches are made to the DOE or to major investors. The real problems of conflict between partners, and the distress created by government policy on public services, are put to one side. There is a danger of a cover-up which marginalizes the acute needs of local communities.

An example of this is the attitude of the DOE to City Challenge. DOE guidelines on City Challenge Implementation Agencies, entitled 'Working Partnerships', recommend that, 'the expectation of the Partnership should be that of a joint venture between primarily three key partners of equal status, albeit with different roles' (DOE, 1992). These three partners are the public, private and voluntary and community sectors. In practice, judging by experiences of community groups in Lewisham and Birmingham City Challenge areas, for example, the status given by the local authority and DOE officials to the business partners is often higher than that given to community partners. What DOE officials want to be assured of by local authorities is that business partners are 'on board'.

Yet paradoxically, local business leaders in the partnership do not necessarily want to be put on a pedestal in this way. They are often more pragmatic and less ideological than ministers and senior DOE officials. In one case in Greenwich, business leaders on a partnership committee stressed that local people were the ones who should decide what happens to their area. 'We don't live here, you do', was one comment.

It will, therefore, be important to monitor implementation agencies set up under City Challenge to see what happens to the balance of power and the prioritization of interests. Other regeneration committees such as the Greenwich Waterfront Development Partnership with local authority, business and community representatives, and 'new style' UDCs, such as Birmingham Heartlands with a 50% local authority representation on the Board, will also need to be monitored.

Changing the Balance

The key issues for inner city communities, faced with partnerships and similar urban policy initiatives, are, firstly, can regeneration be democratized so that local people and their representatives have an equal say, and, secondly, can the objectives of regeneration be bent towards the needs of inner city communities, particularly where unemployment and social deprivation is high?

A major requirement for democratic accountability is to open up the partnership and Development Agency Boards to public scrutiny. The UDCs have not set a good example with their closed boards and confidential papers and proceedings. But the new partnerships can break out of this fear of open government and set a new standard of openness and accountability.

A further issue is representation. Partnership committees, like the Greenwich Waterfront Partnership, have three-way representation on the Board. In this case, the local authority has three seats, the business community has four seats, community groups four seats, town centre development agencies four seats and Thamesmead Town Trust one seat. The local authority representation is limited by legislation to 20% of the votes.

Such a spread of representation aims to be as equitable as possible, and with elections taking place for community representatives, it takes local accountability very seriously. In doing so, it is a model of how partnership can be forged. But it is early days and the partnership will have to work hard to maintain the trust of the community. Many local people in the inner cities take a sceptical and often hostile view of local authorities and government departments.

Another contentious problem is the perceived representativeness of community people on the Board. Very often community representatives do not fully represent the range of interests of the community. Typically, women and people from black and ethnic minorities, and young people are underrepresented. Forging a balanced structure for partnership boards is thus only half of the battle. Genuine representativeness matters just as much.

The second change needed is to give a higher priority to the social dimension of urban regeneration. Affordable housing, improved public services, better training, increased job opportunities and community facilities are often the elements of urban regeneration that are neglected, marginalized or simply starved of resources and attention compared with commercial and private housing objectives. Simply to give these social factors a real priority including creating an explicit linkage between commercial objectives and community objectives would be a huge leap forward.

Many schemes attempt to do this, but studies by the Centre for Local Economic Strategies (CLES) and others show that however worthwhile and innovative these schemes are in themselves, they represent only a tiny percentage of urban policy expenditure. For example, only about 5% of total expenditure on UDCs since 1981 can be classified as social expenditure (social housing training and community grants), the remainder being land and property related spending (CLES, 1992). Most urban funding goes into land reclamation and road building. More money goes into promotion and publicity for the UDCs in England and Wales than into their entire community spending programmes.

A radical, but essential, step would be to build public service level objectives into regeneration: to turn away from physical renewal on its own and bring in 'people-based' objectives particularly for existing residents living in public housing in and around the regeneration area. With local authorities playing a leading part in partnership, this in theory is possible. But local authorities and the new regeneration agencies must not only want to challenge the orthodoxy of physical regeneration but also be prepared to demand that resources are provided for balanced development.

Other issues, like crime, personal safety, health care and community transport, must also be built into both the definition and implementation of area-based regeneration. Improving safety on estates, in streets, in parks and play areas is regarded by local residents as just as important, if not more so, than attracting commercial development. But an even greater leap forward would be to expand local and central government main programme spending on housing, health, training and public services. There is no prospect that an urban programme can compensate for, or fill the gap created by, cuts in mainstream public services. At the same time, the property-based concept of economic development that has dominated urban regeneration for a decade must be reassessed. Other dimensions of economic development, particularly industrial investment, public service provision, and community enterprise must be brought in.

People-Based Regeneration

At the present time, regeneration still means to most people, and to the government, physical renewal. Property-led schemes dominate, and are continuing to do so in spite of the recession. There is little acceptance by government that there needs to be a change in strategy. Government believes the property market will eventually revive as part of the general recovery of the national economy. Thus, in Docklands, instead of looking for a new strategy that deals with the reality of recession and the over-provision of office space in London, the vision of the government and indeed the local authorities, is limited to 'saving' Canary Wharf.

Where community-led development is taking place up and down the country, it is often quite small and becomes marginalized compared with the prospect of enticing in large-scale commercial projects – usually regarded as the 'real' engine of urban regeneration. This is compounded because community-led developments such as training schemes, community enterprises, affordable housing or recreational facilities are non-profit making and are seen as a direct cost to the public purse.

For inner city communities to benefit from urban regeneration, government must drop its prejudices about local authorities and public services. And in order for working class communities in the inner cities to get anywhere near the centre of power and decision making, government, local authorities and business interests must be prepared to give away power and redirect resources. Crucially, government must also use urban regeneration as part of a broader strategy to reduce unemployment and poverty. At the moment, these are not the aims of regeneration. Unless they are, inner city deprivation under existing social and economic policies will get worse.

Local residents, and local authorities, will need to be highly organized and determined over a long period to win these battles. It can be done, though on a small scale, as community developments at Coin Street, Finsbury Park, and Spitalfields demonstrate. The burgeoning of 'Planning for Real' exercises where communities draw up detailed plans for their areas and then come up with schemes to implement the plans (for example in large council estates at Meadowell on Tyneside and Nechells in Birmingham) also show that local communities are demanding more control over their own environments and localities.

The depth of the 1990s property recession is itself a boost to grass-roots initiative because market forces cannot afford to develop sites and need to have public sector partners to get anything going. Communities can take advantage of the recession to press their claims for alternative forms of regeneration, and for real participation. Residents groups in London Docklands are attempting to do this following the vacuum left by the collapse of Canary Wharf.

Community campaigns are important, but increasingly community groups feel they need to produce practical schemes that demonstrate how local needs can be met. But where there are such community schemes, the problems of getting funding for community developments or of bending government programmes into community need are immense. Most community projects have found it very hard to get funding from either the public sector or from the banks for large scale community buildings, affordable housing or major enterprise or training initiatives.

Urban policy has changed its appearance and form since the 1980s. But little has changed for inner city residents. The plethora of new initiatives such as City Challenge and Partnership mean little to most people. Indeed, there is every danger that they will create a new stratum of urban committees that will not be representative of inner city communities, and will be unable to deliver significant benefits to those communities. At this stage, most of these committees do not constitute a 'development elite'. But as long as inner city communities are starved of resources and power, 'people-led regeneration' is as far away as ever.

The task of moving urban policy towards 'people based' objectives and mechanisms is immense. This is now the real challenge for the inner cities, far greater than building, or rescuing, a hundred Canary Wharfs.

12

URBAN DEVELOPMENT CORPORATIONS: POST-FORDISM IN ACTION OR FORDISM IN RETRENCHMENT?

Paul Burton and Mo O'Toole

Introduction

This final chapter attempts to build on the foundations laid in the preceding chapters to offer an account of the future directions that urban policy might take as we move towards the millennium. It begins with a brief consideration of the main factors that have driven urban policy over the last fifteen years and the particular role played by Urban Development Corporations (UDCs) as the policy flagship of the era. We then examine the effect that the UDCs have had on urban policy development during the 1980s and the 1990s, what trends they have initiated or intensified and what pressures they have responded to. In the third section we are concerned with the perspectives on the UDCs, the way in which the UDC story is now being told. Finally we will examine the continuity and discontinuities that prevail in current urban policy. It appears that UDCs have been relegated from the position of flagship to frigate in the hierarchy of urban initiatives. We question how the role of UDCs has changed, particularly in the light of City Challenge as (ostensibly) the new flagship. The chapter finishes by analysing the extent to which City Challenge and the Urban Regeneration Agency in particular as well as other policy vehicles are capable of meeting the enduring problems of urban policy. The question implicit in our analysis is how better equipped are we in the 1990s to tackle these problems and what if anything have we learned from the recent experimentation in the processes of citymaking.

What Has Driven Urban Policy over the Last Fifteen Years?

As Chapter 1 has noted, looking back over the last two decades, we can see a significant shift in the analysis of urban problems. In the 1960s the so-called 'rediscovery of poverty' led to the identification of pathologically inadequate local communities, caught up in self-sustaining cycles of deprivation. These communities were nevertheless seen to be susceptible to state intervention. Policy responses took the form mainly of positive discrimination measures which targeted small areas with additional resources, using such vehicles as the Urban Programme (administered then by the Home Office), Education Priority Areas annd General Improvement Areas. The consensus surrounding this approach began to break down through the work of the Community Development Projects, established in 1969, which developed a powerful critique of the scope of small scale experiments in social engineering. The Inner Areas Studies carried out in Liverpool, Birmingham and London during the early 1970s continued to shift the focus of attention onto the structural problems facing cities as they struggled to cope with rapid economic, social and demographic change, and fed directly into the White Paper *Policy for the Inner Cities* published in 1977.

The Inner Urban Areas Act of 1978 embodied this new analysis of urban problems and adopted a much broader approach by way of response. The traditional Urban Programme was recast under the control of the Department of the Environment and the resources at its disposal increased significantly from £35 million in 1978 to £165 million in 1980. The existence of multiple deprivation within many cities and conurbations was to be tackled by partnerships of central and local government in which main spending programmes would be 'bent' in the direction of the most deprived inner city areas. Alongside environmental and social improvements, the local economic base of each of the target areas would be strengthened through direct support to local firms as well as the provision of land and premises for new business development.

While this potted history emphasizes the development of analysis, understanding and awareness in policy change we should not forget the underlying political struggle. This struggle was (and continues to be) between the dispossessed minorities trapped within the 'inner city' and the representatives of the relatively privileged majority. In a sense it was an expression of the historic tension between the threats and promises of cities. The social, economic and political opportunities offered by urban life have long been contrasted with the threat of violence and social unrest associated with urban concentration (Keith and Rogers, 1991). In the second half of the twentieth century this contrast has been most apparent in the distinction between a suburban ideal and an inner city problem.

Nor should we forget the racial dimension of this struggle (Indian Workers' Association, 1987). Enoch Powell's 'rivers of blood' speech in 1969 was, however, as much of a precursor of the Urban Programme as academic analyses of poverty and we should remember David Donnison's remark that 'a riot makes a much bigger impact on government thinking than any amount of earnest and accurate research'. From across the Atlantic the American experience of serious civil disorder between 1964 and 1968 fuelled fears that British cities might suffer a similar fate (Sills, Taylor and Golding, 1988; MacGregor and Pimlott, 1990).

The conventional wisdom, expressed in the 1977 White Paper, characterized the inner city problem in the following terms. Economic restructuring in general and deindustrialization in particular led to a major reduction in manufacturing jobs, with little in the way of service sector replacement. Alongside this a serious skills gap opened up so that many inner city residents were unable to compete for any other job opportunities. Large areas of dereliction were created as investors sought out more attractive and profitable greenfield sites outside the conurbations, and this in turn made the inner areas

even less attractive to prospective developers. In this deteriorating environment many people who were able to chose to leave, again for more attractive
settings (including the new towns), leaving behind the poor, the old and
relatively recent migrants from former colonies. Local authorities were then
faced with a population requiring comparatively high levels of support but a
dwindling local tax base.

What Has Driven UDCs as the Flagship of Urban Policy?

It is important to remember that special agencies in the form of development
corporations have been an important feature of British urban policy delivery
for most of the postwar years. The new town programme relied on corporations
not just to assemble the necessary talent and expertise to put the programme
into effect, but to ensure the implementation of a national policy interest in the
face of anticipated local opposition (Thomas and Cresswell, 1973).

By the early 1970s the accelerated closure of the Port of London's upstream
operations, in what became known as Docklands, created enormous problems
of deindustrialization but also the opportunity for the wholesale redevelopment
of an area close to the heart of the capital. While there was intense debate
over the type of redevelopment needed (public or private sector housing,
manufacturing or new service sector employment and so on) attention also
focused on the most appropriate organization needed to take these plans
forward in the most effective manner.

The debate soon polarized into two main camps. On the one hand were the
proponents of a special development agency constituted along the same lines
as a new town development corporation, and on the other hand, were the
advocates of a partnership of existing local authorities. The development
corporation lobby stressed the need for additional powers of land acquisition
and a degree of insulation from local electoral politics. They pointed to the
inevitable rivalries and disputes that would arise in any grouping of existing
local authorities (five boroughs and the GLC) and argued strongly for a body
that could transcend these local pressures and act in the national interest. The
riparian boroughs and the GLC took a more localist line and pressed for a
statutory joint committee which would reflect the interests and aspirations of
East Enders in particular and Londoners in general. Local needs and local
accountability therefore underpinned this approach.

The establishment of the Docklands Joint Committee in 1974 represented an
acceptance of the localist case, although it must be said that the pragmatism of
Geoffrey Rippon (Secretary of State for the Environment at the time) was
probably more significant than the balance of the political argument. When the
Conservative government took office in 1979, the new Secretary of State for
the Environment, Michael Heseltine, launched a review of the policy measures
inherited from his predecessors. While accepting that the partnerships established
under the new Urban Programme had a continuing role to play in the
regeneration of most inner city areas, he took a different view in relation to
London and Merseyside, highlighting the practical capacities of special
agencies, their single-mindedness and market orientation, *vis-à-vis* groupings of
local authorities. It is an argument that was deployed during the lengthy

inquiry into the establishment of the London Docklands Development Corporation (LDDC) carried out by a Select Committee of the House of Lords and subsequently during debates over the extension of UDCs to other parts of the country.

But there are at least two other arguments that can be used to explain the emergence of UDCs and their position as flagships of Conservative urban policy. The first is party political and the second may be termed structural. Party political arguments begin with the fact of thirteen years of Conservative government and their mission, *inter alia*, to eradicate socialism at national and local levels. Although, as we noted above, Michael Heseltine was prepared to accept many elements of urban policy which flowed from Labour's 1977 White Paper he was also keen to bypass Labour-controlled authorities in London and Liverpool. Indeed he went so far as to say in the course of a Commons debate on UDCs that, 'It was not red tape and inaction, but pure, prejudiced socialism that was broken through by the LDDC' (Heseltine, M. 1982).

Any careful analysis of the actual plans and operations of the Docklands Joint Committee (DJC, the predecessor of the LDDC) reveals the fallacy of Heseltine's accusation, but this is not to disregard entirely the significance of an anti-Labour strand to Conservative urban policy development. When we take into account the concerted attack on the powers and autonomy of local authorities, especially those controlled by Labour administrations, then we can see a party political agenda. Solesbury (1987) however notes that the breakdown in consensus over the nature of urban problems in the late 1980s was driven as much by an assortment of clerics, academics, business groupings and local authority associations as it was by the main political parties, who remained strangely silent.

UDCs: The Results

There is little doubt that the UDCs have made a significant impact on the recent implementation of urban regeneration policy. It is more problematic to disentangle their precise influence in the 'patchwork quilt' which now delivers this policy. We look at five themes in an attempt to do so; the interaction between the UDC and macro-economic processes, policy styles and the UDCs, the UDC and place marketing, alliances to promote cities, and, finally, the development process. There are two points to bear in mind when attempting to evaluate the UDCs long-term contribution to urban policy making. The first is that the overview comprises evidence gathered from a range of reports that reflect diverse opinions; to date no comprehensive survey of UDCs has been published. The second lies in the specificity of the examples; it is difficult to draw a general lesson from the UDCs, either as a success or as a failure.

Macroeconomic Cycles and the UDCs

It is not within the scope of this chapter to probe the current debate on the nature of macro-economic cycles, but one cannot enter into a discussion of the latter years of UDC policy without recognizing the influence of such cycles on Western economies, though there is discussion as to their length and their precise impact (Elliot, 1992). However they are defined, it would seem that a combination of the cycles inherent in the development process, together with the longer and deeper movements in the global economy, are profoundly threatening to the transient, property- and consumption-led development corporations. A short life span, and a property-dependent programme, have conspired to increase the vulnerability of the UDCs to the negative effects of such fluctuations (Healey et al, 1992). The latest cycle, resulting in a vicious recession, has had a manifold impact on the plans of UDCs, but two outcomes are striking. In the short term, development and land sales have massively declined. Even where significant development has taken place, such as Trafford Park in Manchester, or, in the Newcastle Business Park of Tyne and Wear's Urban Development Authority (UDA), UDCs have failed to buck the overall downward trend in the development market. Law (1989) has described how the oversupply in office space in Trafford is aggravated by cycles. These have ultimately restructured plans which the Trafford Park Development Corporation had prepared for their flagship development.

As the pace of development has slowed, and capital projects have encountered difficulty, so the Corporations have moved in new directions. There has been an increasing emphasis upon training and community development activity. The Black Country Development Corporation has invested heavily in under-fives provision and creche development (BCDC, Annual Report, 1990). Brownill (Ch. 3) has described the increasing community and training activity which LDDC undertook as the decade moved to a close. Simultaneously, UDCs have become more reliant on public sector finance as a primary source of funding, leverage ratios have declined, and grant-in-aid has peaked way above original estimates. For instance, since 1987, UDCs have received £2 billion of grant-in-aid, with the largest proportion pouring into the LDDC (Independent 25 June 1992).

It would appear that the supply-side approach of the new regeneration strategies are significantly more speculative than the Keynesian strategies which predated them. But are the Corporations any better equipped to deal with the vicissitudes of the macro-economic environment than local government planning or economic development departments? In the context of inter-urban competition, the UDCs have influenced the capacity of the locality to engage in capital capturing activities. Returning to Trafford, the UDC has been pivotal in working to attract the Olympic Games (interview Trafford Park, 1989). Similarly the repackaging of cities in which UDCs have engaged with vigour has prompted a wider acceptance of an entrepreneurial approach to economic development (Bianchini et al, 1988).

But UDCs have been unable to assist cities to engage in strategic responses to downturns in the market. Interurban competition relies on winners and losers; as the stakes have been raised in global competition so the strategies have become even more high risk and the losses more significant. UDCs have gamely put in place strategies to win, but have been less than successful in dealing with the increasing pace of competition and the unsuccessful spatial and social projects that are bound up with this competition.

Policy Styles and the UDCs

Perhaps most conspicuously the UDCs have been successful in popularizing a way of doing things. The process of regeneration, indeed of city governance, now corresponds to a model promoted by the UDC. Partnerships, fast tracking and streamlining are all part of the public sector entrepreneurial kitbag, although they do coexist with more traditional professionalized approaches to urban regeneration. The many unprompted reorganizations that have taken place alongside more radical legislative change in local government departments are a testament to the hegemonic hold that the managerial culture of the UDC has over the public sector (Stoker, 1990).

Yet the model does not really correspond to the reality. Kirklees is one of many authorities to have undertaken a reorganization which introduces similar executive decision-making structures to those of the UDC. UDCs however remain predominantly reliant on the existing organizational networks of their cities. Meegan in this volume has emphasized MDC's adherence to the Structure and Local Plans of Greater Merseyside. Tyne and Wear UDC (TWDC) have been very aware of the effect that local political networks have had on their plans and have sought to accommodate the wishes of the established regional political hierachy within the proposals for their flagship developments.

A quick response to developer interest was an essential part of the rationale for establishing UDCs and it would indeed appear that they have more room for manoeuvre in development decisions than local authority planning departments. But, as UDCs work within the present planning framework, they have inevitably been tied up with public inquiries and lengthy consultation processes such as in the Bristol Spine Road or the Tyne and Wear East Quayside projects. Both inquiries spread over a two year period, pushing up costs and prompting serious development problems because of changes in the market.

Perhaps the most notable feature of the UDCs decision-making process is the extent to which they are now mimicking old-style local authority procedures in the field of inner city policy. This is particularly true of their community development work. Corporations have found it necessary, and many have found it desirable, to develop sophisticated consultation networks to appease local hostility or accommodate local desires. Residents monitoring panels at Tyne and Wear are one such example of this process of consultation (TWDC, 1991). There have therefore been some unexpected outcomes of this process. It has breathed new life into the debate on the nature of democracy within planning. The level of dissatisfaction with local authority procedures in some areas appears no greater than discontent around UDC procedures. To some extent the presence of the UDC has allowed us to define what the planning processes should be about, particularly in the case of Docklands. The more established bureaucratic and community networks and their agendas have remained, altered but not eradicated. In most cities, a mutual accommodation has been negotiated, in many as a result of a recognition that both styles of regeneration have merit. This recognition is explicit in City Challenge where submissions that do not have evidence of a true partnership are discarded by the DOE (DOE, 1991).

Place Marketing

Place marketing is now firmly embedded in the vocabulary of urban regeneration (for a fuller account see Wilkinson, 1992). It is used as a technique by economic development and inward investment strategists to create or illustrate the niche in the world of interurban competition which their city occupies. The marketing of cities in the context of global capital movements has become an essential prerequisite to the economic resurgence of the locality. But how does place marketing relate to the UDC? UDCs have popularized the repackaging of declining industrial cities, peripheral regions and specific sites within cities. At one end of the spectrum Canary Wharf signifies the new uses for London's East End; other examples litter the UDAs, the business sites on redundant arms factories and shipbuilding yards in Tyne and Wear, the wharfside developments at Trafford Park and elsewhere, and the museums and galleries of Merseyside. But physical developments in themselves do not amount to a marketing strategy. What UDCs have done is to consolidate and, in some places, create an ethos of marketing place.

The UDC's approach has converged with that of the locality in the quest for new jobs and new populations. This has meant establishing a common sales pitch for local elites, it has required that urban infrastructure fit the new needs of the area and it has meant that training strategies should be similarly matched. Above all, it has required good publicity, whether this be in the form of glossy brochures or in undertaking damage limitation exercises when bad publicity visits the area in the form of a riot or a disturbance. New campaigns have emerged from the pens of specialized consultants and new alliances or partnerships head the promotions. Without the UDC, UDC-type processes such as place marketing would have taken much longer to ingrain itself on the consciousness of the city. While UDCs have, therefore, been unable to live up to the expectation of catalysing wholesale regeneration, they have provided a demonstration of the implements needed to sell cities. It is their separation from the local democratic process which has allowed them to do this. But, as we shall argue in our conclusion, it is that same separation which may be the undoing of their strategies.

Public–Private Sector Partnerships

A plethora of new alliances have been forged during the decade of the UDCs. In most cities the UDC represents one part of a matrix of overlapping elites and organizational, commercial and professional interests. Frequently, the board members rotate around new institutions having sprung from established ones. UDCs have also become synonymous with the new type of partnership that now presides over what was previously public policy making in a new configuration of roles and responsibilities.

But is the UDC integral to the formation of the new alliances that are being struck up in the interest of reclaiming cities and city regions? A number of examples suggest not. For instance, the Sheffield Economic Regeneration Committee was originally established to pre-empt a development corporation. In other areas, such as Manchester and Liverpool, the UDC forum was but one element of the decision-making jigsaw. In Birmingham most notoriously,

but countless other examples exist, partnerships thrive without UDC intervention in any form, though it must be acknowledged in this latter example
that resistance to the imposition of a UDC acted as a catalyst for the creation
of the Heartlands project.

Despite this almost intangible relationship between UDCs and new alliances
it does appear that the UDC has popularized the notion of blurring the
divisions between public and private sectors that can result in the success of
regeneration strategies. The UDC represents only one form of partnership, but
it has assumed a flagship role in promoting the concept. What is common to
both partnerships and to UDCs is an apparent credibility, premised on three
things; a privatized decision-making environment, the involvement of the
private sector in policy formulation rather than simply being the instruments of
implementation and the relegation of the respective local authorities in the
development arena.

The Development Process

The term regeneration has produced much argument, and, for many, it suggests
a brief beyond physical redevelopment (CLES, 1990b; Lawless, 1991). Within
this broader meaning, UDCs have failed to produce long-term regeneration in
terms of jobs and infrastructure. But physical development has taken place,
and in many environments where it previously would have been unthinkable.
The problem about these developments is that they are not necessarily
matched to the requirements of the immediate locality, even if they are
suitable for the long-term redevelopment of the area.

The dispute between TWDC and Shepards, a local scrapdealer· in the east
end of Newcastle, serves to illustrate this point. TWDC have been diligent in
their sensitivity to housing needs for social purposes. But in siting an executive
housing development at St. Peter's Basin, a site overlooked by a Shephards
scrap metal mountain, we see the mismatch of needs that can occur in UDAs –
developers and promoters of new uses for derelict areas, and local employers
and employees who engage in traditional uses on the sites. There are, of
course, more significant examples all of which illustrate the chasm between
necessity and aesthetics, between profit and social justice which urban policy
seems to underscore. More importantly, especially in relation to infrastructure,
they show how the fragmentation of the institutions involved in regeneration
has resulted in less than satisfactory responses to a city wide or a regional
planning strategies.

Securing leverage was seen originally as a means to capture private investment
at the same time as limiting public expenditure. Alas, as reports have shown
(*Independent* 21 June 1992) leverage ratios are strikingly uneven and universally
disappointing. The built environments of UDAs remain persistently dependent
on public finance. The UDCs have been, in effect, a tacit agreement to redirect
and repackage development expenditure between central government and the
development industry.

Perspectives: What Has Really Happened?

So far, we have looked at how we arrived at the UDCs and the key issues to have emerged from them as we have progressed through the quagmire of Thatcherite urban policy. But it is equally important to look at the range of views that now interpret the UDCs and how they might usefully serve us in sorting out where we go next in inner city policy. There are perhaps as many perspectives on what UDCs are about as perceptions on what they have achieved. Although we have categorized them within five frameworks which encompass the thrust of UDC experiment, we recognize that they are not discrete agendas, that there is in fact considerable overlap. Nevertheless it is valuable to distinguish between the key perspectives as they begin to draw a distinctively post-Fordist view of the process of urban governance and regeneration.

The new right has spawned two elements within the UDC agenda, the limitation of public sector bureaucracies alongside an unfettered property market. Although the left, and certainly the left in local government, has perceived the UDC firmly within the boundaries of this philosophy there has always been an ambiguity within central government circles. The criticisms emerging from The Adam Smith Institute, among others, have had a significant impact on the post-Thatcher impasse in UDC policy (Adam Smith Institute, 1991). The free market approach to urban regeneration, pragmatically espoused by Margaret Thatcher and Nicholas Ridley, considered the UDC to be an instrument that would disentangle bureaucracy from the urban landmarket. The critique which subsequently developed and which has, in part, been directed at that other proponent of UDC policy, Michael Heseltine, suggests that the UDCs have gone 'native', that they now represent the worst element of interference in the market place and that they have become a captive of the public sector.

This is extremely pertinent to studies of locality. There is a good deal of evidence to suggest that UDCs have gone 'native' in many of the cities in which they have been located. They meet regularly in joint public sector forums, their decisions have been in line with other public sector organizations in many localities. The extent of their conversion to local values varies; Bristol, for instance, representing a striking example of the failure to establish a trusting relationship and joint working practices. But, in other sub-regions, like Tyne and Wear, or in cities like Sheffield, board member networks, built up through sectoral and historical relationships, ensure a greater coherence with the whole. In other areas traditions of working amongst UDC personnel have the same effect. But ultimately the Corporations are bound by their remit to regenerate an area, and in turn very much subject to the views of the Secretary of State and their Board on what the appropriate method of regeneration might be. This has often resulted in conflict between the Corporation and established interests already involved in the UDAs over the preferred uses for development sites.

In sketching some suggestions as to why the new right should engage in this critique we are also challenging the critics of the left who see the process of the imposition of UDCs as a one-dimensional inorganic process. The UDCs have ensured that we can no longer underestimate the power of locality as a structured force of resistance to a nationally imposed policy. Locality, working through institutional and culture alliances, is so powerful that it would require more than the central resource and corporate plan controls that have been exercised by central government.

The second critique of some importance is that of the democratic pluralist. At one level, this view is most clearly espoused by the Audit Commission or the House of Commons Select Committee on Employment (NAO, 1989). But there are equally cogent arguments ranged against the UDCs by both academics and local government representatives (Batley, 1989; CLES, 1990b, 1992; Imrie and Thomas, 1992). The democratic pluralist critique hinges on the definition of regeneration, and upon arguments about accountability in the planning process. It argues, on the one hand, that efficiency, effectiveness and economy, or value for money, should be indicative of policy success, and, on the other hand, that a commitment to quality and accountability can facilitate such success. Equally, it sees local government as being equal to the task of regeneration if given similar resources with which to work. Whereas the new right theorist views the UDC as an instrument of the market, the democratic pluralist sees it as a mechanism to deal with market failure.

The democratic pluralist interpretation is also significant in our third strand, the local government view. This has its roots in the tension between central and local government. Over the decade the increasingly hostile and polarized stance of these protagonists spawned a number of competing, and sometimes overlapping, views within a central–local state framework. There has been a stream of criticism emanating from local government associations, local councillors and opposition members in Parliament since the introduction of the UDCs, asserting the potential damage in local–central relations. But the local government agenda, which was profoundly party political, also had an important intellectual backdrop. These range from the views of social theorists, such as Saunders and others, who developed the dual state thesis, distinguishing theoretically between the central and local elements in state intervention processes and identifying UDCs as examples of local corporatism (Cawson, 1988 and Saunders, 1988), or Batley (1989), who asserted that they were examples of central corporatism operating locally.

There is considerable continuity between the views of the democratic pluralist, and those of the defenders of local government in the planning process. But the local government perspective is clearly committed to the appropriateness of an evolving local and accountable structure, a structure not unlike that which co-exists with the development corporation but is, they would argue, decidedly more neutral.

The community and labourist perspective achieved its nadir during the mid 1980s. It is a view that is rooted in communities who continue to struggle against the demise of the manufacturing economy and the Keynesian management systems associated with that economic paradigm. The production processes which mark the era of Fordism were accompanied, it has been argued, by associated modes of social and cultural development. While the front line of resistance to the dramatic restructuring has taken place within those industries, there has been corresponding resistance within communities. These communities and their cultures have remained somewhat stubborn in the face of post-Fordist and post-modern renewal and within the context of a democratic planning process they have utilized both institutional and non-institutionalized forms of protest. The culture is influenced by a public sector that is local and accountable or at least if not accountable, intelligible to local constituents. The criticisms, of CLES (1990b), and of Byrne (Ch. 6), reflect this. They are not alone, as one northern MP recently commented:

> *Effectively we are paying through the nose for a policy that has done nothing to regenerate Britain's manufacturing base ... The overall effect is to concentrate resources on a few flagship projects ... while the manufacturing regions go to the wall.*

(Independent 16 July 1992)

UDCs were not established to regenerate the manufacturing base, nor would they in themselves be capable of this or a suitable vehicle for it. What is interesting about this view and the communities who hold it is the extent to which they have been able to secure progressive gains from the development corporations.

Finally there is a more all encompassing critique that places the UDC firmly within the debate on Fordism and post-Fordism, and correspondingly modernism and post-modernism. Within this field there is argument about how completely one should embrace the notion of post-Fordism (Amin and Robins, 1991) and there are nuances amongst those who broadly agree, but we would argue strongly that the views of three authors, Meyer (1991), Harvey (1989c) and Stoker (1991), have captured the mechanisms of transformation in Western cities and in doing so have revealed and contextualized the work of UDCs more instructively than anybody else. Our synthesis of their work is perhaps a little vulgar but they broadly conceive of UDC mechanisms as being part of a complex power struggle for control of the new urban governance; they are about an agenda for change, about managerialism versus entrepreneurialism and they are about a transformation in rules and values on which a new stage in capitalist development is predicated (Harvey, 1989a).

Whilst Harvey's emphasis has always been the spatial dimension of urban policy development, Meyer (1991) and Stoker (1991) add to his analysis by concentrating on other imperatives. Meyer's conception of the dual city explains the interrelationship between the idealized city of the UDCs publicity brochures and that of the urban underclass eschewed by the mainstream, as both a precondition of a post-Fordist agenda and a potential for progressive struggles within the arena of the state (Meyer, 1991). Stoker, like Meyer, has utilized the regulation approach (Aglietta, 1982) to analyse the transformation in urban governance which the UDCs represent. He is equivocal about how far we have progressed into a post-Fordist regime but he does view the state as providing the necessary institutional backdrop, a regime of regulation for the transition to a more successful mode of accumulation. He sees the vehicle of urban governance as developing three characteristics to deal with the transformation: firstly it internalizes the methods of production, operating service delivery and policy development in accordance with the dominant mode of production; secondly, that both left and right have evolved strategies for dealing with the transition and that this makes the decision arena a live and active one where disputation, shifting ground and constant repositioning take place; finally, he argues that the inner city package did not have any coherence until the post-election period of 1987 and then the coherence was in the form of marketing and rhetoric rather than in substantive policymaking (Stoker, 1989).

When used to analyse the changing nature of UDCs, and the mounting problems they now face, this analytical stance is fruitful. UDCs have been forced to compromise on their initial position. They have begun to realize that social, as well as physical, infrastructure is needed for effective regeneration; they have found that public involvement (if not outright accountability) tends to facilitate better quality proposals as well as defusing local political unrest; and they have found that local needs cannot be ignored or left to the alleged trickle down of benefits from an unfettered market. As the property market has moved from boom to bust in the 1990s the tensions which prompted this drift have become even more exposed, to the point that UDCs now seem likely to be squeezed between the return to partnership embodied in City Challenge and the single-minded approach of the proposed new Urban Regeneration Agency (URA).

Whither Urban Policy?

The future of the UDCs is a matter of interesting and somewhat tentative speculation. Overall, we have suggested that they have had a more significant ideological, and organizational, impact than in the matters of physical regeneration and inner city redevelopment. There was much speculation in the late 1980s about their potential as a post-modernist spearhead in a post-Fordist society, yet post-modernism has taken a severe critical denting in recent times while the UDCs are now being challenged by new policy initiatives, particularly City Challenges and the URA. In this section we will look at what may happen and why these new initiatives have emerged before finally going on to say what we believe needs to happen in urban policy in Britain in the 1990s.

The urban policy debate of the 1980s consisted of five main questions: whether to concentrate on stimulating growth or access to and the distribution of the benefits of growth; whether to focus on problems or on opportunities; whether to invest in people or in places; whether to rely on market or bureaucratic/political means to effect change; and whether to use agents or develop partnerships for the delivery of policy (Solesbury, 1987). To a great extent, the UDC approach involved a clear answer to each of these questions – investment in places by centrally-appointed agents would stimulate markets and lead to self-sustaining growth, the benefits of which would eventually trickle down to everyone. City Challenge marks a break with this tradition in many if not all respects. All the areas invited to submit bids are deemed to be experiencing a wide range of serious problems, but their proposals must show how they plan to grasp local opportunities for regeneration. Indigenous economic growth remains an important goal but great weight is now given to the development of mechanisms which links these new opportunities to local people.

Investment in human resources – not just in skills training for employment, but in the more nebulous notion of 'capacity building' – is now well established, alongside investment in physical infrastructure. The development of effective partnership arrangements is now given more attention than ever before, with proposals scrutinized rigorously for signs of genuine rather than superficial partnerships. Finally, market mechanisms have been given most prominence in the competitive element of the whole challenge process. Areas are now forced to compete openly for scarce resources and there is some evidence that this has sharpened up the preparation of regeneration strategies following a period in which the urban programme management initiative had succeeded in stifling much local initiative. City Challenge, therefore, reflects a shift in symbolic acronym – from the three Es (efficiency, economy and effectiveness) of the 1980s to the three Cs of the 1990s (co-operation, concentration and competition) (DOE, 1992).

Solesbury (1987) identified two additional issues in the urban policy debate of the late 1980s. The first was whether urban problems would continue to be addressed directly or tangentially through other policy measures, and the second concerned the criteria that would be used in making the inevitable choices between the competing claims of different urban areas. The second of these can be seen to have been 'resolved' through the competitive process of City Challenge. Areas or authorities are forced to play a game in which there will be a limited number of winners. The option of deciding not to play exists in principle but in practice no one has yet taken that step. In fact, during the first round of bidding, a handful of authorities threw their stake money onto the table without receiving an invitation!

The issue of whether urban problems will continue to be tackled through explicit, dedicated, urban policy measures remains somewhat clouded. The launch of Action for Cities in 1987 was widely interpreted as little more than an exercise in repackaging, pulling together a battery of existing policies and programmes into a glossy document with a preface by the Prime Minister. Academic commentators revelled in the opportunity to apply the critique of 'symbolic policy' to this, adding a twist to Mrs Thatcher's oft-quoted remark, 'We must do something about those inner cities', so that it became, 'We must appear to be doing something but it doesn't really matter what'. Moreover, since the early 1980s a plethora of developments had been taking place on the broader policy stage which impinged, positively and negatively, on the quality of life and opportunities in the inner cities. The establishment of Training and Enterprise Councils (TECs) as relatively autonomous agents of labour market planning, the introduction of local management in schools, compulsory competitive tendering in the provision of local services and the sale of council houses illustrate the diversity of influential non-inner city policies.

At the time of writing (summer 1992) the future of an explicit, dedicated policy for the inner cities is very uncertain. A recent report from the Policy Studies Institute (PSI) has demonstrated the failure of 15 years of intervention in closing the gap between inner city areas and the rest of the country; civil disorder has erupted in many towns and cities, often in areas that have been targeted with special measures; the outer estates are now seen as suffering similar problems to inner areas; and the notion of an 'underclass' is used extensively to describe the source and cause of the most pressing social problems of the day.

Ministers appear to be casting around for something new with which to tackle the inner city problem and so far have come up with plans for a new

URA. This seems little more than a peripatetic development corporation designed to avoid the problem of getting bogged down, expensively, in certain locations. It represents a return to the single-mindedness thought so important when UDCs were first launched, the (re)creation of a specialist property development machine following the diversification of activities seen in the second and third generation UDCs.

What does all this tell us about the tractability of urban or inner city problems and the capacity of the state to intervene effectively? Drawing again on the lessons of the new towns we can say that large-scale redevelopment schemes require a lot of time, money, expertise, careful planning, political will and luck if they are to succeed. More ambitious aspirations to achieve comprehensive social and economic regeneration require the same mix but on a greater scale. Perhaps it is a deep seated recognition of our relative ignorance of the underlying dynamics of urban change and development which makes us all susceptible to the attraction of quick fixes. The more we criticize existing measures the more we increase the pressure to produce dramatically better alternatives. And these must be seen to work not over a period of decades but within the lifetime of parliaments.

We must begin to recognize the scope for effective urban policy measures in the context of broader social and economic change. This means making realistic assessments of the likely impact of spending programmes measured in tens of millions of pounds and doing this in comparison with the total budgets of local authorities and other agencies. It means examining the potential of local job creation programmes in comparison with the scale of job growth (or loss) in the economy at large. It means assessing the scope for countering discrimination in inner city labour markets against a wider backdrop of racism, sexism and other forms of discrimination. The UDCs have only served to emphasize these needs, but they have also illustrated the necessity of other policy mechanisms; for instance, the importance of an integrated strategic plan for the urban region, linking social and economic considerations as well as the polarized populations who now inhabit the same territory.

Flexibility in programme development based upon clearly developed and understood entrance and exit strategies should also be built into all urban initiatives. This would serve to improve continuity for local populations and assist in their capacity building process. Above all, local government should be able to capitalize on this enforced reorganization to perform a new and crucial role in inner city policy, one which can accommodate UDCs and City Challenges. This would be to co-ordinate the now disparate functionaries of the urban infrastructure, TECs, locally managed schools, contracted out services and Housing Action Trusts (HATS), within a framework that is strategically linked and operationally consistent.

REFERENCES

Aglietta, M. (1982) World capitalism in the eighties. *New Left Review* 137, pp. 5–42.

Agnew, J. and Duncan, J.S. (eds.) (1989) *The Power of Place: Bringing Together Geographical and Sociological Imaginations.* Unwin Hyman, Boston.

Alterman, R. (1988) Developer obligations for public services, American Style. Paper presented at Land and Property Development Processes Seminar, Newcastle University, September 22–24.

Ambrose, P. (1986) *Whatever Happened to Planning?* Methuen, London.

Amin, A. and Robins, K. (1991) The re-emergence of regional economies? The mythical geography of flexible accumulation. *Environment and Planning D: Society and Space*, 8, 1, pp. 7–34.

Anderson, J. (ed.) (1983) *Redundant Spaces in Cities and Regions.* Academic Press, London.

Anderson, J. (1991) Business associations and the decentralization of penury: functional groups and territorial interests. *Governance*, 4, 1, pp. 67–93.

Anon (1992) Charter for training. *Making Waves in the Bay*, March, p. 1.

Askew J. (1991) Partnership – a refusal to be marginalised. *Local Government Chronicle* Supplement, February, pp. 16–18.

Association of London Authorities and Docklands Consultative Committee (1991) *How the Cake Was Cut.* ALA, London.

Association of Metropolitan Authorities (1986) *Programme for Partnership: an Urban Policy Statement.* AMA, London.

Atkinson, M. and Coleman, W. (1992) Policy networks, policy communities, and the problems of governance. *Governance*, 5, 2, pp. 154–180.

Audit Commission (1989) *Urban Regeneration and Economic Development: the Local Government Dimension, London.* HMSO, London.

Barber, A. (1992) BCDC aims high for homes target. *Birmingham Post*, 8 August 1992, p. 7.

Barnekov, T. *et al* (1990) *US Experience in Evaluating Urban Regeneration.* Department of the Environment, London.

Batley, R. (1989) London Docklands: an analysis of power relations between UDCs and Local Government. *Public Administration*, 67, 2, pp. 167–187.

Bell, D. (1992) Metro cash delay blow. *Birmingham Evening Mail*, 24 July 1992, p. 19.

Bennett, R. and Krebs, G. (1991) *Local Economic Development: Public–Private Partnerships.* Belhaven, London.

Bennington, J. (1986) Local economic strategies: paradigms for a planned economy? *Local Economy*, 1, 1, pp. 7–24.

Bianchini, F., Dawson, J. and Evans, R. (1988) Re-imagining the City, unpublished paper available from Mo O'Toole, SAUS, University of Bristol.

Birmingham Evening Mail (1992) Coal plan go-ahead. 22 May 1992, p. 17.

Birmingham Post (1991) Renewal will take 35 years – expert. 11 January 1991, p. 6.

Black Country Development Corporation (1989) *Corporate Plan 1989*. BCDC, Birmingham.

Black Country Development Corporation (1990) *Corporate Plan 1990*. BCDC, Birmingham.

Black Country Development Corporation (1991a) *Annual Report, 1990–91*. BCDC, Birmingham.

Black Country Development Corporation (1991b) *Corporate Plan Summary 1991*. BCDC, Birmingham.

Blunkett, D. and Jackson, K. (1987) *Democracy in Crisis: The Town Halls Respond*. The Hogarth Press, London.

Boddy, M., Lovering, J. and Bassett, K. (1986) *Sunbelt City? A Study of Economic Change in Britain's Growth Corridor*. Clarendon Press, Oxford.

Boyle, R. (1987) The price of partnership. Paper presented to International Housing Conference, 'City Renewal Through Partnership', 27 August 1987.

Boyle, R. (1988) Private sector urban regeneration: the Scottish experience. In: Parkinson, M., Foley, B. and Judd, D. (eds.) *Regenerating the Cities: the UK Crisis and the US Experience*. Manchester University Press, Manchester, pp. 74–93.

Boyle, R. (1989) Partnership in practice: an assessment of public–private collaboration in urban regeneration – a case study of Glasgow Action. *Local Government Studies*, 15, pp. 17–28.

Braddon, D., Kendry, A., Cullen, P. and Dowdall, P. (1991) The Impact of Reduced Military Expenditure on the Economy of South West England, Final Report. Bristol City Council, Bristol.

Brayshaw, P. (1990) Urban Development Corporations and Enterprise Boards revisited: a survey of current policies and practice. *Local Economy*, 5, 3, pp. 214–224.

Brindley, T., Rydin, Y. and Stoker, G. (1989) *Remaking Planning*. Unwin Hyman, London.

Bristol City Council (1989a) *Bristol Development Corporation Strategy: A Vision for Bristol*. Report of the City Planning Officer to the Planning and Traffic Committee, BCC, Bristol.

Bristol City Council (1989b) *Bristol Urban Development Corporation*. Report of the City Planning Officer to the Planning and Traffic Committee, BCC, Bristol.

Bristol City Council (1989c) *Bristol Development Corporation: Draft Code of Consultation*. Report of the City Planning Officer to the Planning and Traffic Committee. BCC, Bristol.

Bristol City Council/University of Bristol/Confederation of Shipbuilding and Engineering Unions (1989) *BAe in Bristol. What Future?* BCC, Bristol.

Bristol Development Corporation (1989a) *The Vision for Bristol*. BDC, Bristol.

Bristol Development Corporation (1989b) *The Corporate Plan*. BDC, Bristol.

Bristol Development Corporation (1990a) *Development Strategy*. BDC, Bristol.

Bristol Development Corporation (1990b) *Temple Meads/Kingsley Village Area Framework*. BDC, Bristol.

Bristol Development Corporation (1990c) *Report on Public Consultation*. BDC, Bristol.

Bristol Development Corporation (1991) *Central Development Area Framework*. BDC, Bristol.

Bristol Evening Post (1988) Rags to riches in three years. 1 January 1988.

Bristol Evening Post (1991) Double rap over inner city delay. 3 March 1991.

Brookes, J. (1989) Cardiff Bay renewal strategy – another hole in the democratic system. *The Planner* 76(1), pp. 38–40.

Brownill, S. (1988) The People's Plan for the Royal Docks; some contradictions in popular planning. *Planning Practice and Research* No. 4, pp. 15–21.

Brownill, S. (1990) *Developing London's Docklands; Another Great Planning Disaster?* Paul Chapman Publishing, London.

Brownill, S. (1991) Beyond Dichotomies. Paper presented to AESOP Conference, Oxford, July 1991.

Burgess, J. and Wood P. (1988) Decoding Docklands: place advertising and decision-making strategies of the small firm, in Ayles, V. and Smith, D. (eds.) *Qualitative Methods in Human Geography*, Polity, London.

Burton, P. (1986) Planning theory and public policy: an analysis of policies for London's Docklands. Unpublished PhD thesis. School for Advanced Urban Studies, University of Bristol, Bristol.

Byrne, D. (1989) *Beyond the Inner City*. Open University Press, Milton Keynes.

Byrne, D. (1992) The city. In: Cloke, P. (ed.) *Policy and Change in Thatcher's Britain*. Pergamon, Oxford.

Cabinet Office (1988) *Action For Cities*. Cabinet Office, London.

Cambridge Econometrics (1988) *Regional Economic Prospects*. Cambridge Econometrics, Cambridge.

Cameron, G. (1990) First stages in urban policy evaluation in the United Kingdom. *Urban Studies*, 27(4), pp. 475–495.

Campbell, M. (1990) Introduction. In *Local Economic Policy*. Cassell, London.

Cardiff Bay Development Corporation (1988) *Cardiff Bay Regeneration Strategy – The Summary*. CBDC, Cardiff.

Cardiff Bay Development Corporation (1990a) *Cardiff Bay – The Opportunity*. CBDC, Cardiff.

Cardiff Bay Development Corporation (1990b) *Building a Quality Environment*. CBDC, Cardiff.

Cardiff Bay Development Corporation (1991–92) *Annual Report*. CBDC, Cardiff.

Cardiff City Council (1984) *Statistical Atlas*. City Planning and Development Department. CCC, Cardiff.

Cardiff City Council (1988) *Cardiff Bay Regeneration Strategy: the City Council's Response*. CCC, Cardiff.

Carley, M. (1991) Business in urban regeneration partnerships: a case study in Birmingham. *Local Economy*, 6, 2, pp. 100–115.

Cawson, A. (1985) Corporatism and Local Politics. In: Grant, W. (ed.) *The Political Economy of Corporations*, Macmillan, London.

Centre for Local Economic Strategies (1989) *Urban Development Corporations. Interim Report* September 1989, CLES, Manchester.

Centre for Local Economic Strategies (1990a) Building a people's Europe? *Local Work: Monthly Bulletin of the Centre for Local Economic Strategies*, 21.

Centre for Local Economic Strategies (1990b) *First Year Report of the CLES Monitoring Project on UDCs*. CLES, Manchester.

Centre for Local Economic Strategies (1992) *Social Regeneration – Directions for Urban Policy in the 1990s*. CLES, Manchester.

Champion, A.G. and Townsend, A.R. (eds.) (1990) *Contemporary Britain: a Geographical Perspective*. Edward Arnold, London.

Champion, A.G. and Green, A. (1988) *Local Prosperity and the North/South Divide*. University of Warwick, Warwick.

Church, A. (1988) Urban regeneration in London's Docklands; a five year policy review. *Environment and Planning C: Government and Policy*, 6, pp. 187–208.

Clapham, C. (ed.) (1982) *Private Patronage and Public Power: Political Clientism in the Modern State*. Frances Pinter, London.

Clavel, P. and Kleniewski, N. (1990) Space for progressive local policy: examples from the United States and the United Kingdom. In: Logan, J. and Swanstrom, T. (eds.) *Beyond the City Limits*. New York, Temple University Press.

Cleveland County Council *et al* (1992) *Teesside Urban Development Progress Report No. 5*. CCC, Middlesbrough.

Collins, T. (1992) Board has let the jobless down. *Birmingham Evening Mail*, 24 April 1992, p. 11.

Cooke, P. (1980) Capital relations and state dependency: an analysis of urban development policy in Cardiff. In: Rees, G. and Rees, T (eds.) *Poverty and Social Inequality in Wales*. Croom Helm, London, pp. 206–229.

Cooke P. (1985) Class Practices as Regional Markers. In: Gregory D. and Urry J. (eds.) *Social Relations and Spatial Structures*, Macmillan, London.

Cooke, P. (1987a) Britain's new spatial paradigm. *Environment and Planning A*, 19, pp. 1289–1301.

Cooke, P. (1987b) Clinical inference and geographic theory. *Antipode*, 19(3), pp. 69–78.

Cooke, P. (1988a) Modernity, postmodernity, and the City. *Theory, Culture, and Society*, 5, pp. 475–492.

Cooke, P. (1988b) Municipal Enterprise, Growth Coalitions and Social Justice, *Local Economy*, 3(3), pp. 191–199.

Cooke, P. (1989a) Locality – theory and the poverty of 'spatial variation'. *Antipode*, 21(3), 261–273.

Cooke, P. (1989b) *Localities*. Unwin Hyman, London.

Coopers and Lybrand (1987) *Lower Don Valley: Final Report*. Sheffield Economic Regeneration Committee, Sheffield.

Coulson, A. (1990) Flagships and flaws: assessing the UDC decade. *Town and Country Planning* 59, 11, pp. 299–302.

Crick, M. (1986) *The March of Militant*. Faber and Faber, London.

Crilley, D. *et al* (1990) *New Migrants In London's Docklands*. Department of Geography, Queen Mary College, University of London.

Dabinett, G. (1990) Local economic development strategies in Sheffield during the 1980s. *Centre for Regional Economic and Social Research Working Paper*, 10, Sheffield Hallam University, Sheffield.

Dalby, S. (1990) Heseltine's vision of land regeneration takes shape. In Urban Development in the Thatcher Era, *Financial Times* Survey, 30 October, pp. 6–7.

Darwin, J. (1990) The enterprise society: regional policy and national strategy. *CLES Research Study* 5, Centre for Local Economic Strategies, Manchester.

Daunton, M.J. (1977) *Coal Metropolis: Cardiff 1870–1914*. Leicester University Press, Leicester.

Dawson, J. and Parkinson, M. (1990) Urban Development Corporations: the Merseyside experience 1981–1990; physical regeneration, political accountability and economic challenge. *Centre for Urban Studies Working Paper* 13, University of Liverpool, Liverpool.

Deloitte, Haskins and Sells (1989) *Business Action Plan Study*. Report for the Sheffield Development Corporation.

Department of the Environment (1979) Inner cities policy: statement by Michael Heseltine, Secretary of State for the Environment. *Press Notice No. 390*. DOE, London.

Department of the Environment (1988) *Action for Cities*. HMSO, London.

Department of the Environment (1990) *Public Expenditure on the UDCs*, DOE, London.

Department of the Environment (1991) *City Challenge: Draft Guidance*. DOE, London.

Department of the Environment (1992) *The Urban Regeneration Agency: a Consultation Paper*. DOE, London.

Docklands Consultative Committee (1989) *The Docklands Experiment*. DCC, London.

Docklands Consultative Committee (1991) *The Heseltine File – A Blue Print for Urban Policy?* DCC, London.

Docklands Consultative Committee (1992) *All that Glitters is not Gold: a Critical Assessment of Canary Wharf*. DCC, London.

Docklands Forum (1988) *Minutes and Agenda July 1988*. DF, London.

Docklands Forum (1990) *Employment In Docklands*. DF, London.

Duncan, S. and Goodwin, M. (1988) *The Local State and Uneven Development*. Polity, London.

Duncan, S., Goodwin, M. and Halford, S. (1988) Policy variations in local states. *International Journal of Urban and Regional Research*, vol. 12, no. 1, pp. 107–127.

Duncan, S. and Savage, M. (1989) Space, scale and locality. *Antipode*, 21(3), pp. 179–206.

Duncan, S. and Savage, M. (1991) New perspectives on the locality debate. *Environment and Planning (A)*, 23(2), pp. 155–164.

Dunleavy, P.J. (1981) *The Politics of Mass Housing in Britain, 1945–1975: a Study of Corporate Power and Professional Influence in the Welfare State*. Clarendon Press, Oxford.

ECOTEC (1987) *The Black Country Development Corporation. A Strategy for Development 1987*. ECOTEC, Birmingham.

Edelman, M. (1977) *Political Language: Words that Succeed and Policies that Fail*, Institute for Research on Poverty, Monograph Series, Academic Press, New York.

Edwards, N. (1983) Statement to the House of Commons, 10 February, *Hansard*, Column 1176.

Edwards, N. (1986) Speech to the Welsh Development Agency. Urban Renewal Seminar, Cardiff, 5 December 1986.

Eisenstadt, S. and Lemarchand, R. (eds.) (1981) *Political Clientism, Patronage and Development*. Sage, New York.

Elcock, H. (1986) *Local Government: Politicians, Professionals and the Public in Local Authorities*, Methuen, London.

Elliot, L. (1992) *The Guardian*. 24 August 1992.

Estate Times (1988) *Are Urban Development Corporations getting regeneration right*, 30 September.

Evans, C., Dodsworth, S. and Barnett, J. (1984) *Below the Bridge*. National Museum of Wales, Cardiff.

Fainstein, S., Gordon, I. and Harloe, M. (eds.) (1992) *Divided Cities: New York and London in the Contemporary World*. Blackwell, Oxford.

Financial Times (1986) Special Survey on 'Merseyside', 20 November 1986.

Foley, P. (1991) The Impact of the World Student Games on Sheffield. Paper to the Institute of British Geographers Conference. Sheffield.

Francis, W. (1992) Foreword in *Presentation Abstracts*. Euroco 1992, European Urban Regeneration Conference, Birmingham 12–13 February 1992.

Gellner, E. and Waterman, J. (eds.) (1977) *Patrons and Clients in Mediterranean Societies*. Duckworth, London.

Goldsmith, M. (1992) Local Government. *Urban Studies*, 29, 3/4, pp. 393–410.

Goodwin, M. (1991) Replacing a Surplus Population: the policies of the London Docklands Development Corporation. In: Allen S. and Hamnett C. (eds.) *Housing and Labour Markets: Building the Connections*, Unwin Hyman, London.

Graham, J. (1988) 'Post-modernism and Marxism'. *Antipode*, 20(1), pp. 60–66.

Gregan, P. (1992) Slump hits pace of regeneration. *Birmingham Post*, 8 August 1992, p. 7.

Gregory, D. and Urry, J. (eds.) (1985) *Social Relations and Spatial Structures*. Macmillan, London.

Gurr, R. and King, D. (1987) *The State and the City*. Macmillan, London.

Gyford, J. (1985) *The Politics of Local Socialism*. Allen and Unwin, London.

Hansard (1981) Merseyside Development Corporation. Parliamentary Debates, Sixth Series, Volume 1, Session 1980–81, 19 March, cols. 511–530.

Hansard (1982) Parliamentary Debates, 6th Series, Volume 22, Session 1981–2, Oral Answers, col. 265.

Hansard (1987) Urban Development Corporations (Financial Limits Bill). Parliamentary Debates, Sixth Series, Volume 121, Session 1987–88, 4 November 1987, col. 943.

Hansard (1989) Parliamentary Answer, UDC Spending on Community Projects, May, col. 265.

Hansard (1992a) Sixth Series, Volume 210, Number 38, Session 1991–92, 29 June, Written Answers, col. 367.

Hansard (1992b) Sixth Series, Volume 210, Number 35, Session 1991–92, 24 June, Written Answers, col. 196.

Hansard (1992c) Sixth Series, Volume 210, Number 47, Session 1991–92, 9 July, Written Answers, cols. 307–310.

Hansard (1992d) Sixth Series, Volume 210, Number 48, Session 1991–92, 10 July, Written Answers, col. 390.

Harding, A. (1991) The rise of urban growth coalitions, UK-style? *Environment and Planning C: Government and Policy*, 9, pp. 295–317.

Harvey, D. (1987) Three myths in search of a reality in urban studies. *Environment and Planning D: Society and Space*, 5, 367–376.

Harvey, D. (1989a) *The Condition of Post-modernity*. Basil Blackwell, London.

Harvey, D. (1989b) *The Urban Experience*. Basil Blackwell, Oxford.

Harvey, D. (1989c) Transformation in urban governance in late capitalism. *Geografiska Annaler*, 71(B), 3–17.

Haughton, G. and Roberts, P. (1990) Government urban economic policy 1979–1989: problems and potentials. In: Campbell, M. (ed.) *Local Economic Policy*. Cassell, London.

Hayes, M. (1987) *Urban Development Corporations: the Liverpool Experience*. Liverpool City Council, Liverpool.

Healey, P. and Barratt, S. (1990) Structure and agency in land and property development processes: some ideas for research. *Urban Studies*, 27, 1, pp. 89–104.

Healey, P. (1991) Urban regeneration and the development industry. *Regional Studies*, 25, 2, pp. 97–110.

Healey, P. (1992) Urban policy and property development. Paper presented to the 6th AESOP Congress, June 3–6, Stockholm, Sweden.

Healey, P., McNamara, P., Elson, M. and Doak, J. (1988) *Land Use Planning and the Mediation of Urban Change. The British Planning System in Practice*. Cambridge University Press, Cambridge.

Healey, P., Davoudi, S., O'Toole, M., Tavsanoglu, S. and Usher, D. (1992) *Rebuilding the City, Property-led Urban Regeneration*. E&FN Spon, London.

Heseltine, M. (1979) Parliamentary Debates (Hansard) Session 1979–80, September 13, House of Commons, HMSO, London.

Holland, P. and Fallon, M. (1978) *The Quango Explosion: Public Bodies and Ministerial Patronage*. Conservative Political Centre, London.

House of Commons Select Committee on Employment (1989) Third Report. The Employment Effects of UDCs, HC 327 I and II. HMSO, London.

House of Lords Hybrid Instruments Committee (1989) The Bristol Development Corporation (Area and Constitution Order). HMSO, London.

House of Lords Select Committee (1988) Minutes of the Hearing of The Bristol Development Corporation (Area and Constitution Order). HMSO, London.

Hudson, R. (1989) *Wrecking a Region*. Pion, London.

Imrie, R. (1993) Urban Policy Processes and the Politics of Urban Regeneration. Paper presented to the session on Urban Governance, Institute of British Geographers, Conference, Royal Holloway University of London, January 5–8.

Imrie, R. and Thomas, H. (1992) The wrong side of the tracks: a case study of local economic regeneration in Britain. *Policy and Politics* 20(3), pp. 213–226.

Imrie, R. and Thomas, H. (1993a) The new partnership: the local state and the property development industry. In: Ball, R. and Pratt, A. (eds.) *Industrial Property: Policy and Economic Development.* Routledge, London.

Imrie, R. and Thomas, H. (1993b) The limits of property-led regeneration. *Environment and Planning C: Government and Policy,* 11(1), pp. 87–102.

Independent 21 June 1992.

Independent 25 June 1992.

Independent 13 July 1992.

Independent 16 July 1992.

Indian Workers' Association (1987) *The regeneration of racism: the hypocrisy of inner city policies.* IWA, 112a The Green, Southall, Middlesex, UB2 4BQ.

INLOGOV UDC Workshop (1991) *Report of UDA Monitoring Exercise 1988–1990,* prepared by the Tyne and Wear Research and Intelligence Unit.

Johnson, R.W. (1925) *The Making of the River Tyne.* Reid, Newcastle.

Jones, M. and Craig, J. (1987) Battle in the Black Country. *Sunday Times,* 15 March 1987, p. 3.

Kapp, F.W. (1978) *The Social Costs of Business Enterprise.* Spokesman Books, Nottingham.

Keith, M. and Rogers, A. (eds.) (1991) *Hollow Promises? Rhetoric and Reality in the Inner City,* Mansell, London.

King, D. and Pierre, J. (eds.) (1990) *Challenges to Local Government,* Sage, London.

King, R. (1985) The political practice of the local capitalist association. In: King, R. (ed.) *Capital and Politics.* Routledge and Kegan Paul, London, pp. 107–131.

Kirkham, S. (1990) *Sheffield Development Corporation and the Lower Don Valley. A Study for the Joint Initiative for Social and Economic Research.* Sheffield Business School, Sheffield.

Kirkstall Valley Campaign (1990) *Kirkstall Valley Development Plan.* Kirkstall Valley Campaign, Leeds.

Knowsley Metropolitan Borough Council (1989) *Urban Renewal Programme Submission 1989/90.* Knowsley Metropolitan Borough Council, Knowsley.

Lane, T. (1987) *Liverpool–Gateway of Empire,* Lawrence and Wishart, London.

Lash, S. and Urry, J. (1987) *The End of Organized Capitalism.* Polity, Cambridge.

Law, C.M. (1989) Inner City Policy on the Ground: the Manchester experience. *Cities,* 4, pp. 336–346.

Lawless, P. (1986) *Severe Economic Recession and Local Government Intervention: A Case Study of Sheffield.* Working Paper. School of Urban and Regional Studies, Sheffield Hallam University.

Lawless, P. (1989) *Britain's Inner Cities.* Paul Chapman Publishing, London.

Lawless, P. (1990) Regeneration in Sheffield: from radical intervention to partnership. In: Parkinson, M. and Judd, D. (eds.) *Leadership and Urban Regeneration.* Sage, London.

Lawless, P. (1991) Urban policy in the Thatcher decade: English inner-city policy, 1979–90. *Environment and Planning C: Government and Policy,* 9, pp. 15–30.

Lawless, P., Ramsden, P. and Smith, Y. (1990) Labour supply and demand in Sheffield, Part 3; Census of businesses in the Sheffield Development Corporation area. *A Report for the Sheffield Development Corporation.* Centre for Regional Economic and Social Research, Sheffield Hallam University.

Leach S. (ed.) (1992) *Strengthening Local Government in the 1990s.* Longman, Harlow.

Leeds City Council (1992) *Leeds Unitary Development Plan Written Statement.* LCC, Leeds.

Leeds Development Corporation (1988) *Strategic Plan*. LDC, Leeds.
Leeds Development Corporation (1992) *Annual Report*. LDC, Leeds.
Leigh, C., Stillwell, J., Wilson, A. and Monck, C. (1990) *Yorkshire and Humberside: Economic Development and Future Prospects*, Leeds, Yorkshire and Humberside Development Association.
Lewis, N. (1992) *Inner City Regeneration*. Open University, Milton Keynes.
LGLPA (1980) *Local Government, Land and Planning Act*. HMSO, London.
Liverpool City Council (1991) *Economic Development Plan 1991/92*. LCC, Liverpool.
Loftman, P. and Nevin, B. (1992) *Urban Regeneration and Social Equity: A Case Study of Birmingham 1986–1992*. Faculty of the Built Environment, Research Paper 9, University of Central England in Birmingham; Birmingham.
Logan, J. and Swanstrom, T. (eds.) (1990) *Beyond the City Limits*. Temple University Press, New York.
London Docklands Development Corporation (1982) *Annual Report and Accounts*. LDDC, London.
London Docklands Development Corporation (1987) *Annual Report and Accounts*. LDDC, London.
London Docklands Development Corporation (1989a) *Annual Report and Accounts*. LDDC, London.
London Docklands Development Corporation (1989b) *Community Services Division Presentation*. LDDC, London.
Lovering, J. (1989) Post-modernism, Marxism and locality research: the contribution of critical realism to the debate. *Antipode*, 21(1), 1–12.
Lukes, S. (1974) *Power: A Radical View*. Macmillan, London.
Lyons, M. (1989) Experience with an uninvited guest. *Local Government Chronicle*, 8 September 1989, pp. 22–3.
MacGregor, S. and Pimlott, B. (1990) Action and inaction in the cities. In: MacGregor, S. and Pimlott, B. (eds.) *Tackling the Inner Cities: the 1980s Reviewed, Prospects for the 1990s*. Clarendon Press, Oxford.
Marks, S. (1988) The regeneration game. Perceptions of the Bristol Urban Development Corporation. Unpublished MA dissertation, School for Advanced Urban Studies, University of Bristol, Bristol.
Massey, D. (1984) *Spatial Divisions of Labour*. Macmillan, Basingstoke.
Massey, D. (1985) New directions in space. In: Gregory, D. and Urry, J. (eds.) *Social Relations and Spatial Structures*. Macmillan, London.
Massey, D. (1991) The political place of locality studies. *Environment and Planning A*, 23(2), pp. 267–282.
Massey, D. and Allen, J. (eds.) (1984) *Geography Matters*. Cambridge University Press, Cambridge.
Mayer, M. (1989) Local politics: from administration to management. Paper presented at the Cardiff Symposium on Regulation, Innovation, and Spatial Development, University of Wales, September 13–15.
McConaghy, D. (1972) SNAP 69/72: *Another Chance for Cities*. Shelter, London.
Merseyside Development Corporation (1981) *Initial Development Strategy Merseyside Development Corporation: Proposals for the Regeneration of Its Area*. August. MDC, Liverpool.
Meadowhall Retail Academy (1991) Breakdown of Meadowhall Privilege Cardholders' post codes. (Unpublished Report).
Meager, N. (1991) TECs: a revolution in training and enterprise or old wine in new bottles. *Local Economy*, 6, 1, pp. 4–20.
Meegan, R. (1989) Paradise postponed; the growth and decline of Merseyside's outer estates. In: Cooke, P. (ed.) *Localities: the Changing Face of Urban Britain*. Unwin Hyman, London.
Meegan, R. (1990) Merseyside in crisis and in conflict. In: Harloe, M., Pickvance, C.

and Urry, J. (eds.) *Place, Policy and Politics: Do Localities Matter?* Unwin Hyman, London.

Meyer, M. (1991) Politics in the post Fordist city. *Socialist Review*, 91, 1, pp. 105–123.

Moore, C. and Richardson, J. (1989) *Local Partnership and the Unemployment Crisis in Britain.* Unwin Hyman, London.

Morgan, D. (1992) *Local Government Initiatives versus Central Streamlining.* A paper given at the Royal Town Planning Institute, National Planning Conference and Exhibition, Birmingham 9–11 June 1992.

Murray, R. (1991) *Local Space: Europe and the New Regionalism.* Centre for Local Economic Strategies, Manchester and South East Economic Development Strategy, Stevenage, Herts.

National Audit Office (1988) *Department of the Environment: Urban Development Corporations.* Report by the Comptroller and Auditor General. HMSO, London.

National Audit Office (1989) *Regenerating the Inner Cities.* HMSO, London.

Nevin, B. (1991) *The Black Country Development Corporation and the Sandwell Housing Action Trust: An Impact Assessment of Central Government Initiatives on the Local Urban Policy Frame.* Research Paper No. 7, Birmingham Polytechnic, Birmingham.

Nevin, B. and Loftman, P. (1992) *The Black Country Development Corporation: An Evaluation of the Corporation's Strategic Planning and Economic Impact 1987–1992.* A paper given at the seminar: Urban Development Corporations and Local Authorities, University of Birmingham, 22 September 1992.

PA Cambridge Economic Consultants (1987) *An Evaluation of the Enterprise Zone Experiment.* Inner Cities Directorate, Department of the Environment. HMSO, London.

Pacione, M. (1990) What about people? A critical analysis of urban policy in the United Kingdom. *Geography*, Vol. 75(3), No. 328, pp. 193–202.

Parkinson, M. (1989) The cities under Mrs Thatcher; the centralisation and privatisation of power. *Centre for Urban Studies Working Paper 6*, University of Liverpool, Liverpool.

Parkinson, M. (1990) Urban leadership and regeneration in Liverpool: confusion, confrontation or coalition? *Centre for Urban Studies Working Paper 14*, University of Liverpool, Liverpool.

Parkinson, M. (1990) Political responses to urban restructuring: the British experience under Thatcherism. In: Logan, J. and Swanstrom, T. (eds.) *Beyond the City Limits.* Temple University Press, Philadelphia.

Parkinson, M. and Evans, R. (1988) Urban regeneration and development corporations: Liverpool style. *Centre for Urban Studies Working Paper 2*, University of Liverpool, Liverpool.

Parkinson, M. and Evans, R. (1989) Urban development corporations. *Centre for Urban Studies Working Paper 3*, University of Liverpool, Liverpool.

Parkinson, M. and Evans, R. (1990) Urban development corporations. In: Campbell, M. (ed.) *Local Economic Policy.* Cassell, London.

Parkinson, M. and Wilks, S. (1985) The Politics of Inner City Partnerships. In: Goldsmith, M. (ed.) *New Research in Central–Local Relations.* Gower, Aldershot. pp. 290–307.

Pickup, J. (1988) Cardiff Bay – The Way Forward. In: Evans, E. and Thomas, H. (eds.) *Cardiff Capital Development*, Cardiff City Council, Cardiff, p. 10.

Pickvance, C.G. (1985) Spatial policy as territorial politics: the role of spatial coalitions in the articulation of 'spatial' interests and in the demand for spatial policy. In: Rees, G. *et al* (eds.) *Political Action and Social Identity.* Heinemann Education, London, pp. 117–142.

PIEDA (1988) *Leeds Urban Development Corporation: The Potential for Development*. PIEDA, Reading.

Polytechnic of Wolverhampton (1988) *The Foundry and Drop Forging Sectors in Sandwell*. A study jointly commissioned by the Black Country Development Corporation and Sandwell MBC.

Potter, S. (1990) Britain's Development Corporations, *Town and Country Planning*, 59, November, pp. 291–298.

Prisim Research Ltd. (1991) *Black Country Monitoring Report*, September, Birmingham.

Public Accounts Committee (1989) *Twentieth Report: Urban Development Corporations*. HMSO, London.

Redclift, M. (1987) *Sustainable Development: Exploring the Contradictions*. Routledge, London.

Redwood, J. (1992) Interview on Radio 4, *The World This Weekend*, Sunday, 16 August 1992.

Rees, G. and Lambert, J. (1981) Nationalism as legitimation? Notes towards a political economy of regional development in South Wales. In: Harloe, M. (ed.) *New Perspectives in Urban Change and Conflict*. Heinemann Educational, London, pp. 122–137.

Reeves, R. (1987) On the waterfront. *Radical Wales* 15, pp. 11–12.

Regional Science Research Group (1991) Socio-economic impacts of developments at Liverpool Airport: an extended input–output model for Greater Merseyside. *Regional Science Research Group Working Paper*, Department of Civic Design, University of Liverpool, Liverpool.

Richards, P.G. (1963) *Patronage in British Government*. Allen and Unwin, London.

Roberts, P. (1990) *The Origins and Recent Experience of Public–Private Partnership in Local Economic Development in the UK*. IIR, Vienna.

Roberts, P. and Whitney, D. (1991) Strategic behaviour of the public sector in negotiating public–private partnership solutions in the UK. Department of Regional Planning, Royal Institute of Technology, Stockholm.

Robinson, F. and Shaw, K. (1991) Urban regeneration and community development. *Local Economy*, 6, 1, pp. 61–72.

Robson, B. (1988) *Those Inner Cities*. Clarendon, Oxford.

RSPB (1989) *The Living Waterfront Scheme: Information Note*. RSPB Wales Office, Newtown, Powys.

RSPB (1992) *RSPB/MORI Poll of Public Opinion on the Cardiff Bay Barrage Proposal: Supplementary Data on points of detail*. RSPB, Sandy, Bedfordshire.

Runciman, W.G. (1989) *A Treatise on Social Theory*. Volume 2, Cambridge University Press, Cambridge.

Sandwell MBC (1987) *An Economic Development Strategy for Sandwell: Problems and Issues*. Sandwell MBC, Sandwell.

Sandwell MBC (1988) *Sandwell Trends 1988*. Sandwell MBC, Sandwell.

Sandwell MBC (1990a) *Sandwell Trends 1990*. Sandwell MBC, Sandwell.

Sandwell MBC (1990b) *Sandwell Poverty Study 1990*. Sandwell MBC, Sandwell.

Sandwell MBC (1990c) *Industrial Land and Premises Strategy and Programme 1990*. p. 30, Sandwell MBC, Sandwell.

Sandwell MBC (1990d) *Annual Report and Accounts 1989/90*. Sandwell MBC, Sandwell.

Sandwell MBC (1992) *Tipton City Challenge*. Sandwell MBC, Sandwell.

Sassen, S. (1991) *The Global Cities: London, New York, Tokyo*. Princeton University Press, Princeton.

Saunders, P. (1985) Corporation and Urban Service Provision. In: Grant, W. (ed.) *The Political Economy of Corporation*, Macmillan, London.

Sayer, A. (1991) Behind the locality debate: deconstructing geography's dualisms. *Environment and Planning* (A), 23(2), pp. 283–308.

Seyd, P. (1990) Radical Sheffield: from socialism to entrepreneurialism. *Political Studies* Vol. 38(2) pp. 335–344.

SGCC (1986) *The Regeneration of South Cardiff*. Proposals for an Urban Development Corporation, SGCC, Cardiff.

Shaw, K. (1990) The Politics of public–private partnership in Tyne and Wear, *Northern Economic Review*.

Sheffield City Council (1986) Urban Programme – City of Sheffield 1986–89. SCC, Sheffield.

Sheffield City Council (1988) *Major Development Proposals in Sheffield*. Planning Information Bulletin 15. Department of Land and Planning. SCC, Sheffield.

Sheffield City Council (1990a) *The World Student Games Economic Impact Study Report: Part 1*. Department of Employment and Economic Development. SCC, Sheffield.

Sheffield City Council (1990b) *Sheffield 2000: Phase One*. Report of the Sheffield Economic Regeneration Committee, SCC, Sheffield.

Sheffield City Council (1991a) *Urban Programme – City of Sheffield 1991–94*. Chief Executive. SCC, Sheffield.

Sheffield City Council (1991b) *The Vision – Sheffield City Challenge 1991*. SCC, Sheffield.

Sheffield City Council (1991c) *Sheffield Economic Bulletin: Summer 1991*. Department of Employment and Economic Development. SCC, Sheffield.

Sheffield Development Corporation (1989) *A Vision of the Lower Don Valley: A Planning Framework for Discussion*. SDC, Sheffield.

Sheffield Development Corporation (1991) Report and Accounts 1990–91. SDC, Sheffield.

Sherwood, M. (1991) Racism and resistance: Cardiff in the 1930s and 1940s. *Llafur. Journal of Welsh Labour History* 5(4), pp. 51–70.

Shields Weekly News, 17 November, 1975, p. 6.

Short, J.R. (1989) *The Humane City*. Basil Blackwell, Oxford.

Sills A., Taylor, G. and Golding, P. (1988) *The Politics of the Urban Crisis*. Hutchinson, London.

Skinner, P. (1990) Public Participation in Planning and the Voluntary Sector. Unpublished manuscript available from Nick Oatley, University of the West of England, Bristol.

Smith, N. (1986) Gentrification, the frontier and the restructuring of urban space. In: Smith, N. and Williams, P. (eds.) *Gentrification and the City*. Allen and Unwin, London.

Smith, N. (1987) Dangers of the empirical turn: some comments on the CURS initiative. *Antipode* 19(1), pp. 59–68.

Smith, Y. (1991) The World Student Games, Sheffield 1991: an initial appraisal. *Regional Review* Vol. 1(3), pp. 8–10.

Soja, E.W. (1989) *Post-modern Geographies: the Re-assertion of Space in Critical Social Theory*. Verso, London.

Solesbury, W. (1987) Urban policy in the 1980s: the issues and arguments. *The Planner*, June, pp. 18–22.

Solesbury, W. (1990) Property development and urban regeneration. In: Healey, P. and Nabarro, R. (eds.) *Land and Property Development in a Changing Context*, Gower, Aldershot, pp. 186–194.

Stewart, M. (1990) Urban Policy in Thatcher's England. School for Advanced Urban Studies, Working Paper No. 90, University of Bristol, Bristol.

Stewart, M. (1991) 'Exit' strategies for urban development corporations. Paper for the CLES/DCC Conference on Urban Regeneration for the 1990s, London, April, School of Advanced Urban Studies, University of Bristol, Bristol.

Stillwell, J. (1992) Census 1991: the preliminary count. *The Regional Review*, 1, No. 3, pp. 15–25.

Stoker, G. (1989) Urban Development Corporations: a review. *Regional Studies*, 23, 2, pp. 159–173.

Stoker, G. (1990) Regulation theory, local government, and the transition to Fordism. In: King, D. and Pierre, J. (eds.) *Challenges to Local Government*, Modern Policy Series 28. Sage, London.

Stoker, G. (1991) *The Politics of Local Government*, Macmillan, London.

Sutcliffe, A. (1986) The Midlands Metropolis Birmingham 1890–1980. In: Gordon, G. (ed.) *Regional Cities in the UK 1890–1980*, Harper and Row, London.

Swingler, P. (1992) Scandal of Lost £36m. *Birmingham Evening Mail* 13 July 1992, p. 1.

Thomas, H. (1992a) Redevelopment in Cardiff Bay: state intervention and the securing of consent. *Contemporary Wales*, forthcoming.

Thomas, H. (1992b) The local press and urban renewal: a South Wales case study. *Working Paper 134*, School of Planning, Oxford Polytechnic.

Thomas, H. and Imrie, R. (1989) Urban redevelopment, compulsory purchase and the regeneration of local economies: the case of Cardiff Docklands. *Planning Practice and Research* 4(3), pp. 18–27.

Thomas, H. and Imrie, R. (1993) Industrial change and conflict in urban redevelopment: the case of south Cardiff. In: Meyer, P. (ed.) *Comparative Studies in Local Economic Development. Problems in Policy Implementation*. Greenwood Press, Westport, CT.

Thomas, R. and Cresswell, P. (1973) *The New Town Idea*. Open University Press, Milton Keynes.

Thompson, R. (1990) Economic regeneration: trickling downwards or growing upwards? *The Planner*, February 23, pp. 40–42.

Thornley, A. (1991) *Urban Planning under Thatcherism*. Routledge, London.

Town and Country Planning Association (1979) *Inner Cities*. TCPA, London.

Townroe, P. (1992) Yorkshire and Humberside. In Northern Ireland Economic Research Centre and Oxford Economic Forecasting, *Regional Economic Outlook*, Northern Ireland Economic Research Centre, Belfast.

Turok, I. (1991) Policy evaluation as science: a critical assessment. *Applied Economics* 23, pp. 1543–1550.

Turok, I. (1992) Property-led urban regeneration: panacea or placebo? *Environment and Planning A*, 24, 3, pp. 361–380.

Turok, I. and Wannop, U. (1990) *Targeting Urban Employment Initiatives*. Department of the Environment Inner Cities Research Programme. HMSO, London.

Tyne and Wear Chamber of Commerce (1990) *Contact*, August. TWCC, Newcastle.

Tyne and Wear County Council (1979) *Tyne and Wear Structure Plan*. TWCC, Newcastle.

Tyne and Wear Development Corporation (1990) *A Vision of the Future*. TWDC, Newcastle.

Victor Hausner and Associates (1992) *City Challenge: Working Partnerships – City Challenge Implementing Agencies; An Advisory Note*, prepared for the DOE, February 1992.

Walker, D. (1989) What's left to do? *Antipode* 21(2), pp. 133–165.

Walsall MBC (1987) Black Country Development Corporation *A Strategy for Development: Report to the DoE by ECOTEC*. Report to the Policy and Resources Committee, 1 July 1987. Walsall MBC, Walsall.

Walsall MBC (1990) *Walsall Draft Unitary Development Plan 1988–2001*, Walsall MBC, Walsall.

Walton, D. (1990a) *Cardiff Bay Development*, paper delivered to the Town and Country Planning Summer School, University College of Wales, Swansea.

Walton, J. (1990b) Theoretical methods in comparative urban politics. In: Logan, J. and Swanstrom, T. (eds.) *Beyond the City Limits*. Temple University Press, Philadelphia.

West Midlands Enterprise Board (1987) *Labour Market Briefing June 1987* Birmingham, WMEB Consultants Ltd.

West Midlands Enterprise Board (1991) *Labour Market Briefing December 1991* Birmingham, WMEB Consultants Ltd.

Western Daily Post (1987) Minister raps inner city wasteland. 16 December 1987.

Whitney, D. and Haughton, G. (1990) Structures for development partnerships in the 1990s: practice in West Yorkshire. *The Planner*, 76, No. 21.

Wilkinson, S. (1992) Towards a new city? A case study of image improvement initiatives in Newcastle upon Tyne. In: Healey, P., Davoudi, S., O'Toole, M., Tavsanoglu, S. and Usher, D. (eds.) *Rebuilding the City, Property-led Urban Regeneration*. E&FN. Spon.

Willmot, P. and Hutchinson, R. (1992) *Urban Trends 1: A Report on Britain's Deprived Areas*. Policy Studies Institute, London.

World Commission on Environment and Development (1987) *Our Common Future*. Oxford University Press, Oxford.

Wynn Davies, P. (1992) Docklands given more urban aid than the regions. *Independent*, 26 June 1992.

INDEX